The Origins of Nonviolence
Tolstoy and Gandhi in their Historical Settings

Also by Martin Green

The von Richthofen Sisters
Children of the Sun
The Challenge of the Mahatmas
Dreams of Adventure, Deeds of Empire
Tolstoy and Gandhi

THE ORIGINS OF NONVIOLENCE

*Tolstoy and Gandhi
in their Historical Settings*

Martin Green

THE PENNSYLVANIA STATE UNIVERSITY PRESS
UNIVERSITY PARK AND LONDON

Dedicated to Lin Haire-Sargent, Lucilia Valerio,
and other fellow students of Gandhi

Library of Congress Cataloging-in-Publication Data

Green, Martin Burgess, 1927–
The origins of nonviolence.

Includes bibliography and index.
1. Gandhi, Mahatma, 1869–1948.
2. Tolstoy, Leo, graf, 1828–1910.
3. India—Politics and government—1765–1947.
4. Soviet Union—Politics and government—19th century.
5. Soviet Union—Politics and government—1894–1917.
6. Pacifists—Soviet Union—Biography.
7. Statesmen—India—Biography.   I. Title.
DS481.G3G732   1985   320.5′5   85–12138
ISBN 0–271–00414–2

Contents

Preface

This book tells how the modern version of nonviolence—and satya-graha, and war-resistance, and one kind of anti-imperialism, even— were in effect invented by Tolstoy and Gandhi. It studies the two men's lives, showing how their ideas evolved from different starting points, and via different experiences, to come to a common climax. But the stress falls on the historical forces to which they were reacting, in Russia and India; and on the heritage of resistance (largely religious resistance, inherited from earlier crises of imperialism) which they were able to make use of. Russia and India were, in the lives of Tolstoy and Gandhi, respectively, on the periphery of the expanding world system centered in England, and the two men foresaw, and rebelled against, a future of modernizing imperialism. Thus, the book relates the two men to each other and to the Western world of the last hundred and fifty years. And in order to tell this story, it creates a historical background that is common to both the nineteenth-century Russian novelist and the twentieth-century Hindu politician, and a point of view which brings Tolstoy's Russia and Gandhi's India into a common focus, as occupying the same moment in history.

Note on the Notes and Bibliography

The edition of Gandhi used most often is the Navajivan *Collected Works of Mahatma Gandhi*, of which eighty-five volumes have so far appeared. They are referred to in the footnotes as Gandhi's *Collected Works*, with volume and page numbers. But some of his works are referred to in other editions. For Tolstoy, I have used mainly the Sobranie Sochi-nenii, which appeared in Moscow in twenty volumes; this is listed under Tolstoy, with volume and page numbers. But I read Tolstoy first in English (I have gone back from the English to the Russian, most often), and the fullest edition available to me was that published in Boston in 1904, edited by Leo Wiener. I have identified this by putting Wiener in parentheses.

In other cases, the author's name and the page reference alone are given in the footnote, and fuller detail is to be found in the bibliography, except when two books by the same author are in the bibliography, and then a brief form of the title in question is included in the footnote.

For Tolstoy's major fiction, I have trusted to the modern translations because translating Tolstoy has been a consistent and, in some sense, collaborative venture for nearly a century now, and the new versions have the benefit of considerable critical scrutiny. The non-fiction, however, has been translated more rarely and with less scholarly scruple, since it was meant for immediate social effect. And a lot of letters, journals, and some essays have never been translated. In these cases I have tried to go back to the Russian originals and re-translate, with the help—which I much appreciate—of Dina Birman. This was not possible in all cases, however, because some of the major sources gave no clue of their sources. In these cases I have not gone behind the English-language sources.

Acknowledgments

Of the institutions which have in various ways supported my work on this book, I want to acknowledge Tufts University, where I teach; the Woodrow Wilson International Center for Scholars, where I spent the year 1980–81; and the Guggenheim Foundation.

I wish to acknowledge the Navajivan Trust for permission to reprint excerpts from the *Collected Works of Mahatma Gandhi*, volumes 1 through 85.

I
Empire versus Religion

I had ended this two years' labour, when, on the ninth of September, I happened to travel on a train to a locality in the Governments of Tula and Ryazan, where the peasants had been starving the year before, and were starving still more in the present year. At one of the stations the train in which I was travelling met a special train which, under the leadership of the governor, was transporting troops with guns, cartridges, and rods for the torture and killing of those very famine-stricken peasants.[1]

So read the young Hindu barrister called Mohandas Karamchand Gandhi, some time in 1894, when he was living in Pretoria, in the Transvaal, in South Africa. He was in exile from his homeland of India to another part of the British empire. Having trained as a lawyer in London, he was equipped to parlay that privilege into fame and fortune anywhere in the lion's share of the globe ruled by England. But on his way to Pretoria from Durban, he had been thrown out of the first-class railway carriage for which he had bought a ticket, because a white passenger complained about having to share it with a colored man; and on the stagecoach continuation of his journey, he had been physically beaten by the agent for refusing to give up his seat.

The peasant tried to beg for mercy, but when he saw that this was useless, he made the sign of the cross and lay down. The policemen rushed forward to hold him down. The learned doctor stood by, ready to offer learned medical aid. The prisoners, spitting into their hands, swished the rods and began to strike. However, it turned out that the bench

was too narrow and that it was too difficult to keep the writh-
ing, tortured man upon it. Then the governor ordered
another bench to be brought and to be cleated to the first.
Putting their hands to their visors and muttering: "Yes, your
Excellency," some men hurriedly and humbly fulfilled the
commands; meanwhile the half-naked, pale, tortured man,
frowning and looking earthward, waited with trembling jaws
and bared legs. When the second bench was attached, he was
again put down, and the horse-thieves began to beat him
again. The back, hips, and thighs, and even the sides of the
tortured man began more and more to be covered with wales
and bloody streaks, and with every blow there were heard
dull sounds, which the tortured man was unable to repress.
In the surrounding crowd were heard the sobs of the wives,
mothers, children, relatives of the tortured man and of all
those who were selected for punishment.[2]

Gandhi was reading Tolstoy's *The Kingdom of God is Within You*, sub-
titled "Christianity Not As A Mystical Teaching But As A New Concept
of Life," which Tolstoy had published the year before in Russia; it
was immediately suppressed, but two English translations appeared
in 1894 and—also immediately—a friend in London had sent Gandhi
the one by Aline Delano. Tolstoy was a Russian count, in 1894 sixty-
six years old, and a great novelist with an international reputation.
Gandhi was a Modh Bania, twenty-five years old, notable only for his
timidity and ineffectuality. But the act of communication begun by
Tolstoy was completed by Gandhi, and he sealed himself the other
man's son and heir. Gandhi read on:

Fate, as though on purpose, after my two years' tension of
thought in one and the same direction, for the first time in
my life brought me in contact with this phenomenon, which
showed me with absolute obviousness in practice what had
become clear to me in theory, namely, that the whole structure of our life is not based, as men who enjoy an advanta-
geous position in the existing order of things are fond of
imagining, on any juridical principles, but on the simplest,
coarsest violence, on the murder and torture of men.[3]

In the moment of Gandhi's reading those lines, we may say, his movement of nonviolence was born, the most striking single case in an
otherwise amorphous world movement for peace and social justice.

It was in 1881 that Tolstoy's life had been shattered—his successful and productive life as novelist, landowner, husband, and father. He had, of course, been uneasy in that privileged position before, but two events of 1881 made it finally intolerable to him. One was the new tsar's condemnation to death of the revolutionaries who assassinated his father; the other was the Tolstoy family's move from the country to Moscow. One confronted him with the issue of violence, the other with that of social injustice—for living in the city, where the sound of factory sirens woke him instead of the song of birds, Tolstoy had to know the misery of the proletariat. He took part in the Moscow Census of 1881, to see their conditions for himself; he wrote *What Then Must We Do?* about what he saw; he wrote pamphlets and books attacking the Russian church's version of Christianity and the Russian government's version of justice. *The Kingdom of God is Within You* was one utterance in a long series.

Gandhi's life, on the other hand, had been shattered in an opposite way, by acts of ambition. He had left the land of his forefathers, and their way of life, to go to London to become an imitation Englishman; and having come home, he had left again for South Africa. He had learned to wear English clothes, to eat English food, to read English books, to sit and talk and think English; and he had forced similar changes on his family. He had participated in the betrayal by the Indian intelligentsia in general of their native culture. His life, too, was shattered, but he only half-knew it; he needed Tolstoy to tell him what had gone wrong.

After 1894 Gandhi remained profoundly aware of Tolstoy. *The Kingdom of God is Within You* had overwhelmed him, he says in his autobiography, and he gradually read most of those writings of Tolstoy after 1881 which were translated into English. It was not until 1906, however, that Tolstoy's power to radically influence his behavior became undeniably clear. During that year Gandhi began his campaign of satyagraha (firmness in truth); in January 1908 he started going to South African jails. Then he re-read *The Kingdom of God is Within You*, partly because only in jail did he have time for reading, but more because he was then launched on the kind of radical protest that Tolstoy had incited him to. In 1908, when Tolstoy was eighty, Gandhi sent him a message of congratulation. And in 1909, when Gandhi was in London, he read Tolstoy's *Letter to a Hindu*, which had an even more profound effect upon him. In this *Letter* Tolstoy warned Indian revolutionaries against employing terrorist methods of agitation, and urged them to stay true to their native traditions of nonviolence.

In that year Gandhi was ripe for conversion to even the most extreme of Tolstoy's ideas. He hated London, the modern metropolis, on this visit; he hated the parliamentary procedures in which orthodox politics involved him. But he was steadfastly opposed to the terrorists who were capturing the minds of Indian youth; and, in a triumph over his old inhibitions and debilities, he had given birth to a new self by means of a mental and physical regimen he associated with Tolstoy—vegetarianism, nature cure, and the simple life.

He wrote to Tolstoy with great enthusiasm, describing the work he was doing in South Africa, and Tolstoy replied with equal warmth. Gandhi sent the older man his manifesto, *Hind Swaraj* (Indian Home-Rule), which he wrote immediately after reading *Letter to a Hindu*, and Joseph Doke's 1908 biography of Gandhi: both of which Tolstoy read. And so, miraculously, in the last months of Tolstoy's life, he learned to know the very remote figure who was to be his heir. The last long letter Tolstoy wrote was to Gandhi.

Gandhi returned to South Africa, and in 1910 he and his friend Kallenbach set up Tolstoy Farm, near Johannesburg, as a place for the families of satyagrahis. There they experimented with the simple life—with vegetarianism, fasting, reformed dress, physical labor, nature cure, and so on. Gandhi often said afterwards that his time at Tolstoy Farm was his period of greatest "faith," when he felt able to do things, and asked other people to do things, which later (as earlier) would have terrified him. By comparison, his work in India was marred by compromise and caution.

But in India, and elsewhere, up to the end of his life and after his death, extraordinary things were brought to pass by means of this "faith," the faith in nonviolent action and self-simplification, which Tolstoy passed to Gandhi, like a torch from one runner to another. What did these men have in common that made this act of communication and communion possible?

Both were youngest sons, with a single sister, and defined themselves at first against their elder brothers. Both were married, but Tolstoy at the age of thirty-four and to a girl half his age; Gandhi at the age of thirteen and by his father's will. Tolstoy chose marriage as his destiny, with the greatest excitement, whereas Gandhi had it imposed on him. Both came to profound antierotic disillusionment, but along a different emotional curve. Indeed, their lives can be put side-by-side as wholes, very profitably.

But if one is concentrating on their achievements in nonviolence, then the story begins in 1894, and what they have in common is that they were both citizens of great empires, but believers in radical religion. Theirs was the kind of religion that denies the lust for power of a state, of a ruling class, of a religious sect, of a racial majority; it opposes the tendency toward self-expansion, which lies at the root of most of the achievements of civilization and culture. It values peace and reason, simplicity and self-limitation, suffering and meekness.

This was what Tolstoy called "Christianity as a New Concept of Life." It is a kind of religion to be found *within* Christianity and Buddhism and Islam, and the great world religions. But it is there mixed up with opposite tendencies, for instance, pagan celebrations of erotic life, and liberal celebrations of the humane and the humanist. Radical religion bites at the root of empire, and all splendor, including cultural splendor, is imperial to some degree. Tolstoy and Gandhi were comparatively liberal exemplars of this religion, but, of course, they were dismayingly radical by general standards.

They resisted the imperialist spread of the modern world system, and in this book I will describe that spread as well as their reaction against it. My concern with the system, however, will show itself mainly in what may look like a blatantly English or Anglo-American point of view. I shall sometimes translate Tolstoy and Gandhi into Anglo-Saxon terms, explain them by Anglo-Saxon references, quite crudely; this is partly because my concern with them is existential and I am English, and partly in order to make them comprehensible to my readers. My ultimate reason is that England was always there for them, even when not named; that England was always involved, however implicitly, in their approval and disapproval of things in their own countries; that both men were always reacting to England or America— to the force embodied primarily in the Anglo-Saxon countries. The kind of marriage in which Tolstoy put so much faith could be called English marriage; Gandhi's kind of nationalism could be called English, as we shall see.

To take one simple example, the communication between Tolstoy and Gandhi passed through England. Gandhi read Tolstoy in English translation; he read him while living in an English colony; he was prepared to understand him by his experience with vegetarian and religious reformers in London; they wrote to each other in that language; and so on. All the lines of communication between them, from Russia to India, and vice versa, ran first to London, and then on. And those lines of communication can represent for us all the other lines of force—economic, political, military, and so on—that spanned and penetrated into the world, and set the cultural bedrock stirring and heaving beneath them. Their stories were two strands in a single rope of world history, in which the Anglo-Saxons were dominant, and that is why I keep evoking the pressure of England and America by my commentary.

Finally, the book draws a parallel between Tolstoy and Marx, on the one hand, and between Gandhi and Lenin on the other. Both pairs of lifelines ran rather close at some points, though widely divergent at others: Gandhi and Lenin, for instance, were born in almost the same year and around 1920 were leading the two greatest revolutions in the world; but, of course, one revolution was violent and the other nonviolent. Marx and Tolstoy were born in the same decade and produced their massive works, *Capital*, volume I, and *War and Peace*, also in one decade. *Capital* finally appeared in 1867, *War and Peace* was concluded in 1869, the year Gandhi was born; but, of course, they recommended opposite routes for social salvation. And then there are cross-connections, for Lenin, as a Russian revolutionary, had to confront Tolstoy; indeed, his essays on Tolstoy as artist and as ideologue are still the controlling model for Russian scholarship on those topics.

It seemed worth the risk of confusion or overcomplexity to include Marx and Lenin, because they are the greatest rivals to Tolstoy and Gandhi. One of the essential dimensions of religious radicalism is its difference from political radicalism; to put it as sharply as possible, the main issue dividing the two pairs from each other, and determining our response to both, is violence. Tolstoy and Gandhi are scandalous ultimately because they renounced violence; and their renunciation of pleasure and art and civilization and sex is all secondary to that—in both senses of *secondary*. Those other renunciations can all be seen as consequent upon the first one; and, ultimately, the reason most people resent and resist Tolstoy and Gandhi, even intellectuals who themselves shudder when they pick up a gun, is that Tolstoy and Gandhi declare that men could live without violence. Of course, men could only have peace by giving up many other things and many other powers, but it is the promise as well as the price which disturbs us. So we must keep Marx and Lenin in focus, too, as we study and judge Tolstoy and Gandhi.

In *Fire in the Minds of Men* James H. Billington says of political revolution: "The theater was Europe of the industrial era; the main stage, journalistic offices within great European cities."[4] Religious revolution, on the other hand, occurred in countries on the perimeter of Europe, just being engulfed by European civilization. Tolstoy and Gandhi are not to be pictured in journalistic offices, or, indeed, in cities at all; they belong to the village and the ashram. Tolstoy's educational journal, *Yasnaya Polyana*, was published from his home; Gandhi's *Indian Opinion* was—to use his own phrase—the village industry of his ashram in South Africa. And the symbolism of *theater* is much less appropriate.

Billington also makes clear the important role played in the French Revolution by the Palais Royal—an enclave of cafes and entertainments, of sexual license and pornography, in whose heat the dreams of total freedom hatched—and the comparable importance in other political revolutions of the release of desire. There is no equivalent for Tolstoy and Gandhi. They stood for the flight from the city, and the restraint of desire.

Finally, the image of fire is important in political revolution. Billington says: "The industrial revolution was permitting men to leash fire to machines—and to unleash fire-power on each other—with a force undreamed of in earlier ages. In the midst of these fires appeared the more elusive flame that Dostoevsky described in *The Possessed* . . . 'The fire is in the minds of men, not in the roofs of buildings.' "[5] The key image in Tolstoy and Gandhi is certainly not fire, and is quite often the opposite element, water. Tolstoy's diary for 10 March 1884 says: "Rose early, swept out room. Must be like water, as Lao Tse says."[6] And for 27 March 1895: "The earth does not stand. It and we are all a flowing."[7] Still, it was a revolution that they proclaimed and led; no one was or is more radical than they.

"Religious radicalism," however, brings together two powerful ideas, each with a number of facets, so that the phrase could mean many things. What I mean by *religion* here is, in effect, the opposite of empire: that which binds people together and motivates the group not at or from the peak of its pyramid, but from its base; not for conquest, but for resistance; not in pride of greatness, but in solidarity of faith. This definition is obviously not objective or value-free, but partisan and tendentious. I would not in other arguments deny the name of "religion" to the kind of vision that inspired the Crusades or militant Islam, but here I mean something quite different from that. *Empire* here means a complex of technology and ideology (the rationalism, democracy, and economic enterprise of the West) which often offers itself as anti-imperialist, but can be seen by underdeveloped peoples as dominative. And so *religion*, as the opposite and the opponent of empire, means the resistance to all those things.

Empire and Adventure

The idea of empire and its energizing myth of adventure were to be found in the Hindu and other Indian cultures, in Russia, and in England. They are featured, with varying degrees of prominence, in all great states and proud cultures. Gandhi, however, met them in their British form. He thought of his own culture as predominantly meek, religious, and sacrificial (though he was certainly not unaware of its other strains), and he saw empire and adventure as British.

Those ideas were embodied in a number of forms at the end of the British Empire. (I shall assume that the First World War marked the end of England's expanding imperialism even though the contrary movement of dissolution did not begin till after the Second.) One of those forms was the books by a Wesleyan minister, the Reverend William E. Fitchett, who wrote *Deeds That Won the Empire, Fights for the Flag, Tales of the Great Mutiny, How England Saved Wellington's Men,* and *Nelson and His Captains.* C. F. Andrews, who became as a man one of Gandhi's lieutenants in resisting the empire, was as a boy given *Deeds That Won the Empire* to read, and tales of the great Indian soldiers, like Outram and the Lawrence brothers. As a young clergyman, before he went out to India, he ran the General Gordon Club for Boys, in a working-class town, and told the boys tales of African adventure and South Seas cannibals. He was—however unconsciously—spreading the cult of empire. Later he spread the opposite idea.

There were close parallels for England's Indian soldiers in nineteenth-century Russia, too, in figures like Ermolov and Skobelev. Indeed, Russia had its own tradition of adventure-for-empire, a good example of which is the story of Yermak, the sixteenth-century conqueror of Siberia—a story Tolstoy retold in his School Reader. Yermak led his Cossacks across the Urals to conquer new lands for the tsar, at just the same time as Raleigh and Drake were establishing the British Empire.

This adventure had a very familiar ring to the readers in Kipling's England, as is made clear in this summary by John F. Baddeley, who wrote in 1919 that the story of Yermak

> ... was just such an one as all mankind has ever loved to hear; the story, that is, of an outlaw, leader of a robber band, who after some more than usually desperate outrage has fled the vengeance of the law, and in doing so found a kingdom. . . . the sudden opening of a door into another world, a world known to exist, indeed, but hitherto impenetrable . . . rivers full of fish, forests full of game, arable land . . . best of all, sables . . . Yermak's name can never die. For many generations of Russians he has not been merely the conqueror of petty Sibir, but of all Siberia. The cut-throat of the Volga has been metamorphosed into a knight-at-arms, sans peur et sans reproche, a happy mixture of Herman Cortes and King Arthur. . . .[8]

And the Russians themselves saw their heroes as belonging to the same tribe as Cortes and King Arthur—they treated all European imperialism as their heritage.

This is the most familiar version of imperialism, the idea of empire on which anti-imperialism most often focuses; and most people are anti-imperialist in this sense nowadays. The energizing myth of empire, however, was carried—and still is carried—by other images more importantly than by these explicitly imperial ones. Of all the implicit images, the most important and most effective is that of Robinson Crusoe, the white man alone (typically on an island) who met all the challenges of nature and barbarism, and by solitary effort and courage rebuilt a miniature replica of his native civilization—and now in his readers' minds rebuilds a pride and faith in our native culture. This extremely widespread myth has been carried, not by our generals and administrators, but by our explorers and adventure-story heroes.

The actual term "Robinson Crusoe" turns up quite often, and in important places, in the thinking (and in the lives) of Tolstoy and Gandhi. In some of those places it is a clear symbol of adventure (and, therefore, in the long run, of empire) which they nevertheless endorse—for both men were enthusiasts for empire in their youth and manhood—and their references to Robinson Crusoe extend out to adventure and adventurers in general. In Tolstoy's case we can point to his early novel, *The Cossacks*, which refers to Cooper's Natty Bumppo (a modified version of Crusoe), and to Tolstoy's adventurous life in the Caucasus (a mountainous area in the southwest of Russia), which is reflected in that novel. In the story "A Prisoner in the Caucasus" (written in 1870), the Russian prisoner of the Muslim tribesmen is a hero of Western technology, who mends clocks and pistols for his primitive captors, and cures them by Western medicine. And after finishing *Anna Karenina*, Tolstoy intended to write a novel about the migrant movement east of the Russian people, with a "Russian Robinson Crusoe of the steppes" (Tolstoy's terms) as central character.

I shall argue that it is important to understand Gandhi as a colonial—that his South African experience of freedom from Hindu cultural rules stimulated his development. In his *Autobiography* he tells of taking his nephews out from India to South Africa, because he believed that enterprising youth ought to emigrate, in order to become self-reliant.[9] And when he describes the poor situation of the Indians in Johannesburg, he says that if they had all been Robinson Crusoes, theirs would have been a different story. But they were just ignorant, pauper agriculturists; and he adds regretfully that we do not know of a single emigrant colony of Robinson Crusoes anywhere in the world.[10] In the Gujarati version of the autobiography he does not use the term "Robinson Crusoe," but when he says "If those who went there had all been men who could transform a desert into a garden or convert dust into wealth . . . ,"[11] he offers his version of the Crusoe idea. He and Tolstoy in their early years both saw Crusoe—and the modern system he represented—as innocently creative.

In late life Tolstoy and Gandhi were anti-imperialist (and, indeed, they were so in their youth concerning some aspects of empire) and so antiadventurist, too. But they did not turn entirely against Robinson Crusoe, or the related myths of self-help (the young Gandhi was a great admirer of Samuel Smiles, who wrote *Self-Help* in 1859) and self-discipline (the young Tolstoy kept a Benjamin Franklin diary for several years, and both were prodigiously hard workers in the Franklin mode). This may seem two-faced on their part; however, images of Crusoe and self-help, though they were the moral fuel of the modern system's engine, were significantly anti-imperialist at the same time. They were opposite in tendency to established and hierarchical grandeur—to an imperial court like the tsar's or the viceroy's or (to pass to religion) to the Kali temple at Calcutta or the Shiva temple at Madurai, or a Russian Orthodox service, all mystery, sacredness, and aesthetic splendor. From this point of view, Defoe, Franklin, and Smiles are natural allies of another seventeenth-century Englishman, Bunyan; and it is worth noting that *Pilgrim's Progress* was a favorite of Gandhi's, and when that book reached Russia (only at the turn of the twentieth century), it seemed to some Tolstoyans akin to Tolstoyism. The modern system did embody, in its origins, a turning away from splendor to virtue, from inheritance to self-help, from mystery to rational moralism. To that heritage Tolstoy and Gandhi stayed loyal. They tried to develop those virtues towards an anti-imperialist culture.

Another myth of empire that was important to Tolstoy and Gandhi was the myth of the martial race. Tolstoy was fascinated by the Cossacks and later by the Chechen, one of the mountain peoples of the Caucasus, about whom he wrote in *Hadji Murat* at the end of his life. Gandhi was fascinated by the Pathans, who represented the opposite of everything he himself stood for in Hindu culture, and in the 1930s and 1940s he wanted to settle down in a Pathan village on the North-West Frontier, to see if he could make his values prevail there. Both these tribal peoples were already favorites with Kipling and his readers. Of course, the fascination felt by Tolstoy and Gandhi was not exactly the same as that felt by British empire administrators, since it was attached to the other, anti-imperialist tendencies. But it was sufficiently like theirs to mark all these people off together in distinction from the modern orthodoxy amongst historians, which does not believe in, or pay heed to, martial races.

By and large, we may say that political radicals, at least of the Marxist kind, do not believe in such categories, and religious radicals do. In this, political radicals are more closely allied to the "serious" novel, and the others to the adventure. The "serious" British novel of the nineteenth century may be represented by *Jane Eyre*, in which the heroine rejects a first suitor, St. John Rivers, a missionary who represents the adventure tradition at its most moral, in favor of Mr. Rochester, who is a hero of erotic values and so represents the opposite. Of Rivers, Jane Eyre says:

> This parlour is not his sphere, I reflected: the Himalayan ridge, or Caffre bush, even the plague-cursed Guinea swamp, would suit him better. Well may he eschew the calm of domestic life; it is not his element: there his faculties stagnate— they cannot develop or appear to advantage. It is in scenes of strife and danger—where courage is proved, and energy exercised and fortitude tasked—that he will speak and move, the leader and superior. A merry child would have the advantage of him on this hearth. He is right to choose a missionary's career—I see it now.[12]

Thus Bronte firmly relegates the adventure virtues to the periphery of the moral world. But she does not deny them; the idea of empire, as the expansion of British power and British beliefs, pervaded the whole of British literature, serious as well as light; and that literature influenced the rest of the world. We can take from Tolstoy examples that represent the hegemony of that example in private life, and from Gandhi, examples of public life.

Tolstoy wrote a short novel called *Domestic Happiness*, or *Family Happiness*, in the first person singular, which plainly owes much to *Jane Eyre*, in both form and content. Moreover, when he courted Valeria Arseneva in 1856, he sent her copies of *Vanity Fair* and *Nicholas Nickleby*, and his moral advice to her was Victorian-English—in fact, it could have come straight out of those novels. She must work hard; if they married, they must avoid debts; they must improve themselves every day: "You will see what a calm and great pleasure it is to say to oneself every day; today I have been better than yesterday."[13] And again: "But in order to give oneself up to the pleasures of music, one must first check oneself, labour, work, and, believe me, there is not a delight in life that can be had without work."[14] When he advises her about personal elegance, he is speaking out of *Jane Eyre*.

> There is another kind of elegance; modest, afraid of the unusual and gaudy, but very particular as to such details as shoes, collars, gloves, cleanliness of the nails, tidiness in doing the hair, etc., about which I am firm as a rock.[15] . . .That is why I am so afraid of marriage, because I regard it too strictly and seriously. . . . I do not love tender and lofty things, I love honest and good things.[16]

His idea of marriage was very English. He called it "family happiness," and when he wrote his short novel with that title, he was foreseeing his own marriage, imagining it in terms of the English ideal. When he did marry, he taught his wife English so that she could read Dickens; they hired an English nurse for their children—Englishwomen allowed more freedom of the right kind, and they understood hygiene better (their nurse introduced cold baths at Yasnaya Polyana); and, according to Stepan Bers, Tolstoy referred to his wife as "The Prime Minister." In 1872, when he was put under temporary house arrest and had to suffer the Tula bureaucrats' interference in his life, he declared he would emigrate. "And away to England, for there alone personal freedom is protected from every kind of outrage, and there alone it is possible to lead a tranquil and independent life."[17] Privacy and marriage were two of the great English ideas.

Gandhi, on the other hand, in his early years in South Africa, often used the term "un-British," and when he heard of the death of Cecil Rhodes, "that true friend of the Empire," he wept. An article of 21 January 1904 begins:

> Sacrifice is the law of life. It runs through and governs every walk of life. . . . No race or community has ever achieved anything without the communal spirit. . . . Earnestness commands success anywhere. It does so much more in the British Dominions.[18]

Earnestness was one of the key Victorian virtues. Whereas in India princes wear diamonds, dress like women, are carried everywhere, and pass their days with wine and opium, in England even the king's grandson eats simple food and goes to school with ordinary boys.[19] "Why do the Dutch and the British both hate us? We believe the root cause is not the colour of our skin, but our general cowardice, our unmanliness and our pusillanimity."[20] That British culture, at least British politics, was uniquely manly, that was a lesson Gandhi never tired of teaching.

On his way to England in 1906 (as a deputy, to represent the Natal Indians in Whitehall), Gandhi wrote an article entitled "Tyler, Hampden and Bunyan," in which he said: "The chains that bind us would certainly snap if even a single person from among us did in South Africa one hundredth part of what these men did for their country. . . . A people that has produced such a trinity—why should it not enjoy self-rule?"[21] And having described the Englishmen aboard his ship, and comparing them with those he had seen in the army during the Boer War, he said the Englishman excelled not only in the enjoyment of wealth but also of power.

> He alone knows how to give orders; and he knows too how to take them. . . . He knows how to earn money and he alone knows how to spend it. . . . The man I observed during the war seems to be an altogether different person now. Then he did all his work himself, trekked over long distances and felt happy with dry bread. Here on board the ship he does not do any work. He presses a button, and an attendant stands before him. . . . All this becomes him, but he does not lose his balance. Like the sea, he can contain all within himself. . . . Why indeed should such a people not rule?[22]

Gandhi even made a notable use of adventure language in beginning his satyagraha movement. "Going to gaol is a great adventure"; so now is the time to stop debating and become firm in resolve. His article, entitled "The Transvaal Struggle," begins with a stanza from a Gujarati poet: "Forward ye all to battle, the bugles sound / Raise the cry and take the plunge, for victory's around"; and then follow five lines that say "through adventure did Alexander / Columbus / Luther / Napoleon / and Scott /" (the last for paying off his huge debts) achieve what they did. Gandhi went on to explain what the adventure was in each case, thus providing a summary of the modern system's adventure ideology.[23]

Later on, when he came to regard both England and Indian imitation of the West as a nightmare, Gandhi reacted against adventure, too. We can see this in an essay entitled "The Curse of Assassination," of 27 December 1928, which is about the influence of adventure models on revolutionary politics.

English books have taught us to applaud as heroic deeds of daring, even of free-booters, villains, pirates and train-wreckers. Newspapers fill columns with exciting stories, real or, in their absence, imaginary, of such deeds. Some of us have successfully learnt this art of applauding as heroic anything adventurous. . . . This cannot be regarded as anything but a bad omen. Surely there is nothing heroic about a cold-blooded robbery. . . . [He is thinking of the means by which Indian terrorists like M. N. Roy financed themselves and impressed their message on the public.] The building of the British Empire is not itself wanting in deeds of valour, adventure and sacrifice. . . . But it is time we began irrespective of nationalities to regard deeds with mean motives or meaner consequences with nothing but horror. . . . I know that this means a new valuation of such terms as heroism, patriotism, religiousness, and the like.[24]

As for Tolstoy, the English ideal of marriage and family happiness is precisely what he attacks in "The Death of Ivan Ilych" and "The Kreutzer Sonata," where he shows that the poetry of eroticism cannot transform even the sexual relation between man and wife, much less the institution of bourgeois marriage, with all its luxury, anxiety, and competitiveness. And the larger idea of English respectability and virtue, of which family happiness was the center, came to seem to him a network of hypocrisy and egotism and moral tepidity in which the soul—as he came to understand it—must stifle. It was from the imitation of England that he wanted to save Russia and—in *Letter to a Hindu*—India. As Lenin said, the future development of Russia was something Tolstoy foresaw in the form of a bogy, which he called "England."

Let us now glance at the political radicals. Lenin was himself an anti-imperialist, of course, but the state he founded was within twenty-five years of the founding as much of an empire as tsarist Russia had ever been. As Billington says in *Fire in the Minds of Men*, the Russian empire absorbed Marxism in much the same way as the Roman empire under Constantine absorbed Christianity. In both cases the new ideology was anti-imperialist in intention, but it was chopped up and swallowed down in a form that renewed the vitality of the old empire. The omen was there to be read in Marx's article "The British Rule in India" in the *New York Tribune*, on 25 June 1853, in which he said:

England, it is true, in causing a social revolution in Hindu-
stan, was actuated only by the vilest interests, and was stupid
in her manner of enforcing them. But that is not the question.
The question is, can mankind fulfil its destiny without a fundamental revolution in the social state of Asia? If not . . .
England . . . was the unconscious tool of history in bringing
about that revolution.[25]

Marx followed Hegel and Montesquieu in seeing "oriental despotism"
as absolutely immobile in history (quite different from the sequence
of development in western societies), and even the villages Gandhi
loved were to Marx the "solid foundation" of that despotism which
"restrained the human mind within the smallest possible compass,
making it the unresisting tool of superstition, enslaving it beneath
traditional rules, depriving it of all grandeur and historical energies."[26]

The idea which succeeded to the old enthusiasm for the modern
system, in the minds of most intellectuals, was an enthusiasm for the
development of political societies according to Marx's scheme, above
all by the means of revolution. It was naturally, therefore, this idea
which claimed the heritage of adventure. The great modern adventure is revolution. Jawaharlal Nehru, Gandhi's heir but the destroyer
of the Gandhian heritage, found the romance of the world embodied
in the French and Russian revolutions more vividly than anywhere
else, and "adventure" was a central word in his vocabulary. In *The
Discovery of India* (1946) he asks what had been the cause of the decay
of the old Hindu empire, and answers: "The urge to adventure and
the over-flowing life which led to vast schemes of distant colonization
. . . all these fade away and a narrow orthodoxy taboos even the cross-
ing of the high seas."[27] The concept of life there is closely related to
adventure (and romance and revolution), and Nehru contrasts this
with Buddhism and Jainism (which were strong influences on Gandhi). "Buddhism and Jainism rather emphasized the abstention from
life, and in certain periods of Indian history there was a running away
from life on a big scale. . . ."[28] Nehru's book ends with a quotation
from Lenin.

Anti-imperialism has therefore often been treacherous; in the
sense that when an imperial structure or ruling group has been displaced as "imperialist," often the new group or structure continues to
direct the old operation under a new banner and a new slogan. Tolstoy
and Gandhi are the greatest of anti-imperialists, to repeat, because
they found the sources and roots of empire outside politics—roots

which include, with varying degrees of importance, almost any kind
of cultural triumphalism, or excited grandeur, or dominance and
splendor in life. So that the only root of effective anti-imperialism is
asceticism. And the only men who in this period said no to life with
any degree of authority are Tolstoy and Gandhi.

Asceticism and Religion

"Saying no to life" is Nietzsche's phrase for Schopenhauer, which he
uses in the preface to his *Genealogy of Morals*; and Nietzsche was one
of the greatest prophets of that moral expansion of the self which
Tolstoy and Gandhi denied. Nietzsche speaks of "the instincts of pity,
self-abnegation, self-sacrifice, which Schopenhauer had gilded, dei-
fied, and projected into a beyond for so long that at last they became
for him 'value-in-itself,' on the basis of which he *said No* to life and
to himself."[29] Of course, it was not only Schopenhauer who valued
those instincts of pity, self-abnegation, and self-sacrifice so highly; the
great world religions, like Christianity, Buddhism, and Hinduism, also
sprang up to deny the world empires, as did Tolstoy and Gandhi.
Nietzsche's Yes to life and to himself was one of the determining
models of modern morality; it has its own radicalism, including aspirations to oppose political empire, but it goes directly counter to religious radicalism.

Of course Tolstoy and Gandhi did not reject every kind of pleasure or every kind of power; but out of the immense range available
to civilized men (that is, to first-class citizens of great empires), they
rejected so great a quantity that there is a qualitative difference between
them and other political philosophers.

Tolstoy's religion was essentially kenotic, self-emptying. Amongst
the prayers he composed in his diary, one finds many exclamations
like, "Help me, Lord, to purify myself spiritually, so that you may live
in me, that I may live by you"; or, "Help me, help me, my God, before
I die, to live only before you, always with you and by you." In his
book of philosophy, *On Life*, Tolstoy puts this idea more theoretically.
"His animal personality is for man the spade given to a rational being
to dig with, and in digging to blunt and sharpen and use up. . . .
'Whoever shall seek to save his life shall lose it.' "[30] An anecdote from
his biography will make clear his desire to become a *yurodivi*—a "fool
in Christ." On 30 June 1908, Tolstoy went to pay a call on a blind

peasant, called Rozov, who he knew had called him a hypocrite. Tolstoy said he held no grudge for being insulted, shook Rozov's hand, and left the house to get into the carriage, where his wife was waiting. (It would not have been her kind of visit.) But Rozov followed him out angrily, saying he'd been temporarily confused, and had taken Tolstoy's hand by mistake, for he would never shake hands with such a scoundrel, a pharisee, a hypocrite, and so on. Sonia was furious at the scene, and commanded the coachman to drive on; Tolstoy, however, hung out of the window as they left, saying he loved Rozov and crying: "Oh, if only it could be like this with everyone."[31] He was glad to be a fool.

Morally, he believed in strenuous effort. In "The First Step," an essay of 1892 that was one of the first things Gandhi read by him, Tolstoy says that to be good without fasting is as impossible as to walk without standing. And he generalizes the point by saying that "consecutiveness" (steady moral self-discipline) has been forgotten because Christianity, as it displaced paganism, discredited all the pagan virtues, teaching infinite perfection in the place of finite. We want the higher qualities without the lower, love without self-renunciation, humanitarianism without abstinence. Socrates called abstinence the first virtue; but nowadays we think we can and must develop our passions, and so become dependent on hundreds of habits.

Thus, Tolstoy's stress was on negation, on discipline, on death. We should congratulate our friends on being ill because only in suffering is the spiritual world born; and in his diary on 31 December 1894 he wrote that the young, who in other ways agreed with him, always avoided his basic idea (they called it exaggerated) that one should consume less, demand less, diminish oneself. To his closest disciple, Chertkov, he said: "[T]he very best state for one's soul is—not to be guilty but to feel guilty."[32]

We find exactly the same stress in Gandhi. Suffering is the badge of the human race, not the sword; after seeing a beautiful crucifix at the Vatican in 1931, he wrote: "I saw there at once that nations like individuals could only be made through the agony of the Cross and in no other way."[33] Like Tolstoy, he relied on prayer. "Prayer has been the saving of my life. Without it I should have been a raving lunatic long ago."[34]

Like Tolstoy, Gandhi was not interested in the historical Jesus, or the historical Krishna. Tolstoy hoped to have it demonstrated that Jesus was a myth, and Gandhi said the Jesus of history was not the same as the Jesus whom Christians adore. The mystical incarnations were living ideas—more real than earthly existences. Religion could

never be based on history, for if it were so based, faith could be
undermined.

Gandhi, too, was in love with death. Pyarelal tells us that after
prayers at the Ashram one day he told the others how much he looked
forward to the day when they would fall before a shower of bullets—
when the trees around them would remain alone as witnesses to the
supreme sacrifice. And in 1924, having given a vivid description of
some starving people, their lives ebbing away, he concluded: "They
seem to mock for us the life we live."[35] The knowledge of death
modifies our experience of life. He objected equally to the West's
recklessness about sacrificing life in war and its anxiety about pre-
serving life in sickness.

His stress is on renunciation and the acceptance of deprivation.
"God created nothing finer than the Hindu widow [who does not
remarry]. . . . Self-control has been carried by Hinduism to the greatest heights, and, in a widow's life, it reaches perfection." (Nehru, on
the other hand, preferred the active virtues, as he said, and found it
very incongruous when a journalist compared his melancholy distinction with that of a Hindu widow.)

Gandhi told a friend:

> You were quite right in not coming to Madras [to see him].
> Love must be patient and humble. It is the rich and leisurely
> who can afford to be demonstrative in their love. We humble
> folks have naturally a different and better method of showing
> love. True love acts when it must, meanwhile it grows silently
> but steadily.[36]

This means a renunciation of personality, of heart. Gandhi's closest
religious disciple, Vinoba, writes in *The Steadfast Wisdom* that a palmist
told him he had no heartline on his palm.

> "God be praised," I responded, "if that is so." In my opinion
> a man need have only intelligence, buddhi. It is better not
> to have a heart of the kind described. The heart must be
> assimilated into the mind and lifted out of the unstable flux
> of uncertainty. The heart is a bundle of desires . . . like wrap-
> pings round the heart. Remove them one by one and the
> bundle will disappear entirely.[37]

This religion, then, cuts very deep, to the root of personality
itself; it reaches out to repudiate the heart of civilization. Tolstoy's

son Lev tells us that on one of his visits to Yasnaya Polyana, Turgenev condemned Christianity as fit only for old women and declared himself for civilization. Tolstoy of course made the opposite choice, saying that civilization would burst one day like a waterspout; and in many other places he described it as a bubble, an illusion, which holds men captive in a trance of evil. To free oneself or others from that trance, one must destroy the self. Thus, Tolstoy and Gandhi are enemies of humanism; for them, humanism is a flowering of sensibility possible only to the ruling class of empire. Both laid their axes to the tree of humanist pride—and for that reason they are themselves accused by humanists of spiritual pride. In fact, they did indeed aim at greatness, as much as the generals, industrialists, and dictators, but it was a different kind of greatness—of the soul, not of the self.

The soul is an old-fashioned concept with which we are uncomfortable today. To use modern terms, the soul is something irreconcilably alien to the body, its perceptions always being betrayed by the senses; the self is something inextricably involved with the body, its perceptions always imbibed through and confided to the senses. (The young Tolstoy believed in the self, the old Tolstoy—and Gandhi—in the soul.)

If this dichotomy is accepted, it becomes possible to say that Tolstoy and Gandhi said no to the life of the self—to all those appetites and ambitions—while in the life of the soul they pursued greatness. There is nothing paradoxical in this, according to the traditional consciousness of spiritual religion. Today, however, we have lost contact with that tradition because our consciousnesses are shaped by the self, not the soul. So many people accuse Tolstoy and Gandhi of pride and deny that they are religious at all. Are they not rather moralists? Indeed, it is true that they belonged to no church and acknowledged no theology, no orthodoxy, no authority. The mystical incarnation idea of religion—the stress on the Church—represented by T. S. Eliot can be seen from this point of view as an extension into religious terms of this cult of the self, including the body. (Eliot's kind of religion notably excluded Tolstoy and Gandhi.) It is therefore necessary to justify using the term *religious* for them so portentously.

Their religion was not theological or ecclesiastical but existential. Their sense of the divine was aroused by something they encountered at the further limit of their own experience—their moral experience— not by religious mysteries or miracles, not by temples and rituals, not by creeds and theologies—and not primarily by the beauty of Nature. But that sense of the divine was something they persistently aroused in themselves, and something to which they responded dutifully once it was aroused. They spoke to the Lord and the Lord spoke to them, even though they knew that the divine is not a person. "God is not a person, and so I cannot love him," said Tolstoy; "But I am a person, and so I must."[38] And Gandhi told a friend, "I know your love. God does not live somewhere in the sky. For me, pure love like yours is God, and it is such love that gives me strength to undertake yajnas like the present one."[39] One of Gandhi's most famous formulas was that "Truth is God," and "Satyagraha," his kind of political action, means "Firmness in Truth." In these uses truth means the action that is adequate to the situation, and the situation includes your moral responsibility within it. To be firm in the truth is to transform that situation by bringing out its hidden moral dimension and, by pressing that upon all the other people involved, to overwhelm the resistance vested in their political and economic interests and categories. The Truth is the face of God insofar as we can know it—a mere glimmering, at best, but recognizable as something other than oneself, other than one's own interested reflection, if the scrutiny is serious enough.

Their religion reached to the divine in the depths of man's reason and love, but it was anthropocentric and scarcely theological at all. "Is there a God?" Tolstoy asked in his diary in 1906. "I don't know. I know there is a law of my spiritual being. The source and principle of that law I call God."[40] Yet this piety is also transcendent, not immanent, and so Tolstoy and Gandhi are not religious in the sense of most of the great heretics from Christianity in the last century. Theirs is no cult of the erotic, or the ecological, or the feminine principle, but of that furthest intensification of the moral we call the spiritual. It develops itself by the denial of appetite and the ordinary ego. This religion of spirituality is at the heart of most of the great traditional religions and has manifested itself in a variety of figures; there are the founding fathers of new religions, like Jesus Christ, and the faithful adherents of those religions grown old, like Dorothy Day; and then there are people like Tolstoy and Gandhi, who belong to neither of those categories, being schismatics (they quarreled with their churches but not with the spirituality they preached) but who are equally heroes of religion, achievers of great religious feats, and inspirers of faith in others.

II
Russia and India

Tolstoy and Gandhi were both born in enormous and politically unified land-masses. India was habitually called a subcontinent, as distinct
from a country, and Russia has always been seen, from the perspective
of the nation states of Europe, as colossal and uniform. (Europe feels
itself to have a complex geological structure, an indented sea-line,
and a moderate climate, to correspond to its plural nationalism and
democracy.[1]) At least we can say that this birth offered the two men
a different destiny from birth in Denmark or Java or Iceland or Korea.

They were, moreover, both born citizens of great empires; and
in Gandhi's case I don't mean primarily the British but the Hindu
empire. Although it is true that only the British had territorially united
all of India under one rule, Hindus were, like the Chinese, an imperial
culture. They had been a colonizing people, and their culture had
established itself in many parts of Southeast Asia, the East Indies, and
Africa. Again, the two destinies, and even the ideologies they came
to, might have been different if the men had been born in a tribe or
in one of the kingdoms of Africa or the South Seas. And both countries
were on the periphery of the modern world system, being neither
core states like England or France, nor outside it like China or Japan
before 1850.

A corollary worth noting is that Russia and India were both subject to catastrophes (some natural, some man-made) for which the
core countries had no longer any equivalent. Their towns and villages
were subject to terrible fires (we hear of Tolstoy fighting fires in his
own village); to epidemics like cholera and plague (Gandhi fought
such epidemics in both South Africa and India), the scientific treatment of which was resisted by the sufferers; and to earthquakes and
famine (both men fought famine on a large scale). For Europeans
and Americans such disasters are not a frequent feature of experience,
and their way of thought differs correspondingly; it has a narrower

range of expectation—of disasters—and a narrower sense of reality, one which excludes more possibilities as exaggerated or morbid. It is only nowadays, when the expectation of calamity (of nuclear anni-hilation) again hangs permanently over our minds, that their extrem-ism may again seem plausible or even authoritative to us.

The forces that Tolstoy and Gandhi represented, and those they combatted, operated right across the globe and affected huge masses of people. The Russian and the British were the world's two greatest empires. The Russian, by the end of Tolstoy's life, exceeded 8,660,000 square miles, or a quarter of the land surface of the globe. Its pop-ulation was 74 million in 1859, 120 million in 1897, and 150 million in 1906. The British empire in 1897 was 11,000,000 square miles (ninety-one times the area of Great Britain itself) and its population was 372,000,000. (The Roman Empire in its prime had 120,000,000 people, in 2,500,000 square miles.) Although Christian, the British Empire was also the world's greatest Muslim power (Russia was the second greatest) and of course the greatest Hindu power. These empires had many enemies, internal as well as external—it was the Bolsheviks who brought down the Russian government. But the empire they merely inherited and expanded—the empire found in an anti-imperial ideology its needed infusion of new blood. The principle of empire itself found in Tolstoy and Gandhi its most outright assailants and deadly denouncers.

The Russian and British empires were, by ordinary nineteenth-century standards, quite opposite in character. Russia's was a conti-nental empire, Britain's oceanic. Russia's was a despotism, Britain's a constitutional democracy. Russia was a military power, Britain a naval. The peace-time strength of the Russian army was estimated in 1911 as 1,100,000 men; the war-time strength as 4,500,000. The British could muster, even including the Indian Army, only 400,000 men. Russia was much less fully mechanized and industrialized; the 1911 *Encyclopaedia Britannica* pointed out that the artillery and train service of the Russian army was so inadequate that the boasted 4,500,000 would probably amount to only 2,750,000 in actual war. Meanwhile, the British navy had 330 ships in 1897, with 92,000 sailors; while the French had 95 ships, the Russians 86, the Germans 68, and the United States 56.

At that time all other navies, both military and mercantile, were pale shadows of the British. Thirteen foreign navies used British guns, for instance, and half of the world's shipping flew the Red Ensign; in absolute terms, that was 13,500,000 tons, or twice as much as twenty years before. In 1896 and 1897, 1,000 new British ships were launched, James Morris tells us in *Pax Britannica*.[2] Of every 1,000 tons of shipping that passed through the Suez Canal, 700 were British, 75 German, 63 French, 43 Dutch, 19 Italian, and 2 American. The British Empire was so naval and oceanic that it was not to be estimated in terms of square miles of land occupied. It was a matter of islands, fortresses, and coaling stations strung out along great routes; for instance, the route east, by way of Gibraltar, Malta, Aden, Singapore, and Hong Kong. And it was a matter of investments and influence: Argentina was run on British capital, its agriculture, its industry, its railways, its telephones, and all communications; Siam's foreign trade was all in foreign hands; the Imperial Bank of Persia was British; the advisers to the Sultan of Morocco were British; and so on.

The Russian Empire covered one-fourth of the earth's surface and included a hundred nationalities. Many groups, both national and religious, were excluded from society's centers of privilege and power, or were severely subordinated. This was true not only of the Jews and the Old Believers, of the Poles and the Central Asian tribes, but even of the main agents of Russian imperialism, the Cossacks. Just so in India, the hunters and gatherers who had never known a Neolithic Revolution still lived in the hills and forests (it is estimated that there are still thirty million of them), and even Hindu society proper is very unequal. The Chandalas are supposed to keep far from caste Hindus, to approach them only with shouts of warning, to stick black feathers in their hair (blackening even the head, the center of all honor), to eat off broken dishes, to keep black swine around their houses, and to hang rags of meat to dry from their roofs. (In compensation they are allowed—like the Cossacks—freedom from the moral and cultic prohibitions that hem in the caste Hindus, and freedom for singing and dancing and love-making.) Tolstoy and Gandhi were both born into positions of privilege within these structures of dominance and oppression, and were anxious about the obligations they had thus incurred.

The two great differences between their countries were first that Russia was a hybrid state, half in the modern system and half out, by territory, a quarter European and three-quarters Asian; and, second, that Russia was ruled by Russians, India by Englishmen. The conflict that Gandhi could dramatize as being between India and England (though he was clear as to how many Indians already belonged to the modern system with their minds) had to be felt by Tolstoy as being between Russian peasants and Russian rulers. And so, when we put the two countries side by side, we shall, in treating India, sometimes put forward English names and ideas to compare with the Russians, because the ruling class of India was English.

In *The Icon and the Axe* James H. Billington suggests that these two objects were the primary symbols of traditional Russia.[3] The axe stood for fighting, for building, and for living in the forest, with its dangers of fire and wild animals. (The axe is to Russia what the spinning wheel is to India; out of the forest came the furs which were Russia's typical clothing.) The icon was the primary work of art; Russia was not a literary but a visual and aural culture. The Vladimir Mother of God was its great image, and Andrei Rublev (1370–1430) its great artist.

More exactly, these were the symbols of the Russian frontier. The equivalents for Russian town life were the cannon and the bell. By the sixteenth century, Russia had made the biggest cannon and the biggest bells in Europe. A hundred cannon were fired to announce the anointment of a new tsar, and Boris Godunov's bell-tower dominated the Kremlin. But the biggest bell was too big to hang, and the largest cannon too broad to fire. Modern Russia was to exhibit the same pattern—rivaling and outdoing the West above all in military technology, but exaggerating—because it refused to import the other ideas which in the West went along with the technology. A recent historian ends her study of the Russian middle class by saying: "It is Russia's greatest tragedy that the tools of industrial progress were placed in her hands before she had formulated the concepts which would properly direct their operation."[4]

For India, the equivalent images seem to be two reciprocal rhythms. The first is that of pollution and purification, which is so central to Hinduism and which makes the social procedures of, for instance, eating, so elaborate. The sprinkling of water, the morning ablutions, the holiness of the Ganges, the burning of corpses, the sacrificial fire, which is the heart of the Brahmin religion: all this is purification. And it is the fear of pollution that expresses itself in the physical distance people preserve from other people, the strong feeling against meat and blood, the ritual separation of castes, and, most dreadfully, the excommunication of pariahs. Hindus are forever becoming polluted, by their own and other bodies, and forever having to purify themselves.

The second reciprocal rhythm is that of making and unmaking cloth. "Making" here does not mean only the spinning and weaving but the wrapping and unwrapping of sari or dhoti about the body (cloth and clothes are the same thing in traditional India). And "unmaking" does not mean unraveling, but the beating clean of clothes on river rocks. Always in India one is aware of cloth coming into shape and being beaten flat again, being worn out. This of course gives another dimension to the meaning of Gandhi's spinning, and reminds us of another primary process that the West has locked behind factory walls and lost touch with. Both reciprocal rhythms can be seen at once in the women washing clothes on the banks of the Ganges—or any other river.

In both countries, writers comment on the irregularity with which work is done and duties performed; on the ease and indulgence with which young children are treated; on the imprecision with numbers— in India Carstairs cites "five, seven, ten" as a characteristic number; and on the easy gaiety of the lower castes: noisily demonstrative, Carstairs says, they get drunk, fire off guns, men and women dance together, and husbands and wives express their affection in public, in ways strictly forbidden to upper castes.[5]

Tolstoy thought a lot about India, as his *Letter to a Hindu* shows. It was a part of his general concern for the Orient in the last part of his life, when he wanted to save the rest of the world from the culture of the modern system. And Gandhi thought a lot about Russia, not only Lenin's but the tsar's, while he was in South Africa; partly because many of his friends there were Jews with Russian family connections. Thus an issue of *Indian Opinion* in 1905 makes a comparison of the people of Russia with those of India, in a paragraph on Gorky. And later an article on the 1905 revolution, entitled "Russia and India," says: "The power of the Viceroy is no way less than that of the Tsar. . . ."[6] The difference, it continues, is that our oppressors are more gradual and moderate than theirs; and therefore the Russians, foolishly but heroically, become anarchists and conspirators, even the girls. Russia would remain for Gandhi—as for all Indian revolutionaries—the mother country of terrorism.

Primarily, therefore, he had a strong sense of the difference between the two empires. In 1907 he quotes an English supporter as saying that the Asiatic Registration Bill (a political measure against the Indians by the white settlers) could never become a law of the British Empire—could be passed only in Russia. He saw England as standing for freedom (however ineffectually, so far as Indians in South Africa went) and Russia as standing for despotism. This was how the Russians also saw things. Alexander Herzen, in exile in London, looked back on his boyhood and saw it in terms of a personal oppression by the tsar, Nicholas I (who reigned from 1826 to 1855, the period of Tolstoy's boyhood and youth).

Nicholas—reflected in every inspector, every school-director, every tutor and guardian—confronted the boy at school, in the street, in church, even to some extent in the parental home, stood and gazed at him with pewtery, unliving eyes, and the child's heart ached and grew faint with fear that those eyes might detect some budding of free thought, some human feeling. And who knows what chemical change in the composition of a child's blood and nervous system is caused by intimidation, by the checking or dissimulation of speech, by the repression of feeling.[7]

And this was more than a matter of personal despotism. In Russia the state had always come first. As Valentine T. Bill says, "It was not society which created the state of Muscovy; it was the state which created and controlled Muscovite society."[8] Under Nicholas the civil service grew enormously. The provincial Government of Kostroma had an advisory staff of seven in 1829, but needed fifty-four in 1848. In Voronezh the equivalent group grew from nine in 1829 to fifty-four in 1862. (The population grew by about fifty percent in those years.) During Nicholas' reign the total staff of provincial and district governments grew fourfold to eightfold, and there was a corresponding growth in the bureaucratic center of St. Petersburg. Taxes soared, and most of the income went to pay for the army, which in 1840 absorbed fifty percent of the budget.[9]

Tolstoy wrote to his cousin Alexandrine in 1857, having just returned to Russia from a holiday in Europe and freedom.

If you had seen, as I did one week, how a lady in the street beat her girl with a stick, how the district police officer got me to say I would send him a cart-load of hay before he would provide my man with a legal permit, how, before my eyes, an official almost beat a sick old man of 70 to death because the official had got tangled up with him, how the village elder, wishing to be of service to me, punished a gardener who had been on a drinking spree not only by having him beaten, but by sending him barefoot over the stubble to watch over a herd, and was rejoiced to see that the gardener's feet were covered with cuts—if you had seen all this, and a whole lot more besides, you would believe me that life in Russia is continuous, unending toil and a struggle with one's feelings.[10]

And two months later he wrote:

> It makes me laugh to recall how I used to think—and as you
> still appear to think—that it's possible to create your own
> happy and honest little world, in which you can live in peace
> and quiet, without mistakes, repentance or confusion, doing
> only what is good in an unhurried and precise way. Ridic-
> ulous! *It's impossible*, Granny.[11]

Within the modern system, Russia was the shadow counterpart
of England; one might say that it had rejected the white magic of the
system, which was tied up with various kinds of freedom for the
individual citizen, and had appropriated its black magic of power,
including violence. The white magic, displayed by England, included
free trade and free elections; freedom of the press, of worship, and
of speech; experimental science; and the possibility of social mobility
and of sceptical philosophy. In the core countries, all this seemed
indissolubly tied to their prosperity, their world dominance, their
empire. But the Russian state saw the technology as their true secret,
and as something that could be acquired without the ideology. (One
might cite the great explosives, gunpowder, dynamite, and then nuclear
fission, and the consequent guns, cannon, and bombs, as the sinister
aspects of this technology—the modern black magic.) The Russians
as much as the English had always seen this. Chernyshevsky wrote in
1846:

> Is our mission just to have an army of a million and a half,
> and the power, like the Huns and Mongols, to conquer Europe
> if we so desire? Should we not pity the existence of such
> peoples? They have lived as if they had not lived. They passed
> like a storm, destroying, burning, imprisoning, plundering
> everything—and that is all. Is our mission too to be of this
> kind? To be omnipotent from the military and political point
> of view, and nothing as regards any other, superior aspect
> of national life?[12]

By the standards of nineteenth-century thought, "national life"
was holy, but everything to do with "empire" was unholy. So the
Russian Empire was a proof of the tyrannical and anachronistic character of the tsarist state, and the British Empire was an anomaly, an

accident. The young Gandhi believed in the British Empire because he believed it to be an empire-that-was-not-an-empire.

The respectable political process was nation-building, the progress of the rest of the world following the path blazed by England and France and the countries of Northwest Europe—the countries at the heart of the modern world system. This had been achieved by Germany and Italy in the second half of the nineteenth century, and was helped along by the British and others in countries like Greece and the various Balkan and Middle Eastern possessions of old-fashioned empires like Austro-Hungary and Turkey. This was the process Gandhi engaged in, in South Africa and then in India, expecting to be helped along, and indeed rewarded, by the British themselves, once he had demonstrated the Indians' worthiness—their readiness for nation-building and self-government.

The exemplary success of the modern system, in both economic and political terms, was the United States of America. This country seemed to everyone a living demonstration of the anti-imperialist character of the modern system and of the possibility of a nonimperial greatness. Even reactionaries like the Russian Pobedonostsev thought that America represented the ideal politics, though he continued to insist that it was not for Russians—they were not good enough for it. The Spanish-American War in 1898, and the other beginnings of American imperialism, tarnished the American image after 1900, but it continued to glow. Both Tolstoy and Gandhi were inspired by Thoreau, Garrison, Ballou, and other figures of nineteenth-century New England, and both found many of their most devoted admirers among Americans.

Perhaps the most striking example of nineteenth-century Russia's character as an autocracy was its institution of military colonies, which it inherited from the previous century but which grew under the liberal tsar, Alexander I, and persisted under Nicholas. Military colonies were communities of soldiers, organized and disciplined along army lines, doing agricultural work and including their wives and children—in effect, breeding grounds for recruits. Each marriage was supposed to produce one child a year, and fines were imposed on those who were infertile, or produced still-borns or daughters. By 1824 such villages supplied a quarter of the Russian army's soldiers, and later, the labor for factories and railroad building. Whole lives and generations were lived within a military framework. These colonies were not unique to Russia, but were on a larger scale here than elsewhere, and they were of course more totally opposed to liberal ideas (embodied in English society) than anything else in Russia. They were a caricature of the caste system—Cossacks without their heritage of freedom. (They were abolished in 1857, after Russia had been defeated in the Crimea.) And especially associated with them was the general and minister Aleksei Andreevich Arakcheev, regarded by the gentry in general and Tolstoy in particular as a monster of cruelty— a "wild beast," Tolstoy called him—who legitimized every brutality by his personal devotion to the tsar.

Of the various schemes of ideas abroad in the young Tolstoy's Russia, and important in understanding him, the one most closely connected with state power is that which has been called "Conservative Nationalism."[13] Its slogan was "Autocracy, Orthodoxy, and Nationality," and it meant to unify the variety of the tsar's subjects in loyalty to him and in Russianness. It is particularly associated with the reign of Nicholas I, which covers the first twenty-seven years of Tolstoy's life.

These ideas were close to those of the Slavophiles, who glorified the people of Russia and wanted to defend them against the modernization introduced from above by the state—the bureaucracy. (Tolstoy was generally sympathetic to the Slavophiles, though not a member of their group.) But *they* were *not* adherents of the state. Thus, these two groups gradually drew apart in the 1850s, but both were equally opposed to the Westernizers, who wanted Russia to follow the example of Western Europe.

One of the leading Slavophiles, Konstantin Aksakov (1817–60) wrote about the Russian national character, saying that the Russian people was not a nation; it was humanity; that is, it stood outside the modern scheme of nation-building. This idea both excused Russia for its shortcomings as a modern state (its multiplicity of populations, and its technical and political backwardness) and gave it a higher and more spiritual vocation. Another Slavophile, Khomyakov, said Russians were like Germans, a people who could appreciate and appropriate other people's achievements—absorb them rather than produce their own— as Germany, for instance, had discovered or invented Shakespeare. (It must be remembered that at this time Germany was not a unified state but was in full cultural flowering, as represented by Goethe and Schiller, Kant and Hegel, and that it was the next state westwards from Russia—the last one before Russia to undergo its westernizing transformation. It was an important model for Russia to study.)

An important belief held in common by the Slavophiles and the late Tolstoy, was their judgment against Peter the Great, the modernizing tsar, whom the Romanovs, and Nicholas in particular, claimed as their personal sponsor. For Konstantin Aksakov, Peter was the titan who introduced evil into Russian history, and his city of St. Petersburg was the image of legalism and compulsion. Tolstoy, too, opposed St. Petersburg to Moscow, and made much of the opposition. (He had private, family reasons to feel a strong and guilty identification with Peter the Great, for the founder of the Tolstoy line had been a protégé of the tsar's and had done some of his dirty work.)

In the 1860s these ideas were gradually displaced by others, essentially similar but labeled *pochva*, the soil, and *pochvenniki*, those who believed in the soil or rootedness. (Unlike the Slavophiles, the new men did not have to believe in the aristocracy or in the official church.) Amongst them we find Dostoevsky, the critic Apollon Grigorev, Tolstoy's great friend of the 1870s, Nikolai Strakhov, and—more distantly—Tolstoy himself. In the essay "Russian Literature in 1851," Grigorev defined a historical criticism that understood literature to be the organic product of an age and a people; and in the late 1850s he wrote about nations: "Each such organism is self-contained in itself, is in itself necessary, has in itself full power to live according to laws peculiar to it. . . ."[14] *War and Peace* was to be a great example of organic literature that reflected the organic nationality of the Russian people. These Russian ideas were part of a wider resistance movement, reaching all through the modern system, which built up around concepts like society (and culture) in opposition to the state (and civilization).

In intellectual life, the Westernizing tendency was led by figures like Turgenev in literature, the older Solovev in history, and Chicherin, briefly a friend of Tolstoy. In the 1860s their interpretation of politics and culture was challenged and their leadership usurped by the radicals, led by Chernyshevsky; in the 1880s, by the Marxists, led by Plekhanov. All these groups believed that Russians were like other people, or would be once they underwent the beneficent influences of modern civilization and culture. Though Tolstoy always stood apart from both of these forces, he had more points of contact and agreement with the former, the Slavophiles and the nationalists.

If we turn now to India, we might find the equivalent for Tsar Nicholas' brutal oppression in the overweening racism of British imperialists like Sir Francis Younghusband, the invader of Tibet. An example of his attitude is quoted by R. A. Huttenback:

No European can mix with non-Christian races without feeling his moral superiority over them. He feels, from the first contact with them, that whatever may be their relative positions from an intellectual point of view, he is stronger morally than they are. And facts show that this feeling is a true one.

It is not because we are any cleverer than the natives of India, because we have more brains or bigger heads than they have, that we rule India, but because we are stronger morally than they are. Our superiority over them is not due to mere sharpness of intellect, but to the higher moral nature to which we have attained in the development of the human race.[15]

This racism grew more virulent in the nineteenth century, but already in 1780 Robert Orme had described the Indian as "the most enervated inhabitant of the globe." He continues: "He shudders at the sight of blood, and is of a pusillanimity only to be excused and accounted for by the great delicacy of his configuration. This is so slight as to give him no chance of opposing with success the onset of an inhabitant of more northern regions."[16] We can also look at examples relating to the position of the Indians in South Africa, where Gandhi encountered this racism, most painfully. Lionel Curtis wrote in a letter to the *Times* on 4 May 1907: "Englishmen who believe in the excellence of their civilization cannot really desire to see their Empire used as a means for propagating the society and institutions of the East in new countries, to the exclusion of their own."[17] The Convention of Associations of East Africa declared, " . . . whereas these people follow in all things a civilization which is eastern and in many ways repugnant to ours . . . [we must] avoid a betrayal to the Asiatic of a section of the African peoples whose destinies have fallen into our hands. . . ."[18] Finally, the report of the Economic Commission called the Indian "not a wholesome influence because of his incurable repugnance to sanitation and hygiene. The moral depravity of the Indian is equally damaging. . . . [He brings with him] the worst vices of the East."[19]

England knew a more reputable kind of imperialism, in which Gandhi believed. For instance, on Empire Day, 1906, Gandhi wrote that the ideal of empire is "of producing, as John Ruskin puts it, 'as many as possible full-breathed, bright-eyed, and happy-hearted human creatures.' "[20] Another such imperialist was editor W. T. Stead, who publicly opposed England in the Boer War; Gandi read Stead's *Pall Mall Gazette* regularly when he was a student in London. There was to be much imperialist writing in the 1890s: Sir Charles Dilke's two-volume *Problems of Greater Britain* in 1890, Milner's *England in Egypt* in 1892, and Sir Alfred Lyall's *Rise and Expansion of British Dominion in India* in 1894. All of these books were very widely read, and they exerted a pressure upon non-Europeans—especially those who were subjects of the British Empire, like Gandhi—which can be compared with the pressure of conservative nationalism in Russia.

There was, moreover, a likeness in the pressure of the bureaucracy in both countries. Although England was famous for its liberal
freedoms, India was famous for its civil service—and its military service; the two were conjoined in the famous "Civil and Military Services," which can remind one of the portentous ring of "service" in
the tsar's mouth. Many things were done in the empire that would
have shocked the homeland (until they were introduced there from
the empire), and in India these were typically elaborations of administration and police control. As Morris says in *Pax Britannica*, "India
was different in kind from the rest of the Empire. . . . It was so immense
that it really formed, with Britain itself, the second focus of a dual
power."[21] We have to grasp that political ellipse imaginatively, in order
to compare the British Empire with the Russian.

There were no military colonies in India, but a very distressing
aspect of British rule there, from the Indian point of view, nonviolent
or not, was the Indian Army, which was a British creation. This army
was a large part of the empire's military strength, for it had huge
reserves—the 350,000 men in the armies of the native princes could
be called on in an emergency. Even in peacetime, Gandhi calculated,
the 70,000 British troops in India plus the 140,000 Indians cost the
country £70 million a year—money raised, moreover, by taxing, and
so legitimizing, the trade in opium and toddy (palm wine).[22] Within
six months of the outbreak of war in 1914, seven divisions of Indian
infantry and two of cavalry (plus two brigades) were sent overseas—
altogether 200,000 men. On other occasions, those troops moved into
different countries (for instance, China) and were used "shamelessly,"
as Gandhi said, "to crush other people's freedom. Indeed, India is
the key to the exploitation of the Asiatic and other non-European
races of the earth."[23]

The army was in a sense even less a Hindu institution than it was
an Indian. The soldiers were predominantly Muslims and Sikhs, with
special groups of Rajputs, Dogras, Mahrattas, and Gurkas. Practically
none came from that educated middle class that took part in nationalist politics. But there were seemingly inexhaustible numbers of
recruits in the northern provinces where the martial races lived. In a
way which can again remind us of Russia—of the Russian character
of this part of the British Empire—this army was more pliable to its
commanders' purposes than the British Army proper, for no Mutiny
Act or Members of Parliament defended the soldiers against low pay
or severe punishments.

Finally, it should be noted that although the British had abolished
slavery—and taken a world-lead in doing so—they had subsequently

instituted, as far as Indians went, a kind of serfdom comparable with the Russian. In fact, Hugh Tinker's book on the export of Indian labor overseas between 1880 and 1920 is titled *A New System of Slavery*.[24] In his introduction Tinker says:

> Only gradually did the accumulation of evidence produce the conclusion that indenture and other forms of servitude did, indeed, replicate the actual conditions of slavery. It became apparent that for a period of seventy or eighty years British statesmen and administrators were being confronted with evidence that the planting interest was exploiting Indian workers in ways which could not be tolerated by a decent, humane society; and yet they continued to assure themselves that these wrongs were mere abuses and irregularities which could be amenable to reform.[25]

Between one and two million Indians emigrated to tropical countries between 1830 and 1870, according to Tinker. In the mid-1850s a heavy annual migration to the Caribbean began, and the passage death-rate shot up.[26] About 525,000 indentured men went to the French and British sugar colonies between 1842 and 1870.[27] (Another million and a half went to Ceylon, where about a quarter of a million settled down.) Indentured Indians were often put straight into the Nigger Yards and Camps des Noirs just vacated by the slaves. "The plantation meant the barracks, the huts where the workers spent their scanty hours of rest; and above all the canefields, where the fronded cane waved, as end-product of back-aching toil under the burning sun; and the factory, where the juice was distilled into sugar and rum."[28] Essentially the same things happened in Natal, where Gandhi encountered them, only a little later.

The British Empire did not have its Westernizers, much less its Slavophiles, but there was a conflict of policy towards India which could be compared with that. The utilitarians and evangelicals had Westernizing plans for India. The presence of the British in India was, as Gandhi said, an ideological as much as a political aggression. Even the best of them were determined to change India—for the good as they understood that. This is confirmed by George D. Bearce in *British Attitudes Towards India 1784–1858*. In his introduction Bearce writes: "Antipathy in Britain towards the political and social institutions of India was as much a general disapproval of the medieval and aristocratic society passing away as a failure to understand and appreciate institutions peculiar to India."[29] This disapproval, however, was not felt by all Englishmen. Notably the English aristo-military caste responded appreciatively to the spectacle of the princes and also to the plight of the peasants. (Tod's *Annals of Rajasthan* [1829] is an early expression of that appreciation.)

Representative of the "Westernizers" was Lord William Bentinck, who went out as governor general in 1828, and who worked on reforms with Macaulay and Sir Charles Metcalfe (acting governor general in 1835–36). Bentinck avoided wars and was reluctant to annex new lands. He was a Radical in home politics and, as Bearce describes, ". . . a man of simple tastes, sober dress, and Christian propriety. He looked like a Pennsylvania Quaker . . . , conducted himself with the simplicity of a middle-class gentleman. Calcutta society, which preferred imperial grandeur, and the sense of British superiority, found his modesty and pacifism rather dull."[30] Whenever such reformers found their programs to be not working, they blamed India's lack of a middle class; and they put their hope for the future in the development of modern technology. Bentinck said in 1834, "I look to steam navigation as the great engine of working this moral improvement."[31] Lord Auckland also proclaimed his faith in steam, and William Cabell, a secretary for the Board of Control of the East India Company, wrote in 1837 that the steamboat would "effect a complete moral revolution"[32] once it was launched on Indian rivers. (Naturally, steam was only representative; they also hoped for much from indigo and coffee plantations, cotton mills, iron foundries, and coal mines.) The Westernizers of the 1860s in Russia had spoken more often of science than of technology, but they had had similarly extravagant hopes.

The opposing party among the British in India at its best loved India and appreciated its culture (Kipling is a good though late example) and at its worst was aggressively imperialist. Bearce says: "The revival of imperial sentiment in British attitudes after 1828 came from two principal sources. Anglo-Saxon officers on the frontiers of British India found war and expansion the pathway to personal glory and financial security. . . . "[33] There were imperial spokesmen in London, like Lord Ellenborough, who was president of the Board of Control from 1828 to 1830, from 1834 to 1835, in 1841, and again later. In 1842 he went out as governor general and saw the post as that of a military leader who, "like the ancient caliphs," would "give laws from his stirrup."[34] He wanted the queen proclaimed empress of India, with a viceroy responsible to her alone. Moreover, he saw his task to be to prepare "Britain and India for the inescapable conflict with Russia in Asia and Europe."[35] He had a personal admiration for military officers and a corresponding contempt for civil servants. Like

Tsar Nicholas I, he would have liked to pass all the latter through army training—and, indeed, the whole native population, and for the same reason—to teach them loyalty.

Gandhi, like Tolstoy in Russia, wanted something different from what either of these parties wanted, but he was most unlike the imperialists and had some vivid confrontations with them. One of these confrontations that was particularly long-lasting and resonant was with Winston Churchill. Churchill loved India in the ways typical of his caste. He went there as a subaltern in the Fourth Queen's Own Hussars and stayed for two years, playing polo, hunting tigers, and sticking pigs. In 1947 he was still sending £2 a month to the man who had been his bearer then. But he also had realistic motives for his attachment. "If we lose India, we shall go down, out, and under. India is our bread and butter, that is all."[36] As under-secretary for the colonies, Churchill met Gandhi in London in 1906, but he refused to meet him in 1931 at the Round Table Conference. (Though they never met again, they remained intimately aware of each other.) In February of 1931 he said in Parliament: "The loss of India would be final and fatal to us. It would not fail to be part of a process that would reduce us to the scale of a minor power."[37]

Churchill described Gandhi as "a half-naked fakir" and a troublemaker "of a type well known in the East."[38] These Kipling terms were, of course, those in which most imperialists—including the king, George V—saw Gandhi. Alfred Milner, who had to deal with Gandhi in South Africa, referred to him as "some clever babu"; and Lord Chelmsford and the civil service hierarchy habitually called him a charlatan, at the beginning of his career in India. Lord Wavell, the penultimate viceroy, called him "a malevolent old politician . . . shrewd, obstinate, domineering, double-tongued. . . ." Indeed, all these English attitudes were summarized by Churchill when he said: "Gandhism and all that it stands for must be grappled with and finally crushed."[39]

Churchill fought the idea of giving India independence from 1910 until the end of British occupation there, in 1947. In 1942, at the Lord Mayor's banquet, he declared: "I have not become His Majesty's First Minister to preside over the dissolution of the British Empire."[40] Gandhi was locked up in the Aga Khan's palace from 1942 to 1944, and denied all contact with the outside world. Finally, in February 1947, Churchill said to the House of Commons: "It is with deep grief that I watch the tattering down of the British Empire with all its glories and all the services it has rendered mankind. . . . let us not add by shameful flight, by a premature, hurried scuttle—at least let us not add, to the pangs of sorrow so many of us feel, the taint and sneer of shame."[41]

Looking for an equivalent opponent to Tolstoy on the Russian scene, we might turn to Pobedonostsev, the procurator of the Holy Synod, who engineered Tolstoy's excommunication in 1901 and recommended other forms of punishment. Their confrontation was also long-lasting and resonant, and, in fact, we are bound to see in it a real-life enactment of the Grand Inquisitor's confrontation with Christ in *The Brothers Karamazov*. Moreover, these two men, though they never met, were also intimately aware of each other.

On 15 June 1881 Pobedonostsev wrote to Tolstoy that "your faith is one thing, and mine and that of the Church another, and that our Christ is not your Christ. . . . Mine I know as a man of strength and truth, healing the weak; but I thought I detected in yours the features of one who is feeble and himself needs to be cured."[42] When he read "The Kreutzer Sonata" he was very impressed with the truth of Tolstoy's depiction of modern marriage—he shared, more timidly and discreetly, Tolstoy's black scepticism about modern ideas. But he wrote to the tsar: "Alas, our Count Tolstoy, like all the members of the sects, forgets the words of Holy Scripture: 'man is a lie,' and that is why man must seek aesthetic truth and the authentically ideal, not in the feelings of his own conscience, but outside himself and without himself. . . . Tolstoy is fanatical in his folly and unfortunately he attracts and leads to madness thousands of foolish minds."[43] He told the tsar that "The Kreutzer Sonata" was spreading an epidemic insanity and doing untold harm to students, young girls, and the ignorant masses.

In his *Report to the Tsar* for 1887 he said that Tolstoy's relationship to the peasants had changed for the better, only because his sons were preventing him from giving away his money and because Sonia did not let him engage in secret propaganda. Thus, he intervened in Tolstoy's domestic struggle and made the wife his ally. He contemplated excommunication in 1886, confirmed his intention in 1896, and in the reports of the Synod for both 1899 and 1900 mentioned Tolstoy as dangerous. The decree appeared on 22 February 1901, and in 1902 Tanya Kuzminskaya, Sonia's sister, wrote from St. Petersburg that the Council of Ministers had discussed sending Tolstoy into exile.

If due account is taken of the difference between Tolstoy's cultural activity and Gandhi's—and that between the Russian autocracy and the British Empire—I think these two confrontations will seem cognate. And another symmetry we must perceive, in order to prepare us to understand them, is in the progress of the two empires.

As we have seen, Russia was, like Britain, an expanding power all through the modern period. In the nineteenth century Russian expansion in Central Asia can be seen in conjunction with British expansion in South Asia; the two empires moved towards each other and watched the other's advance uneasily. David Gillard, in *The Struggle for Asia 1828–1914*, notes that between 1798 and 1806 Russia and England developed their Asian empires simultaneously. While the Russians were establishing themselves on the south side of the Caucasus, the British were defeating the Marathis and Mysore in the southern part of India. Thereafter, the two powers began to frighten each other by their policies or suspected policies; Prince Gorchakov, the Russian foreign minister, said in 1864 that politicians are "irresistibly forced, less by ambition than by imperious necessity, into this onward movement where the greatest difficulty is to know where to stop."[44] The British leaders took alarm between 1828 and 1833.

Palmerston took an aggressive line towards Russia between 1833 and 1841. Then came a ten-year lull, during which England was more worried about Canada than India, and about the United States as a possible aggressor. Between 1853 and 1860, an alarmed Russia made every effort to settle the Caucasus revolt, which was absorbing energies (an army of 200,000) that would otherwise have gone into eastward expansion. Between 1860 and 1878, with the Caucasus conquered, the Russians acquired great quantities of Central Asian territory, and England did badly at the Great Game. The hegemony over Central Asia passed to Russia.

The Russian conquest of the Caucasus is important to us because Tolstoy took part in it, but it is also important in the history of Russian and English imperialism. As J. F. Baddeley says, the Chechens "stood, too, though all unknowingly, for the security of British rule in India. . . . 'When once they were swept away, there was no military or physical obstacle to the continuous march of Russia from the Araxes to the Indus.' "[45] Baddeley also describes with enthusiasm the Cossacks' work of conquest and colonization, of "pacifying the frontier." "Russia was only doing what England and all other civilized states have done, and still do, wherever they come in contact with savage or semi-savage races."[46] He tells how the terrified natives composed songs about the Russian general Ermolov—as the tribes of Central Asia were to do about General Skobelev.

Ermolov is an interesting figure, partly because he captured Pushkin's imagination. He claimed to have descended from Genghiz Khan, and boasted that he made the natives tremble at the sound of cannon, which they had never heard before. His system of fighting the Chechen involved the destruction of whole villages—we hear of one destroyed in 1819, leaving only fourteen men alive, and one hundred and forty women and children. Ermolov was disgraced in 1827, but lived until 1861, becoming the incarnation of Russia's great past and the inspiration of many young men. He projected himself as a terrorist, and boasted of it complacently.

Between 1856 and 1860 Russia acquired the Maritime Territory from China, and in 1864, Tien Shan. She also signed treaties with Korea. Most of her advance, however, was in Turkestan, where she acquired enormous territories steadily, defeating khan after khan in a dramatic revenge upon the Mongols for their thirteenth-century conquest of Russia. In 1865 Cherniaev took Tashkent from the khan of Kokand, with a tiny force of a thousand men. The following year Romanovski defeated a force of 40,000 Bokharans and took Khodjent; and in 1868 Kaufmann took Samarkand itself, which left the state of Bokhara only a satellite of Russia. In 1871 part of East Turkestan was seized from China, and in 1873 the khan of Khiva's forces were besieged, defeated, and massacred in Gok Tepe on the Oxus. In Gillard's opinion, Russia won the Great Game and dominated Asia.

But within India, Britain's empire continued to grow. In the 1860s England added 4,000 square miles to her Indian territories; in the 1870s, 15,000 square miles; in the 1880s, 80,000; and in the 1890s, 1,330,000. (During the nineteenth century, one hundred and eleven wars were fought in India; while outside wars, in which Indian troops fought, cost Britain £90,000,000.)

In his introduction Gillard says:

> Empire-building and the conflict of neighbouring empires have been normal ever since the emergence of political units powerful enough for the purpose. . . . There is no way to classify international behaviour as aggressive or defensive, purposive or opportunistic. . . . Until the 19th century, it made sense to distinguish the states system of Europe from the empires and principalities of Asia. It ceased to make sense when two members of the European states system were also the two most powerful states in Asia. . . . [47]

Nation-building turned out to have been imperialist all along. Gillard's point is perhaps made most crisply at the start of his introduction: "International politics are commonly regarded as irrational and unprincipled. . . . From this viewpoint, the celebrated rivalry between the Russians and the British in Asia in the 19th century would seem to be a classic case of futility, mutual misunderstanding, and the arrogance of power. . . . " Thus, Tolstoy and Gandhi were both situated within a single, and classical, confrontation of empires.

III

Russian Literature and Indian Politics: 1828–47 and 1869–88

Into these two great empires Tolstoy was born in 1828 and Gandhi in 1869. Their family circumstances and personal relations will not concern us here; nor will their formal education and first professional formation. Both were students of law, Tolstoy at Kazan University, Gandhi in London at the Inns of Court. But this tentative identity of lawyer was something prescribed for them, and neither one ever felt at ease with it. The field of activity that aroused Tolstoy's deepest imagination and ambition was literature, and for Gandhi the equivalent was nationalist politics.

Neither was interested, in their beginning years, in nonviolence or in the simplification of life. Quite the contrary; each at the age of nineteen made his way to the metropolitan city of his empire, Moscow or London, the centers of wealth and power, of modernization and luxury—of the *elaboration* of life. The fields of action they chose, law, literature, politics, were all parts of the modern cultural system, points at which its pride of life particularly flourished. And before they engaged their energies in one field, they lived as richly (as variously, as distractedly) as young men about town. (In Gandhi's case, that was a brief and tentative episode in London.) Tolstoy did not become a writer or Gandhi a politician in their earliest youth—they were both late developers—but they did become aware, however dimly, of the conditions of the vocation of a writer in Russia in the first half of the nineteenth century, and of a politician in India in the second half.

Literature was represented in the young Tolstoy's Russia above all by Pushkin and Lermontov, who defined many important possibilities both inside and outside literature for him. The dandyism that preoccupied Tolstoy as a student at Kazan (1845–47) and in Moscow later would probably not have had so powerful an effect had not the greatest of recent Russian writers been nobles and dandies themselves.

Dandyism was a serious option for young men, especially nobles, at that time, and all the more serious for its denial of seriousness. Modern institutions, including literature, carried the message that the feudal world had passed away, the aristocracy was a picturesque relic of the past, and serious values were the concern of the middle class. The young noble was invited to assert himself as wickedly frivolous or frivolously wicked—as a dandy. In both Russian society and Russian literature, he did so.

For instance, Alexander Pushkin (1799–1837) came from a family of the nobility not unlike the Tolstoys, but more glamorous and decadent—more Byronic. Five Pushkins had signed the Act of Election that called the first Romanov to the Russian throne in 1613, and the poet was proud of his "six hundred-year-old ancestry."[1] Through his mother, he was descended from Peter the Great's negro—a slave boy the tsar had gotten from the sultan's seraglio in 1706. He made a career in the army, married into the aristocracy, and one of his sons was known to Pushkin, who was the negro's great nephew. But the writer's parents were both feckless, irritable, and unstable socialites. His father was a writer in French, his uncle a better one, and Pushkin himself began as an admirer and imitator of Voltaire and Parny in verse. Famous writers like Karamzin and Zhukovsky visited the house when he was a child.

In 1811 he went as a schoolboy to the newly opened tsar's lyceum, where he displayed great precocity, sexually and poetically and in other ways. The director, a German, disapproved of him as lacking heart and sincerity, and it is true that in some ways Pushkin was a man of the eighteenth century, of *civilization*, in the French sense. He made his friends among the guards officers who had been to Europe in the Napoleonic wars and who later became the Decembrists. Pushkin himself became a duelist, amorist, fencer, and dandy; he wore his nails long, with gold sheaths to protect them. A good deal in his temperament was comparable with Byron's, and he imitated the latter to some degree; he wanted to go to fight for Greek independence in 1821, and he took as a mistress a woman who had been (or said she had been) Byron's. In all this he was more fiercely flamboyant than Tolstoy, less nineteenth century, less attracted to the vocation of helping all nature develop, less Rousseauistic and drawn to domestic tranquility; there was no one in his life like Tolstoy's Aunt Toinette.

And this has something to do with the tragedy that destroyed him. Having been a great seducer who delighted in making husbands jealous, he married a much younger woman who flirted with other men and spent her time at balls. Pushkin got a letter saying he had been cuckolded (and pointing to the tsar as one of her lovers); he fought a duel with a rival French dandy and was killed. (Orwell has shown how like Tolstoy's tragedy was to "King Lear"; Pushkin's was like "Othello.")

As a writer, Pushkin was extraordinarily versatile, and opened up nearly all the possibilities which later Russian writers developed, including Tolstoy during most of his career. Notably, he wrote stories about the Caucasus and the Cossacks, about the frontier and the wild and nature; he found even overt imperialism intoxicating. (This is not to say that he was blind to its ugliness.) Under Nicholas I, as we have said, a big military effort, including Cossack regiments, was mounted to crush the rebellion (it was a classically imperialist war) and gradually it succeeded.

Tolstoy went to the Caucasus in 1851 to visit his brother Nicholas, who was an officer in the Russian army there. He was fascinated both by the Chechens, the rebellious tribesmen, and the Cossacks, amongst whom the Russian regular soldiers were lodged. Tolstoy himself joined the army while he was there and briefly considered a military career, but felt a deeper vocation to writing. The Caucasus had given him something to write about, and his successful change of life had given him a stronger sense of his own powers. In focusing on the Caucasian experience, then, we can see more clearly the link between Tolstoy and Pushkin (and Lermontov).

Pushkin, like Tolstoy later, made himself a Cossack of the imagination; he carried a Cossack whip and lived with a band of Cossacks for a time. Moreover, again like Tolstoy, he translated his enthusiasm into literary form—his living and his writing were interdependent. Some of the best passages of his story "The Prisoner of the Caucasus" (1821) describe the mountains and the life of the Chechens with enthusiasm. The hero of this story suffers from the discontents of civilization (he is disgusted with the restraints of social life and is pining with unrequited love) before he is captured by the Chechens. To help him escape, a Chechen girl files through the prisoner's chains, and, because he doesn't love her, then throws herself into the river. This is one of the classic myths of imperialism to be found in many literatures, and it expresses, however complacently, the guilt of the imperializing power. In his epilogue, however, Pushkin celebrates in anticipation Russia's final victory over the Caucasian tribesmen. His friend Vyazemsky said Pushkin had stained his poem with blood by making Ermolov his hero. "Blood freezes in one's veins and one's hair stands on end, to read that Ermolov: 'Destroyed and annihilated the tribes like a black plague.'"[2] Poetry is not the ally of executioners, said Vyazemsky; we should be educating the tribes, not annihilating them; this is an anachronism.

Tolstoy, too, could be accused of anachronism and atavism in his enthusiasm for the Cossacks. This was because both he and Pushkin refused to trust the modern system's ideological chronology, which relegated all militarism and imperialism to the past, as an atavism or a vestige.

Adventure tales were the part of Pushkin's work that made him most widely famous; and this subject later gave Tolstoy his greatest early success. Pushkin also wrote "The Fountain of Bhaktisaray" (1824), which is about a tragedy of jealousy in a khan's harem. This is another of the erotic myths of imperialism: the pale, blond woman of the west/ north, who is usually passive and spiritual, is, paradoxically, more attractive than the dark woman of the east/south, who is fierce and sexual.

Above all, Pushkin wrote "The Captain's Daughter" (1836), a historical novel about the desertion of the Cossacks to the side of Pugachev in his rebellion against Catherine the Great: "This vast and wealthy province [Orenburg] was inhabited by a number of half-savage peoples who had but recently acknowledged the authority of the Russian sovereigns. Unused to the laws and habits of civilized life, cruel and reckless, they constantly rebelled, and the government had to watch over them unremittingly to keep them in submission."[3] That this reminds us of "The White Man's Burden"—in which Kipling exhorts the Anglo-Saxons to "send out the best ye breed," to rule "A fluttered folk and wild / Your new-caught sullen peoples / Half devil and half child"—was no coincidence. Because Russia and England were imperialist powers all through the nineteenth century, imperialism generated several of the great imaginative truths of those cultures, though they appeared under ban to all but the most recklessly truthful of the poets.

This is one of the links tying Tolstoy to Pushkin, this identity as dandy-poet-warrior-imperialist. Because of the rank they were born into, the ruling caste of a great empire, righteousness was out of their reach. It was going to be a long way back for Tolstoy, from this beginning, to religious nonviolence.

Mikhail Lermontov (1814–41) also had close connections, personal and literary, with the Caucasus. He spent months in the Caucasus as a child, staying with his grandmother's sister, in 1817, 1819, and 1824. This woman's husband had been a friend of Ermolov's, and she chose to live on the frontier, in a sense on the front line, even after his death. Thus, Lermontov, like Pushkin and Tolstoy, knew the Caucasus situation from the inside; he sympathized with the curiously divided Cossacks, who often deserted to the Chechen and were half hostile to the Russians.

Lermontov wrote a verse version of the story Pushkin had told—and which Tolstoy later told—the myth we can call "The Prisoner of the Caucasus." This is one of the stories Anglo-Saxon imperialism also generated, as we see in the case of Pocahontas, and it is a significant link between these three Russian writers.

Lermontov also wrote "Ismail Bey," the story of a Caucasian taken hostage as a boy by the Russians and brought up as a Russian officer and aristocrat. Once he reaches manhood, the hero returns to join his nation and fight against the Russians, until he is shot by his own brother, who distrusts his loyalty. The rhetoric is typically imperialist: the tribesmen and their mountains are celebrated as the incarnation of freedom; but the march of empire is inevitable and is even grander than freedom. "Yield thee, Cherkess," said a Russian officer: "For comes an hour when you yourself shall cry / 'Slave though I be, I serve a prince most high / King of the World'—a new stern Rome comes forth / A new Augustus rises from out the North."

This story was told by English authors about Indian princes who were educated at a British public school and then returned to their princedoms, but who could not forget their taste of true civilization. It was also told by the best-selling Russian novelist Bestuzhev-Marlinsky, who had died in action in the Caucasus just before Lermontov got there. Bestuzhev had led a life as romantic as his novels, and Lermontov drew the illustrations for *Ammalet Bek*, the novel in which Bestuzhev told this story himself. There was thus a close and intense connection between all the dandy-Decembrist-imperialist romancers, including Tolstoy; they studied each other, as men as well as writers.

Lermontov, too, was a dandy and amorist, and made a cult of Pushkin. After a Pushkin-like duel with another Frenchman, he was imprisoned and exiled to the Caucasus. The critic Belinsky, who saw him in the guardhouse on that occasion, described him as a real-life hero out of his own or Pushkin's stories. In the Caucasus he made friends with Pushkin's brother and with Rufin Dorokhov (also one of Pushkin's circle), the man from whom Tolstoy drew the dandy Dolokhov in *War and Peace*. Such figures of insolent aristo-military glamor were very important to all three writers, though of the three, Lermontov came closest to assimilating himself to those originals. He took over the leadership of Dorokhov's troop of irregulars and made himself a Dionysus of war. That is, he gave up washing or cutting his hair, and took to wearing the native shashka; he rejected the stance of a civilized gentleman, becoming a Cossack or Chechen warrior. And, like Pushkin, he died in a duel, one which he brought upon himself by his dandy insolence. He mocked the Chechen costume, weapons, and shaven-head affected by another dandy called Martynov—a costume which claimed, like his own, that its wearer had internalized the savage virtues of the enemy. (We can see this cult of the savage in Tolstoy, too.)

Tolstoy himself ran some risks of meeting a similar death by dueling, in the 1850s, and may be said to have treated Turgenev rather as Lermontov treated Martynov (the man who killed him). Of course, there were many other sides to Tolstoy, and this one was rarely predominant. But he was deeply attracted to a serious and morally committed kind of dandyism; and because the voice in which he tells the stories of his novels does not reveal this (his novelist's voice was liberal-democratic), we must remind ourselves that he was, in behavior, aristocratic. He was also deeply attracted to Pushkin's and Lermontov's purity of taste and energy of invention as writers. This is indeed a related matter—aestheticism and dandyism are natural twins—and a line of succession can be drawn in Russian literature, which runs from Pushkin to Tolstoy to Chekhov to Nabokov.

Another aristocratic writer important to Tolstoy was Sergei Aksakov (1791–1859). His subject was the nonmilitary expansion of Russia against the peaceful Bashkirs in the provinces east of Kazan, and his emphasis was on the fertility of virgin lands and the patriarchal style of the Russian pioneers. He was therefore close to Defoe as well as Scott, to use English terms—close to the pastoral style of imperialist romance. He added to that, however, both an identification with the aristocratic caste and a Rousseauistic interest in sensibility and psychology, which brings him very close to Tolstoy. His writing is autobiographical, and he himself knew the patriarchal pioneer life as a child; but he knew it dialectically, in terms of a tension between his parents.

A sickly child, Aksakov grew up very close to his mother, a woman of remarkable intelligence and sensitivity, but, as an official's daughter, belonging to a different environment. Aksakov disliked his mother's reluctance to enter into the patriarchal system of relationships—she wouldn't manage the household, collect the rents, direct the spinning or the weaving. His father, less developed intellectually and morally, loved that life, but as he loved nature and sports—unconsciously.

> . . . men who had grown up in the country and were *passionate lovers* of Nature, though they themselves were not really conscious of this, never defined the feeling to themselves, and never used any of the words that I have just used about it. . . .

I now sensed within me this new life and became a part of
Nature, though it was only in adult years that in remem-
brance of that time I consciously came to value all the magic
charm of it, all its poetic beauty.[4]

Thus, Aksakov's expansive vision of Nature is counterpointed, in the
nineteenth-century manner Tolstoy followed, against the discontents
of civilization, as felt by a child in parental tensions and authenticated
by a child's point of view and a child's experiences—being teased,
rebelling, being punished, hating school, being locked up in darkness.

In contemplating Tolstoy in his youth, with his destiny as writer
stirring feebly in him, we should see the great shades of Pushkin and
Lermontov standing to the left and right of him, and Aksakov beck-
oning him on. It was not the direction he would later have chosen,
but it nonetheless prepared him for his ultimate destiny. It is important, though, to note also certain more impersonal facts: for instance,
the way Russian nobles could feel that literature was their class
prerogative—which was far from being the case in England, for
instance. In 1825 Pushkin wrote to a friend: "The spirit of our literature depends in part on the status of our writers. We cannot offer
our works to a lord, for by our own birth we esteem ourselves his
equal. . . ." (Bourgeois writers, like Dr. Johnson, asked lords like Ches-
terfield to be their patrons.) And, more defiantly, "The lack of esteem
for one's ancestors is the first sign of wildness and immorality."[5]

This claim that literature and aristocracy were linked in Russia
was far from being simply or absolutely true; much of the writing
and publishing being done in Russia was commercially oriented and
intellectually vulgar, as it was in other places—Pushkin himself wrote
in 1836, "During the last twenty years, Russian literature has developed into an important branch of industry,"[6] and he made bitter jokes
about the price he could get for his poetry. And the real vulgarians
of publishing were naturally people whose names are now forgotten.

But it still seemed possible to Pushkin—as it had been to Pope
one hundred years earlier in England—to claim a part of literature
as the preserve of aristocratic talent (and to reinforce the distinction
by appealing to literally aristocratic criteria). Certain genres were tied
to the aristocracy; for example, it was nobles who wrote the lyrical
autobiographies of childhood, the meditative descriptions of nature,
and the sportsman's sketches. (Turgenev, Aksakov, and Tolstoy himself were famous writers of this sort). Meanwhile, members of the
intelligentsia in the 1860s wrote bitter accounts of the sordidness of
life in the seminaries and roughly sarcastic polemics. Tolstoy complained about the vituperative tone that Chernyshevsky introduced

into *Sovremennik*, as did Herzen and Turgenev, and even the magazine's nominal editor, Nekrasov.

In Pushkin's time, Russian literature was a new growth and was very aware of the long-established literatures to the west. Pushkin, and later Tolstoy, tried to give Russia the dignity of an independent literature, which was a major sign of national independence. He himself founded *Sovremennik*, in 1835, with the aim of giving Russia an equivalent for England's famous *Edinburgh Review*. And Belinsky (the most famous Russian critic of the period just before Tolstoy began publishing) said in 1846 that foreigners were fully entitled to ignore the Russian writers, who were imitative up to Pushkin's time and even after Pushkin were still un-Russian. Pushkin was himself a great imitator of all sorts of Western originals, but he could make an imitation authentically his. But Belinsky said that for Russian writers in general, that was not good enough: "The demands of Europeans in this respect are very exacting. Nor is this to be wondered at: the spirit of nationality of European nations is so sharply and originally expressed in their literature that any work, however great in artistic merit, which does not bear the sharp imprint of nationality, loses its chief merit in the eyes of Europeans."[7] This teaching is, of course, the reflection in literary terms of the political doctrine of nation-building. And the Russians felt they did not measure up to this demand. Turgenev afterwards said that under Nicholas I there was no such thing as literature, and, therefore, no national self-awareness.

But the project of establishing literature in Russia suffered not only from its newness, and from its very limited audience, but also from the repression directed at it by the autocracy. Here again the form as well as the content of literature was a political matter. It was often said (for instance, by the censor Aleksei Nikitenko) that the nations of Europe had *earned* the right to have a literature, as they had earned the right to be politically free. Russian writers said—as did Indian nationalists like Gandhi in South Africa—that their compatriots must demand freedom, seize it, suffer for it, as the free men of England and France had done. In an angry letter to Gogol, who had defended conservative nationalism in 1847, Belinsky said the Russian public saw its writers as its only defenders, its saviors from autocracy, orthodoxy, and nationality. (He told Gogol to base his conservatism, if he must be reactionary, on the church, and not to drag in the name of Christ, who "taught liberty, equality, and fraternity.")

And yet the mid-nineteenth century was a great period of writing in Russia. Ronald Hingley has said that the crucial twenty-five years— the "golden age"—was from Turgenev's short novel "Rudin" (1856) to Dostoevsky's very long *The Brothers Karamazov* (1880).[8] It is a curious coincidence that those are the years of Tsar Alexander II's reign, 1861 to 1881; it is something more than coincidence that they are the years of Tolstoy's career as a novelist. After 1881 he turned against fiction (though he did write some) and even against literature—which shows the profound consonance of Tolstoy's mind with the events of his day, despite the resolution with which he turned his back on them.

Turning now to Gandhi, we may say that nationalist politics in India had a great variety of beginnings, in secret societies, open rebellions, cultural revivals, newspaper polemics, and officially sponsored organizations like Congress. These can be glimpsed in the careers of leading figures—for instance, Balvantra Tilak, Lala Lajpat Rai, and Bipin Chandra Pal—who performed something of a parallel function in Gandhi's life to Pushkin and Lermontov in Tolstoy's. This famous trio of Hindu reformer-revolutionaries, known as Lal, Bal, and Pal, shaped the tradition of political radicalism that Gandhi was to inherit, even though they were very different men coming from different parts of the country. Furthermore, the national politics they represented was very unlike the nonviolent kind Gandhi was later to devise.

Gandhi was not politically precocious, just as Tolstoy was not literarily precocious. Before he left India in 1888, he tells us, he never read a newspaper, and he seems to have taken no great interest in politics before he got to Natal in 1893. But the great radicals, like these three, were there for him, however dimly, and in later years their outlines filled in and they became important to him. As soon as he had established himself as a leader in South Africa, he went back to India and made himself known to the nationalist politicians. Balvantra Tilak (1856–1920) was a Poona Brahmin who began his nationalist work in education. With one or two other teachers, he founded a new school, which became Fergusson College in Poona, and took Jesuits as the model in their school, and called themselves Indian Jesuits. Tilak's basic mythology, however, was Hindu, and he devised a scheme for dating the Vedas by means of the position of the stars mentioned in them. The point of this was to date the Rigveda at 4000 B.C., and thus claim immense antiquity and superiority for the Aryan cultural traditions.

Apart from the Vedic Aryans, his other great enthusiasm in Indian history was the Marathis, and Tilak built his house on Singagahr (a mountain whose name means "the fortress of the lion"), where their great military leader, Shivaji Maharaj, ensconced himself. When in 1881 he began his Marathi magazine, he called it *Kesari*, the lion. Leonine imagery was central to his politics.

Tilak shifted from education to vernacular journalism (in Marathi) and to a revival of Hindu festivals, especially those connected with Shivaji Maharaj (1627–80). This man had, in effect, created the Hindu nation of Maratha, which defied the Muslim emperor of Delhi and in the heyday of the Peshwas (1713–60) became a confederacy of imposing proportions. The Peshwas were Chitpavan Brahmins, who at first advised rulers and then grasped the reins of power themselves, becoming hereditary heads of state. The last one surrendered to the British only in 1818, and the government remained suspicious of Poona, their sacred capital, and of the violence of Maharashtran politics. (Gandhi's assassins were Chitpavan Brahmins.)

In 1881 Tilak began his magazine *Mahratta* (his career henceforth was largely in journalism), and its declared aim was the revival of national feeling. Like Gandhi, he aspired to be both a hero of one kind of Indian (in Tilak's case, the aggressive, would-be imperial, proto-Marathi) and, at the same time, the leader of all kinds of Indians, however remote geographically or psychologically. Soon he was involved in lawsuits, most often against the British or their protégés. Two of his followers, the Chaplekar brothers, committed a terrorist murder in 1897 and Tilak was arrested in 1898. He was condemned to jail, but released six months early on a petition signed by English as well as Indian notables, like Max Müller and Dadabhai Naoroji. He was given the popular title, Lokamanya, "the beloved of the people."

Besides his journalism, Tilak worked to revive popular Hindu festivals. His larger intention was, of course, to revive Indian pride. In 1897 he wrote: "The dwarfing influence of the British raj has turned the backbone of Maharashtra and Konkan, once forming the famous cavalry of the Deccan and the navy of the Konkan, their country's pride, into a mere servile class of field labourers, destined now to work like slaves for the good of the omnipotent bureaucracy. . . ."[9] The British had changed the caste character of the Indian nation; it had been Kshattriya, but now was servile, Shudra. The British themselves, he no doubt would have agreed, had usurped the Kshattriya, or warrior, identity in India. The nationalist leaders, including the early Gandhi, wanted to reclaim that identity for India.

Tilak was not a reformer, in the sense of a Westernizer. The leader of the reforming party was Justice Ranade, whose heir was Gokhale, whose heir, in turn, was Gandhi. This lineage was sharply opposed to Tilak's in every way. In 1887 Ranade founded his National Social Conference, which met annually to report on progress in reforms; he, for instance, defended a girl who was in trouble for refusing to marry the man her dead father had selected for her.

Gandhi would certainly have been on Ranade's side. Tilak, on the other hand, attacked the girl and Ranade, and when in 1891 it was proposed to raise the marriage age from ten to twelve—a cause dear to Gandhi's heart—he objected.

He wanted to renew Hindu pride in Hindu institutions, trusting that that pride would be enough to remove their imperfections. He cared primarily for male/caste/nationalist pride and tradition, and often inspired violent protests to support his causes. He stated: "Individuals as well as institutions are of two kinds; those that take the circumstances as they are and compromise with them, and those that . . . [create] favorable circumstances by robustly and steadily fighting their way up. . . . I cannot accept the compromise."[10]

Between 1891 and 1897 he built up a militant Hindu party in Maharashtra and became its martyr-hero. He revived Ganapati, which had been a family feast for the Peshwa Brahmins, and expanded it to rival Mohurram, the Muslim festival that had been both religions' summer celebration. To take part in Ganapati, the young men of the Hindu lower classses were organized into militant *melas* and marched about in step, carrying lathis.

In 1896 Tilak began Shivaji festivals in Poona and on the mountain nearby, where Shivaji was crowned in 1674. Huge portraits were carried up the mountain by torchlight. Tilak said that hero-worship was the root of nationality, of social order, and of religion. Discussing Shivaji's murder of the Muslim leader Afzal Khan, he said, "[T]he laws which bind society are for common men like you and me. No one seeks to trace the genealogy of a rishi or to fasten guilt upon a king. Great men are above the common principles of morality."[11]

When the government refused funds to schools that were under his sponsorship, a dozen secret societies were founded, including the Mitra-Mela, to which Vir Savarkar (the man who inspired Gandhi's assassination) and his brother belonged. Tilak got Savarkar his scholarship to London, where he studied bomb-making (he sent the manual back to Tilak) and wrote his history of the mutiny, called *India's First War of Independence*.

Arrested in 1908, Tilak spent six years in exile in Rangoon, but on his return had great prestige and in 1916 captured the Congress. At the Amritsar Congress in 1919 he was opposed by Gandhi, who spoke, as always, of Truth. Tilak responded, "My friend! Truth has no place in politics";[12] he quoted the Sanscrit proverb that advised "treat a rogue with roguery"; and in a letter to *Young India*, on 28 January 1920, he wrote, "[P]olitics is a game of worldly people, and not of sadhus."[13] Gandhi, of course, maintained the opposite. But in certain ways—a love of the Indian way, a boldness of style and readiness for dangerous action—Gandhi was Tilak's heir.

By and large, however, Gandhi, the politician of peace and truth, was Tilak's opponent. And, indeed, back in August 1908, when his South African journal *Indian Opinion* reported Tilak's sentence, Gandhi wrote that he was a great man on the wrong track. "Pungent, bitter and penetrating writing was his objective [just the style Gandhi had expressly forsworn for *his* magazine] . . . ; the rulers are justified, from their point of view, in taking action against such a man. We would do the same in their place."[14] Thus, Gandhi and reformers were opposed by the heroic-nationalist line of Tilak-Savarkar.

Bipin Chandra Pal (1858–1932), on the other hand, is the great example of the Indian revolutionary nationalist—he was known for a time as the Danton of Bengal—who lost his faith under the pressure of repression. He began as a reformer, especially in matters of religion. A member of the Brahmo Samaj, he loved Emerson and translated Theodore Parker, and in 1898 he was given a Unitarian scholarship to Oxford. From there he went on to America, delivering speeches against drink. He was one of the great Indian orators; Nehru wrote home from Cambridge to his father that Pal had thundered at his student group as if they had been ten thousand instead of a dozen.

Pal began by writing in praise of Hinduism, which he described as a family of religions while Hindu society was a federation. (This is like the defense of Holy Russia, as being fundamentally different from the *nations* of Western Europe.) But after 1895, and especially after 1905, when Lord Curzon announced that Bengal would be partitioned, everybody became political, including Pal. The resistance to the partition was the cause of all those educated and well-to-do classes who had taken part in the Bengal Renaissance, including the Tagores. Pal preached passive resistance and Swadeshi (the boycotting of all but native produce). In 1907 he went to jail for refusing to testify against Arabindo, who was involved in illegal activities.

In jail, however, he issued a statement that he was a sociologist and not an extremist; this was the first sign of a change in him, and it paralleled a general sense among the well-to-do in Bengal that they were in deeper water, politically, than they had intended. (They were afraid of arousing the mostly Muslim peasants against them.) After his jail sentence, Pal came out speaking of India's duties rather than her rights.

Still a great national hero, he took over as editor of *Bande Mataram* when Arabindo was sent to jail in 1908. However, later that year, he went to England again, his passage paid by Krishnavarma, a London-based Indian nationalist who financed many revolutionaries. While in England, he repeatedly repudiated terrorism and said India should appeal to England's civilized conscience. He was then denounced as a traitor by Krishnavarma. In 1911, when he sailed home, Pal announced that he believed in the British Empire, once it had become a commonwealth.

In India, however, he again took part in the Home Rule movements, as a moderate, and was a member of Congress from 1916 to 1920. In that year, at Barisal, he objected to Gandhi's "pontifical authority" over the nationalist movement, saying *he* believed in logic, not magic; he was interrupted angrily by his audience. Thus, he, too, was defeated by Gandhi, and though he lived another sixteen years, his political career was dead.

Finally, Lala Lajpat Rai (1865–1928) was a Punjabi, whose mother was a Sikh. Trained in the law, he joined first the Brahmo Samaj, the most respectable and Western of the reforming organizations, but then—as would be likely to happen in the Punjab—the idea of "the ancient Aryan culture" became his guiding star, and he joined the rival organization, the Arya Samaj. This was an organization, founded by Swami Dayanand, to reform Hinduism from within, and not in the direction of Christianity. It was fiercer and more virile in its style than the Brahmo Samaj (it went out proselytizing). It was strong in Maharashtra and the Punjab. In introducing *The Story of My Deportation* (he was arrested and deported in 1908 for his part in the Partition protests), Rai said, "[A]s a Hindu, it is my devout prayer that I may be born again and again in this land of the Vedas to contribute my Karma to the corporate Karma of the nation."[15] This is the style of the Arya Samaj.

When Rai moved to Lahore, he found the local branch of the Arya Samaj split between "the cultured" and the more pious, the "mahatmas." He joined the first, for he had never been religious— he was an activist. In fact, he admired the military Rajputs, and the first book he bought after passing his law exam was Tod's *Annals of Rajasthan*; Rai wrote: "the valorous deeds of the Rajputs . . . developed into an irresistible passion."[16] He joined the Congress in 1888, but soon left it, disillusioned by the lack of action there.

Mazzini was his inspiration, and Rai translated his *Duties of Man* and then wrote his biography in 1896. But Garibaldi the soldier was also his hero, and he wrote his biography, too. He himself wanted to be a man of action. He is described by G. M. Birla as "very impulsive and short-tempered."[17] Like Gandhi, Lajpat Rai wanted action, not talk, but his feeling for it was theoretical. Unlike Gandhi, he could not create action for himself.

In 1914 he went to London, and then he spent 1915 to 1920 in America; there he was one of the Berlin Committee for revolutionary conspiracy, some of whom were tried in Chicago and San Francisco. "In Los Angeles," he said, "every Hindu I met was a revolutionary."[18] Returning to India, he opposed Gandhi's policy of noncooperation in 1920 and objected even more to Gandhi's withdrawal from it in 1922, when it was having results. Gandhi was by then a man of peace and was imposing nonviolence on the whole Indian movement. But the initiative had passed to Gandhi, and Rai, too, was outmaneuvered. His death, however, was heroic; he died from wounds received from the police in a political protest.

Of the three areas of India that these leaders represented, Bengal and Maharashtra had the reputation of being centers of revolution. The nonviolent Gandhi was often accused of a sly and sanctimonious Gujarati hostility by brilliant Bengali leaders like Subhas Chandra Bose and fiery Maharashtris like Savarkar. Bengal was considered to be intellectually and educationally superior to the rest of India, and temperamentally more fiery and volatile; Maharashtra kept the militant tradition of the seventeenth- and eighteenth-century Marathis, and felt itself more specifically Hindu and nationalist than other places; Punjab was a land of peasants and Sikhs, and of more recent and British Army soldiering. Images of these kinds clustered around and supported the three leaders and helped make nationalist politics militant.

Discussion of the most impressive of the cultural revivals, the Bengal Renaissance, will correspond to what was said about the situation of literature in Russia and will place Gandhi's cultural propaganda into a somewhat contemporary context. We can take our description of Bengal from J. H. Broomfield's *Elite Conflict in a Plural Society.*[19] In 1900 Calcutta was the biggest city in the empire after London, with a population of more than a million. The British banking and agency houses on Clive Street, along with the Indian merchants in the Burra Bazaar, together financed a coal-and-rail network that brought jute, coal, indigo, and tea from countryside to the port. Government House contained the viceroy, who ruled one-fifth of the world's people; Belvedere contained the lieutenant governor of Bengal, who ruled twice as many people as lived in the United Kingdom.

Slightly more than one-half of Calcuttans were Bengali Hindus, and most of them were doing clerical or professional work. Of the rest, the great majority were Muslims, and in all of Bengal the Muslims were a majority and were growing twice as fast. Only in the towns were the Hindus in the majority, but they were in the positions of privilege. The ruling class, in both town and country, were called Bhadralok, the respectable or gentle folk; they consisted of the brahmin, vaidya, and kayastha castes, and there was a wide gap between them and the rest. Characteristically, they were dedicated to education and literature; in fact, many rich merchants were excluded from the Bhadralok, while people of lower birth but with education could enter it. Lord Curzon's proposed Partition of Bengal in 1905 was an attempt to reduce their power and to save the Muslims from subordination. This was defeated by an effusion of nationalist sentiment, led by the Bhadralok.

The Bengal Renaissance at the end of the nineteenth century consisted of a purification of religion, the most important manifestation of which was the Brahmo Samaj, a society which promoted a rationalized and moralized form of Hinduism. The Brahmo Samaj had links with and a resemblance to Unitarian Christianity. In addition, there was a flowering of the arts, reviving old Indian forms but also practicing new European ones, in which the Tagore family, amongst others, played a large part. The results of this renaissance were even more various, for they included terrorist organizations like those to which M. N. Roy and Arabindo belonged, but also a highly public and oratorical politics, represented by Surendranath Banerji and Bipin Chandra Pal, and religio-politics like the Ramakrishna mission, now called Vedantism.

This was a major revival of Indian culture, not improperly called a renaissance. Its major characteristic was its aesthetic splendor, represented by Rabindranath Tagore, which expressed an aristocratic temperament. In this way Gandhi's work was to be very different, and he had many ideological quarrels with Tagore. There were other elements to the renaissance, however, from which Gandhi was able to learn; for instance, the revival of folk arts, and the religion of Ramakrishna and Vivekananda, which combined strong religious emotion with a desire to come to terms with the achievements of the West.

The great political manifestation of the renaissance was the agitation against the Partition of Bengal in 1905. The agitation was on the whole an unpleasant experience for the Bhadralok, even though they triumphed, because, according to Broomfield, it revealed their unpopularity with other social groups. There followed a general withdrawal of their leaders from politics.

Arabindo retreated to religion, Tagore to literature, and Pal—later—to England and English imperialism. By the time Gandhi got ˙ to India, renaissance politics were over, and its significance for him may have been negative, in a twofold fashion: its failure made Bengal's resistance to his leadership (as a non-Bengali politician and non-Bhadralok) impotent; and it warned him against basing his own movement on middle-class and cultured values.

These two fields of activity, therefore, awaited Tolstoy and Gandhi. Russian literature was there for Tolstoy; not as a single option, of course—he must still choose what sort of book to write—but as a set of options; and Pushkin, Lermontov, and Aksakov represent those he preferred. And nationalist politics were there for Gandhi, also as something both single and multiple; there were many kinds of Indian nationalist, and Bal, Pal, and Lal represented various options out of which he compounded his own.

To keep our sense that a single pattern underlies all this variety, we need to remind ourselves that both Russian literature and Indian politics were modes of action for young men who felt the pressure of a new cultural mode coming upon their country from outside. Literature was one of the most important ways young Russians could assimilate the challenge of the West and respond with a Russian equivalent; could put back that overweening superiority by demonstrating the Russian soul in all its idiosyncracy and authenticity. And political nationalism was the obvious way for young Indians to rouse their countrymen from the humiliated sloth and passivity and dependence of being a subject nation, to show that Indians, too, could be men and nation-builders. These were important motives for Tolstoy and Gandhi individually but also socially; they were to find in these fields of activity inspiring roles to play, which united them with the elites they admired. These beginnings, however, led them away from the values they came to hold and to represent to others later.

IV
Moscow and London:
1847–55 and 1888–94

In this period (the first half of that period I have called youth)—from nineteen to twenty-six in Tolstoy's case, and nineteen to twenty-five in Gandhi's—each of the two young men was finding himself or looking for himself, assuming a number of different postures in rapid succession, looking for the one that best expressed his sense of self. For each of them, a principal setting was a great capital city, Moscow and London; and each of them found himself in a series of false positions, from which he extricated himself as quickly as possible.

Moscow was the capital city of the Holy Russia of the Slavophiles, the mother city of the Russian nobles as opposed to the bureaucrats, the symbol of all that was anciently and organically Russian. But Tolstoy's Moscow was more importantly the paradise of the Russian dandy, where Tolstoy could pursue a young-man's destiny. (Dandyism must be understood to mean more than elegance in dress or manners; it meant a cult of the young man and his youthful beauty, his style and wit and self-assertion, in defiance of the mature values of manliness, fatherhood, manageriality, and responsibility.)

In Moscow the more frivolous products of the modern system were dispensed by French restaurants, hairdressers, glove-makers, and so on, which were frequented by young men like Tolstoy. He also fenced and exercised with Poiret, a Frenchman who kept a gymnasium on the Petrovka, where Tolstoy hoped to become the strongest man in the world. Notably missing from Tolstoy's diary of 1848 is any concern with the revolutions that broke out all over Europe, or with the Russian intervention which set the kings of the *ancien régime* back on their thrones. The lack of entries does not mean a total lack of interest on Tolstoy's part—what went into his diary was what affected his sense of himself, his process of self-formation. Still, one need only think of Marx to realize that what was happening in Europe politically could have affected a young man's sense of himself. In the year 1848 Marx and Engels composed *The Communist Manifesto*; Marx was in Paris for the early rising, then went to Cologne, where he edited the *Neue Rheinische Zeitung*, and was one of the leaders of the revolutionary movement there. It was the moment when Marx most decisively showed his capacity for practical action.

Meanwhile, Tolstoy was thinking things like "[T]he position of a young man in Moscow society partially tends to predispose him to idleness. I say 'a young man' in the sense of one who combines in himself such qualifications as education, a good name, and an income of R10,000 to 20,000."[1] (*R* in sums of money means *Rubles* when the currency is Russian, *Rupees* when Indian.) He goes on to note his need of a countess to get into the right salons. This could be Pushkin's or Lermontov's diary; it represents the consciousness of the young aristocrat in the nineteenth century, squeezed into the villain's role by the tendencies of bourgeois sentiment and bourgeois politics. If such men read novels like *Clarissa* they could see themselves only as Lovelaces, and could portray themselves only as Childe Harold or Don Juan, as Onegin or Pechorin; if they read histories of the French Revolution or the Decembrist Revolt, they could see themselves only as ineffectual rebels—as what the Russians called "superfluous men"—doomed to a romantic death on the guillotine or before the firing squad.

Dandyism can be described as a cultural equivalent of narcissism, and the latter is very prominent in Tolstoy's early work. In a variant of *The Cossacks*, for instance, Tolstoy wrote:

> . . . that people *could* be good and noble if they willed it, Olenin was quite convinced [Olenin is Tolstoy's representative in the story]; his own young soul, he felt, was beautiful, and with that he was content. . . . For my part, I love the amiable inactivity of those young men who survey the scene before them, yet lack the courage to turn their pent-up energies into immediate action. . . . Olenin felt the all-powerful genius of youth was asleep within him, and he instinctively followed his impulses.[2]

In Tolstoy's early fiction, the narrator is usually in love with his young hero—who is also in love with himself.

More prominent in his experience was being in love with other men, but this was equally involved with narcissism. In 1851 he wrote in his diary, "I very often fell in love with men. . . ."[3] He named several, saying the only one he still loved was Dyakov, and adds that they all found it painful to look at him. In *Childhood* he spoke of his terror of displeasing a boy he loved: "Was it because . . . despising my own looks, I valued beauty too highly in others, or, most probably of all, because awe is an infallible sign of affection, that I feared him as much as I loved him? The first time [he] spoke to me I was so taken aback by such unexpected happiness that I turned pale, then blushed, and could not answer him."[4] In consequence, the other boy tyrannized over him.

In his work of the 1850s Tolstoy explored many aspects of this young man's cult of himself. For instance, in the Sebastopol sketches, he dwells on the way a young man is locked within his self-preoccupations and experiences everything in the debased form of "what will impress others." In "Strider" (1863) he puts forward a very dandyish theory of love: Serpukhovskoy was "handsome, happy, rich, and therefore never loved anybody"; therefore, everybody loved him; he, his horse, his mistress, and his coachman, were all handsome and superior—the glamour spread from one to the other—and so love was helplessly attracted to them, and commanded, and deserved, no return.[5] It is an immoralist world Tolstoy analyses, and his later work is a series of attempts to win moral self-respect for himself.

He also worked out some brilliant images for the dandy sensibility, notably the juxtaposition of an older man with a younger man, in which the interest is partly the contrast, partly the relationship, but perhaps most essentially the revelation that the older man is still the younger one in a rougher and gruffer form. The most brilliant example of this occurs in the last of the Sebastopol sketches, in which the younger Kozeltsov brother, Volodya, is described in the most sumptuous, almost cannibal, sensual detail, and the older brother is faded, coarsened, turned stolid by contrast; but we realize that he had been just like his brother and still contains that within himself, able to make that appear on special occasions. That is also the device in "The Oasis," where the subject is a middle-aged woman and the girl she had been, and in "Two Hussars," where the two men are father and son (the moral is different there, but the device is the same, and the device is essential to dandyism). In *War and Peace* the same thing recurs, in the juxtaposition of Petya Rostov, just before he is killed, with Nikolai.

An early story that expresses the conflict Tolstoy felt in these matters is called "Christmas Night" (1853). This begins with a description of Christmas in Moscow, which is so sordid by contrast with the Christmases of one's childhood in the country: because of the poetic sense one had then of the unexpected and of old traditions and of the superstitions of the people.[6] Innocence, therefore, is one of the themes, but innocence necessarily lost and past. We then see the central character, Ivin, go to buy gloves for a ball, from Charles, the dispenser of French fashions in Moscow. There he is accosted by Prince Kornakov, who reappears at the ball to introduce Ivin to the countess he has long adored from a distance. A heavy contrast is drawn between the world-weary but charming prince and the blushing, ardent boy, who is too shy to be anything but clumsy with the lady; when the lady goes home, however, she weeps when her husband touches her, because she has seen what poetic love would be like.

After the ball, Ivin and the Prince are carried off by a very dissipated man to a restaurant, to visit the gypsies, and then to a brothel. This man, Dolgov, is cynical, selfish, and coarse-minded, but he is accepted in fashionable society as a masterful figure because he has style. He fixes Ivin up with a prostitute, and the reader is reminded of the way the Prince had fixed him up with the countess. The dandy experience is glamorous but poisoned.

But dandyism was not purely or even primarily a literary role for Tolstoy. It was embodied in the people he knew, notably in members of his own family. His brother Sergei had served in a smart regiment, but retired from that—abruptly and obstinately—to live in the country, devoting himself to hunting and to the gypsies, that incarnation of the aesthetic element in Russian life. He fell in love with one of the best singers in the Tula gypsy chorus, Marya Shiskin, and took her away from her parents to live with him at Pirogovo, which had been his share of the parental estate. Lev's Yasnaya Polyana was also full of gypsies, for he loved their songs, which were full of the love of freedom and the steppe. He himself, even in later life, used to sing these songs, dressed up in gypsy costume. He learned the gypsy language, and Sergei is said to have nearly persuaded him to marry one of the girls, as he had. Sonya later said, according to Tolstoy's disciple, Biriukov, that the gypsies had turned both brothers' heads.[7]

There was also "Uncle" Kostya Islavin, who was a courtesy member of the family, being a son of Count Nikolai Tolstoy's great friend; he was the brother to Liubov Islavin and so a real uncle to Sonya Tolstoy. He was a talented musician and an attractive man, who got Lev Tolstoy into dissolute ways in St. Petersburg. In 1851, in Tiflis, Tolstoy wrote: "My affection for Islavin ruined a full eight months of life in St. Petersburg for me. Though unconsciously, I only worried about his liking me."[8] (In his diary Tolstoy named Islavin amongst the men he had once been in love with.) But it was his brother Dmitri who was more seriously ruined by Islavin, while Lev was in the Caucasus in the early 1850s. Up to that time, Dmitri had continued in the severely moral and religious ways he had begun at the university in Kazan, and had spent a lot of time with monks and nuns. Under Islavin's influence, then, he began drinking and whoring and gambling, with far less power of self-control or moderation than his brother. An illegitimate son, Islavin had no home and no income of his own, and he played a Mephistophelean role—the role Sheikh Mehtab played vis-a-vis the Gandhi brothers—to the Tolstoy brothers in their youth; Aunt Toinette warned Lev against him in vain; and at the end of his life, in the 1880s and 1890s, he was still a hanger-on of Lev's.

Finally, there was a cousin who was known in fashionable society as "Tolstoy the American" because he had been to Alaska and had had many adventures, including getting himself tattooed. He was famous as a duelist, gambler, amorist, and general blackguard. He was portrayed in Tolstoy's fiction as the first Hussar in "Two Hussars" and as Dolokhov in *War and Peace*. He is mentioned in Griboedov's play, *Woe From Wit*, and he played a part in Pushkin's life. He did not die until 1846, and Lev often visited his house, both before and after his death. Like Sergei, he married a gypsy, and their daughter married a friend of Tolstoy's called Perfilyev. At the end of his life, Tolstoy wrote, "I remember his fine, bronzed face, shaved save for thick white whiskers down to the corners of his mouth, and similarly white curly hair. I should like to relate much about this extraordinary, guilty and attractive man."[9] The dandyism that such men represented to him was not, even when Tolstoy was old, merely bad, but was also something attractive; when he was young they exerted great authority over his moral imagination—though even then, other and opposed ideals challenged theirs.

From his irresolution Tolstoy found a typical temporary relief by an impulsive decision, in April 1851, to go to the Caucasus with his brother Nikolai. The latter had spent the previous four years there, in the army. In this way Lev stumbled into participation in a series of wars, of which this first one was a classic case of imperialism in action.

Russia had annexed Georgia in 1801, and the mountain tribes of the Caucasus had been sporadically fighting against the Russians ever since. In 1826 they acquired a leader of military genius, Shamil, who turned the tribal cause into a holy war of Islam against Christianity, with military leaders who were also holymen, murids. But the Russian writers, whose imaginations were captured by the war, interpreted the tribesmen's cause as freedom, that being a modern system value. Lermontov wrote in "Ismail Bey": "O, wild the tribes that dwell in these defiles; Freedom their God, and Strife their only Law!"[10] It was also, of course, an anti-modern-system cause, the mountains being the refuge of those who would otherwise be disciplined by the armies of the cities. This ambivalence made the subject of the war a richly rewarding one for the writers. In a variant on *The Cossacks*, Tolstoy wrote of his hero, "War was certainly the last occupation he would have chosen; this particular war, in which a hill people, oppressed but bold and chivalrous, were fighting for their freedom, seemed to him monstrous."[11]

The population of the Caucasus was about four million, very mixed in tribe and language. The Tolstoy brothers were stationed at a Cossack stanitsa on the Terek, on the eastern side of the Caucasus, the land of the Chechens. Except when they were led out on expedition, the situation was one of defensive alert, and the aggression was attributed to the enemy. The Cossacks had long been settled in frontier villages beside the Terek, and the Russian troops were quartered—not very welcomely—upon them. The Cossacks represented the element of freedom in Russian life; they were like the gypsies, except that they were a military fighting force, and a politically significant body, used against the enemies of the state.

For Tolstoy, as we can see from *The Cossacks*, they were both a stepping stone and a link between the Russians and the Chechens. The theme of that (autobiographical) story is the attempt of a young Russian noble to incorporate some of the wild freedom that the Cossacks represent (they represent it by borrowing Chechen dress and war-cries and ways of riding, and so on); the noble's imagination does not reach out to the tribesmen themselves, who are entirely outside of civilization, but in imitating the Cossacks, he more remotely imitates the Chechen. The cult of a martial race was a natural extension of dandyism; the young Chechen warriors were called *djigits*, and a *djigitovka*, a display of, first, horsemanship and then gunplay was usual at all festivals. (Tolstoy acquired a young djigit friend, called Sado Miserbiyev.) The djigit was a figure of great glamor; his trophies included the heads or hands of victims, tied to his saddle. In those tribes the women did all the manual work and played a heroic part in their legends; and this was also true of the Cossacks—the Cossack girl in Tolstoy's story is drawn to suggest that.

Cattle-lifting, highway robbery, and murder were deeds of honor among the Chechen; arms and a horse, a man's most prized possession. They embodied freedom from civilized moral restraint, as the Indians did in America, and the Cossacks imitated them, as the frontiersmen imitated the Indians. As long as their forest stood, the Chechen were unconquerable, and Shamil forbade tree-cutting. The Russians subdued them by a long, slow process of tree-felling, and one of Tolstoy's short stories about the war is entitled "The Wood-Cutting."

I have called this a classic case of imperialist war for several reasons. A great empire was advancing its frontier at the expense of some mountain tribesmen. The representatives of civilization were subduing more primitive peoples. The regimental troops of the cities were fighting bands of mountaineers, in wildly beautiful and romantic scenery. Soldiers in uniform, with firearms and cannon, were fighting khans in chain-mail, wielding scimitars and iron maces—their guns and cannon mostly captured from the Russians or bought from English gun-runners. It was a situation about which one was bound to feel strongly, but the ways of feeling were constricted; they had already been explored, and conflicted with each other. Thus, it was a situation that provoked irony. Tolstoy wrote his brother Sergei on 23 December 1851: "With all my strength I will assist with the aid of cannon in destroying the predatory and turbulent Asiatics."[12] Once there, however, he became seriously ambitious for a military career and hoped to become a protégé of the supreme commander there, Bariantinski.

The Caucasus was then one of the four growing points of the Russian Empire. The other three were Alaska, Kazakstan, and the border with China, where Muraviev-Amursky seized the island of Sakhalin. Muraviev-Amursky was a sort of Russian Rhodes or Jackson, convinced that his country had a destiny to control South East Asia. He began his series of voyages in 1847, and in 1851 established a Russian port at the mouth of the Amur. N. P. Ignatiev brought about the Treaty of Peking, which brought Russia Vladivostok and the Maritime Provinces between the Amur and the Usuri. But of all these it was the Caucasus that held the glamor for those not involved. For instance, the Turkestan campaigns between 1864 and 1881, though fought against a cruel and barbarous enemy, and though they added enormous stretches of territory to the Russian empire, never attracted the romantic attention that the Caucasus war did.

As far as the Russian authorities were concerned, it had the safety valve function that frontier wars always have. "The Russian army of the Caucasus led its own separate existence, constantly fighting. It gave the bored and disaffected the chance to escape from the bureaucratic blight which afflicted Russia proper. It gave adventure to those who sought it; oblivion to those who wanted to forget their pasts; the restoration of honour to those in disgrace or under a cloud."[13] In this way the Caucasus will remind us of Britain's North-West frontier wars in India and their bard, Kipling. One of Tolstoy's stories about the army, "Reduced to the Ranks," might have been written by Kipling; and *Hadji Murat* was a subject that would have attracted him.

The most famous writer about the Caucasus was the novelist Bestuzhev-Marlinsky (he wrote under the latter name), who had been one of the Decembrist conspirators in 1825 and served out part of his sentence of exile in the Caucasus. He came there as a hero of aristocratic freedom, and while there he both wrote wildly romantic tales, which were very popular, and lived a wildly romantic life, ending in melodramatic tragedy. But his personal tragedy was socially a stimulating myth. His best-known novel, *Ammalet Bek* (1831), is described in an English translation of 1895 as "a curious picture of war as carried on between the Russians, those representatives of the civilization of the North, and the wild fierce tribes of the Caucasus." The description prepares the English and American reader to find—as he does find—an exotic variation on a staple of his own fiction.

Achmett Khan has stirred up trouble against the Russians in the Caucasus and has involved Ammalet Bek, who loves his daughter, Sultanetta. There is much talk of how the tribesmen live in freedom, like lions, among their mountains; their songs are translated, their customs described, their landscape celebrated. "Wildly beautiful is the resounding Terek in the mountains of Darial. There, like a genie borrowing his strength from Heaven, he wrestles with Nature. There, bright and shining as steel, cutting through the overshadowing cliff, he gleams among the rocks. . . . he bellows and sounds like a wild animal among the imprisoning cliffs; he bursts, overthrows and rolls afar their broken fragments. . . . At one moment he sees its wild and troubled waves raging like infernal spirits chased by the archangel's brand. After them with a shout as of laughter, roll the huge stones. . . ."[14] The mountain scenery becomes the embodiment of freedom.

Ammalet Bek is captured by the Russians and assigned to the personal responsibility of Colonel Verkovsky, a sympathetic and intelligent man, a hero of civilization. In contact with him, Ammalet Bek begins to become civilized himself. He saves Verkovsky's life twice, and loves him; but Achmett Khan demands the Russian's head as the price of Sultanetta's hand, and Ammalet Bek forces himself to kill his friend, only to be cursed by Sultanetta afterwards.

The killing of Verkovsky, and an earlier scene in which a band of Tatars chant a song of resistance as they await their death at the hands of a much larger Russian force, are very similar to scenes in Tolstoy's *The Cossacks* and *Hadji Murat*. The latter has some claims to be considered Tolstoy's finest short fiction, but is after all only a remarkably deromanticized example of the imperialist romance.

Tolstoy took the Cossacks seriously, as a political and social phenomenon that had lessons for organized society. In 1865 he said: "The Russian people repudiate that property which is most stable—

arable land. This truth is not a dream. It is a fact which was imple-
mented in peasant communes. . . . the Russian revolution can only be
based on it." And on 2 April 1870: "All of Russian history was made
by the Cossacks. It is not without reason that the Europeans call us
Cossacks. The people want to be Cossacks. . . . "[15] And he was not
alone in this.

The Cossacks were the front line of the Russian army in the
Caucasus, as elsewhere. At the same time, they were frontiersmen in
the American sense, refugees from the life of the cities, either in
person or by inheritance. They have always symbolized freedom in
Russian culture: Herzen and his revolutionary friends called themselves a "Cossack band." Wilhelm Bervi uses the same image for the
young Socialists at the University of Kazan in the 1840s. Thus, they
were uniquely representative of imperialism in the modern-system
sense, the equivalent in political and military terms of the adventure
tale in literature, and easily translated into Anglo-American experience (though no one group in our history is as richly meaningful as
they). John F. Baddeley, in *The Russian Conquest of the Caucasus* gives
a very British sense of them. They are "the only true colonizers beside
the British. . . . It is to these qualities and to the combination of plough
and sword, mainly in the hands of the Cossacks, that Russia owes
today the extent of her empire."[16]

Shklovsky says that Tolstoy saw in them a model for all Russia—
a peasantry without a gentry—and that the schools Tolstoy opened
around Yasnaya Polyana were model Cossack societies of freedom,
with no serfs, no floggings, and no women in subordination. Tolstoy's
feeling for the Cossacks seems to have been more aristocratic and
romantic than Shklovsky allows—they may have suggested to him,
with their horsemanship, a gentry without a peasantry as much as the
reverse; but there can be no doubt that they were important to him.

Turning now to Gandhi and London, we find that the great
imperial city was in one aspect another paradise of the dandies during
his time there. *The Portrait of Dorian Gray* came out in 1890, as did
the Sherlock Holmes story, *A Study in Scarlet*. And Gandhi himself
had during his stay in London a brief and uncharacteristic period of
elaborate and expensive dress. He wore a top-hat and carried a silver-
mounted cane; he took lessons in elocution, dancing, and violin-playing;
he was developing his personality to match and correspond with the
rich and elaborate world around him. But it would be wrong to suggest
that even in that period he was comparable with Oscar Wilde or with
Tolstoy in Moscow forty years earlier. London was to Gandhi rather
a land of Brobdingnag, in which he moved between the legs of men

and institutions that towered above him like colossi and trembled at bellowing voices far above.

In Gandhi's London, Trafalgar Square had become the arena for manifestations of organized discontent, and John Burns of Battersea was the big Labour leader. The years 1889 and 1890 saw terrible winters, and there was a long strike on the docks, which Cardinal Manning helped to settle. (Gandhi went to congratulate him on his peace-making.)

He began there, as part of his English personality, to take an interest in political matters, and he regularly read three publications, the *Daily Telegraph*, the *News Chronicle*, and the *Pall Mall Gazette*. As for international and imperial affairs, he was in London during the time of the Scramble for Africa, when the European powers were competing and cooperating in the division of the unclaimed parts of that continent. But at that time Gandhi had no political convictions that condemned imperialism. Probably he paid more attention to signs of a new kind of interest in India on the part of Parliament. In 1883 John Bright, one of the great Liberals, gave his approval to the formation of a Parliamentary committee on India and became chairman of its executive; on behalf of this committee, John Slagg, the Member for Manchester, asked for an inquiry into affairs in India. And in 1892, just after Gandhi left England, Dadabhai Naoroji, an Indian economist and ex-businessman Gandhi much admired, was elected a Member of Parliament.

For his legal studies Gandhi joined the Inner Temple on 6 November 1888, but his work left him ample time to look at London and to find within it what was congenial to him. He took, for instance, an interest in Christianity, listening to several famous preachers but preferring always the Nonconformists. He said that Joseph Parker, the Congregationalist who preached at the City Temple, brought him back to theism. And later in South Africa he was friendly with ministers who attended the Keswick Conferences of evangelicals, which owed something to the model of American revivalist meetings. He read the New Testament, and especially the Sermon on the Mount, with enthusiasm, but he rejected the Old Testament. And though impressed by this side of Christianity, he does not seem to have ever been very close to conversion. He found more of what he wanted in the looser doctrine and stricter asceticism of vegetarianism.

We can call the London that was congenial to Gandhi the city of the New Life. This was the city of experiments in life-style, diet, creed, sex, clothes, and so on; the community of Shaw, Carpenter, Havelock Ellis, H. M. Hyndman, and others; the confluence of Tolstoyans, vegetarians, and Socialists. Gandhi was interested in all of this, and sampled a little of each offering. But in order to understand him, we must evoke also that imperial London which surrounded him and struck his imagination through every sense and from every angle. London was then a megalopolis, a world capital, a giant and imperial city; Gandhi's time there was after all in the very decade of Victoria's Diamond Jubilee of 1897, which James Morris has described at length in *Pax Britannica*, with the subtitle "The Climax of an Empire."

Morris lists the territories Britain then ruled, continent by continent. In Africa, for instance, there was Ashanti, Basutoland, British East Africa, Cape Province, Gambia, the Gold Coast, Natal, Nigeria, Nyasaland, Rhodesia, Sierra Leone, Somaliland, Uganda, and Zanzibar. There were forty-three governments within the empire, eleven of them self-governing—since the six Australian colonies were not yet united as one. Then came the Crown colonies, and then the protectorates; Egypt, for instance, had been administered by England since 1882. And this geographical size was reflected in the stature of the individual Englishman, in the eyes of contemporaries—including Gandhi.

England was changing. The journalist W. G. Monypenny said that "empire" and "imperialism" had taken the place that had been held by "nation" and "nationalism."[17] English psychology was now that of a master race. "At that moment of her history, Britain was settled in the habit of authority—authority in the family, in the church, in social affairs, even in politics. It was the last heyday of the patricians . . . the English posture abroad was habitually one of command. To the educated Englishman responsibility came naturally. No other power had been so strong for so long."[18] England's change of character was importantly a matter of its becoming more military. It was, as I have suggested, a change from the bania to the kshattriya caste in its leading representatives. As John Bowle says in *The Imperial Achievement*:

> Anyone looking through the periodicals at the time of the Diamond Jubilee of 1897 will be struck by how military the pattern was: by the quasi-Prussian tropical helmets of the age of Kitchener and Curzon, the professional touch of the new khaki suited to the Northwest Frontier and the Veldt, the bemedalled chests of military magnates, the roar of applause with which the new popular press greeted exploits that made news. If Lord Roberts was the dapper and amiable embodiment of a peculiarly British tradition, Kitchener could hold his own with the most monolithic titan of the German army.

And the fleet, spic and span, with an impeccable tradition and officered by professionals who were almost a caste, was respected and romanticized even by the solid civilian majority to whom the army and the Empire in India appeared more of a class preserve.[19]

Bowle reflects on the curious contrasts within the character of the England that Gandhi knew—the contrasts between what I have called its black magic and its white magic.

Indeed, the Liberal experiment, so civilian and humane, carried out within the island between 1906 and 1914, had been made in contrast with the barbarity of the power politics and armaments of the time, in contrast with the rampant militarism of the Prussian officer caste, the nationalist passions that seethed within the Austro-Hungarian empire, the colossal social upheaval brewing in Russia. It was incongruous with the armaments race, with the great coal-burning battleships with 15" guns, the howitzers, cannon and machine guns. . . .[20]

Kipling was not, of course, sympathetic to that New Age movement of thought within which Gandhi moved; he gave his support to the army and the navy and to those main pillars of the imperial temple which he saw the New Life as undermining. (Ironically, he was probably more in sympathy with the Oriental occult than Gandhi ever was, or at least his late stories suggest that. The rational and moral severity on which England had prided itself was now more the property of the naked fakir than of the bard of empire.) Kipling was certainly one of those writers, some English, some Indian, who made Orientalism an imaginative force in the England of the 1900s. The most famous of the Hindus' attempts to reassert their pride in their cultural heritage, though an attempt led by the non-Hindus, Madame Blavatsky and Mrs. Besant, was Theosophy, which Gandhi got to know in London. This movement, which I have subsumed under the heading of Orientalism, was important to Gandhi and, indeed, to all of London of the New Life.

Some Theosophists introduced Gandhi to Edwin Arnold's very popular verse translation of the Bhagavad Gita, entitled *The Song Celestial*. Thus, the first time Gandhi read this famous poem, central jewel of the Hindu religious and literary tradition, it was in English and was a part of this English Oriental movement. He then met Arnold at the West London Food Reform Society, and for a time he, Arnold, and Josiah Oldfield ran a vegetarian club together in Bayswater. He also read, in 1899, the Bhagavad in the original Sanskrit, and the Arnold verse biography of Buddha, entitled *The Light of Asia.*

Edwin Arnold was a minor poet in the line of Keats and Tennyson, who went out to India in 1857 (at 25) to be principal of the Government College at Poona. When he came back to England, he became a leader-writer for *The Daily Telegraph*, a new daily begun when the repeal of the Stamp Act made it possible to sell newspapers more cheaply. This paper had a generally imperialistic character and financed explorer expeditions like Stanley's three-year voyage from Zanzibar to the mouth of the Congo, which began in 1874. Arnold was much involved in the sponsoring and planning of the expedition, and Stanley named African mountains and rivers after him. Later Arnold went on to translate from the Koran and other Arabic sources, and finally focused his enthusiasm on Japan, where in 1892 he married a Japanese girl who was only in her twenties. (Gandhi always cited Arnold's books as the source of his knowledge of Japan.) He enthusiastically predicted an imperial expansion for Japan—for Arnold was all for expansion and expansiveness, in every sphere of life. His generosity and susceptibility to new moral ideas were genuine enough.

But the most important general truth that Arnold exemplifies is that in those decades people could combine expansive imperialism with experimental Orientalism. It was perhaps from men like Arnold that Gandhi learned to believe in British imperialism as a reaching out to other lands (in both senses of reaching out) on the part of an inordinately energetic people, supremely gifted to organize, control, and administrate, who turned, in the overflow of their energy, to ask other cultures to teach them the ultimate meanings of life. That, after all, is the message of *Kim*: the Lama, with all his unworldliness, has the secret of life, and the players of the Great Game, with all their worldly responsibilities, will always turn to him in the end. Published in 1901, *Kim* is one of the most vivid expressions of this kind of Orientalism.

The experiences of Gandhi's life that correspond to Tolstoy's experiences in the Caucasus took place in South Africa. They were not, of course, the same experiences. The most famous event in Gandhi's biography there, his victimization and humiliation by white racists soon after he arrived, never happened to Tolstoy in the Caucasus. That event should be put in the context of the literature of Anglo-Saxon imperialism, where such incidents are often described, though usually from a white racist point of view.

South Africa, however, meant more than that experience to Gandhi. It meant first-hand knowledge of the expansive process of the modern system—not only imperialism, which was a vivid enough fact in India, but colonialism. And it meant seeing two historical layers of this process, the English and the Dutch. The Dutch Boers in South Africa were, like the French Habitants in Canada, the fossilized driftwood left behind by a first wave of modern empire when that retreated; and in Gandhi's time they were being submerged and smitten by the second wave, the English.

Thus, the Boers were a curiously arrested form of white empire life, fossilized at the cultural stage (roughly seventeenth century) at which the imperialist vitality had died in Holland, when England assumed the leading role in the modern system. In the East Indies the Dutch continued to work their profitable investment, but in a merely commercial spirit, somewhat more contracted than the true modern spirit shown by the English in India, for instance. The other parts of the Dutch Empire gradually lost contact with the mother country and with the European metropolis as a whole. Even the spirit of technological enterprise died in them; their agriculture remained primitive; they hunted and relied on what was, in effect, slave labor. In matters of high culture, they reverted to a premodern style, a ritual as static as that of nineteenth-century India or seventeenth-century Muscovy—a *bitovoye blagochestie*.

At the same time as the Boers trekked north, however, the Bantu ("the people") trekked south, away from the East Africa highlands, where they were being captured and sold into slavery by Arab traders and raiders. For, of course, there have been other empires in the world, brown empires, beside the white. Indeed, among the Bantu were the Zulu—a black warrior race that became imperialist under the leadership of Chaka, the great hero of the Kaffir wars and the Napoleon of the Zulus—who were a black empire.

There were desperate battles between the Zulus and the British even after Gandhi arrived in Natal. He saw Zulus as a martial race, of whom Indians were bound to be afraid. One of the interests of Chaka for us is that his story was told in the best of Rider Haggard's novels, *Nada the Lily*, and as such it became one of the legends of British imperialism at the end of the century, part of the energizing myth of white empire. Haggard had accompanied Sir Theophilus Shepstone when he rode into Pretoria in 1877 and annexed the Transvaal; *Nada the Lily* is dedicated to Shepstone, and presents him as a white and civilized Chaka. Haggard's experiences in South Africa provided him with the stories he told when he returned to England, which were extremely widely read from 1890 on. He and Kipling were two of the most influential writers in Gandhi's England, corresponding to Marlinsky and Lermontov in Tolstoy's Russia. Indeed, Gandhi's close friend Joseph Doke wrote a South African romance, *The Secret City* (1913), which Gandhi much enjoyed, which is quite like some stories by Haggard.

Though imperialist writers, Kipling and Haggard were both in love with non-British races and landscapes. Indeed, both were interested in the occult and both could be called Orientalists; and, as we have seen in the case of Edwin Arnold, imperialism and Orientalism often went together.

In South Africa, Gandhi became the representative of Edward Maitland's Esoteric Christian Union, another example of the Oriental wing of the New Age. (He recommended Maitland's books as a defense against materialism, anarchy, and so on.) Since Gandhi afterwards regretted the destruction of his 1894–97 correspondence with Maitland—it was the only lost correspondence he regretted—a look at this clergyman's son is in order.

Edward Maitland, born in 1824, was brought up a Calvinist but rebelled against the doctrine of original sin. "And I knew that, however weak and unwise I might be, I was not evil."[21] This shift of target from sin to weakness was typical of the times and corresponds, within religion, to the concentration on power and expansion in literature and politics. In itself it announced his unlikeness to Gandhi (and to Tolstoy in his mature phase), for both of them knew evil in themselves.

His most important work was *The Perfect Way*, written with Anna Kingsford and published in London in 1890, but delivered as lectures in 1881. A preface in the revised edition points to Matthew Arnold's "men cannot do without it [Christianity] but they cannot do with it as it is."[22] (Tolstoy also often cited Arnold's religious essays as valuable.) *The Perfect Way* is a kind of gnosticism. "In our day of analysis, research, and criticism, religion has to appeal to the intellectual as well as the devotional side of man's nature."[23] It offers truths discovered by intellectual intuition, like the multiple rebirths of the ego, and sums up its teaching in three propositions: (*a*) Christian dogma are the same as those of earlier religions; (*b*) true belief lies in the mind and heart; and (*c*) Christianity is (when understood this way) a scientific account of man's spiritual history.

"The Perfect Way" is to displace both materialism and what it calls conventionalism (traditional religion). Perhaps what is most striking about it is its stress on women. Woman, we are told, is the crowning manifestation of humanity.[24] Simon Peter, the rock on which the Church is founded, represents Understanding, but woman is Intuition. God is twain, both male and female; He is the Life, but She is the substance. "On the plane of manifestation, as the Soul macrocosmic and microcosmic, She appears as the Daughter, Mother and Spouse of God . . . bearing in Her arms the infant Man, in whom . . . the universe is redeemed."[25] On the physical plane, Man is only Boy till he recognizes Her; on the spiritual plane he is only a materialist till he chooses Her, the soul, as his better half. Maitland and Kingsford had been members of the Theosophical Society and were rivals to H. P. Blavatsky and Annie Besant. The dominance of women in these movements was reflected in their doctrine; sexual revolt was in the air.

Imperialism, and much else in late nineteenth-century culture, was tied to heavily masculine images and values; this is seen in Kipling's work. This kind of mystical feminism was clearly a reaction against that masculine dominance, but, as we have seen in Maitland's case, it was not necessarily anti-imperialist. It was widespread, however, taken up in Russia by Vladimir Soloviev, one of Tolstoy's main ideological enemies, and developed by such disciples of his as Rozanov.

Upon his partner's death, Maitland wrote a two-volume *Life of Anna Kingsford* (1895), in which he presented her as a "contemporary Revelator and Saviour." Always possessed of psychic powers, she married a cousin and bore him a daughter, but seems to have soon ceased to be his wife sexually. Indeed, when her husband had taken orders in the Church of England, she had converted to the Church of Rome and taken the baptismal name of Mary Magdalen, because the famous sinner-saint had appeared to her in a number of visions. When her husband had become a country curate, she had gone to London, bought and edited *The Lady's Own Paper*, and spoken and written as a feminist. In 1873 she had taken up the study of medicine, and in 1875, under Maitland's protection (they met when she wrote him enthusiastically about his novel), she had gone to Paris as a medical student.

The biography unintentionally portrays a neurotic and spiritually ambitious woman, in whom impulses of the most crudely egoistic and self-advertising kind were mixed up with genuine insights and convictions. (Edward Carpenter, who collaborated with Maitland, spoke of Kingsford's gifts as "a considerable literary ability and a generous and undisguised use of cosmetics."[26]) Sexually, she was of the type of Lou Andreas-Salome, the type portrayed in fiction by Hardy as Sue

Bridehead, the emergence of which was a cultural phenomenon of the 1880s. Along conventional lines of thought, her abilities are considerable, but because she did not accept ordinary discipline, the sense she makes is mixed up with nonsense. It is most unlikely that Tolstoy or Gandhi would have recognized any spiritual authority in her. But Gandhi was sympathetic to much that she attempted, as a religionist and an Orientalist.

Gandhi was perhaps deceived by all this imaginative interest in the East, and all the apparent activity in the direction of a New Life. He had, after all, good reason to think that a big change was coming over England, and to think that those prodigious energies which in nineteenth-century England had been put into seizing new lands and developing new industries, would now find expression in more genial and liberal projects. Nearly everyone said that the age of armies and wars was over. There was a promise in the air between 1880 and 1914 that the age of the fathers was over: D. H. Lawrence and his friends and allies were deceived by it, too. We should not use the word *deceived*, however, to imply a blind stupidity in them. The promise of such a change was made, but it naturally provoked a defensive reaction; when that came, England had to choose between the "ideal" and the "real," and on the whole it chose the latter; but it might not have.

Thus, Tolstoy in Moscow and the Caucasus, and Gandhi in London and South Africa, were both on the verge of their careers (their first careers, in literature and politics). They were still more acted upon than acting; their contemporaries certainly did not look upon them as leaders or look to them for great achievements. But we now see that they were accumulating the ideas and the experience they would later put to use. They would first interpret those ideas to energize their participation in the modern-world culture; they would later give them another interpretation, which they would use, each in his own opposition to that culture.

V
St. Petersburg and Johannesburg: 1855–62 and 1894–1906

In the second half of this period I have called "Youth" (between the ages of twenty and forty, roughly), Tolstoy and Gandhi found their ways to literature and politics, respectively, the two fields of activity in which they were to invest most of their energies for most of their lives. But they were still perceptibly testing their wings even at the end of this period, and their great achievements were still to come.

We can associate Tolstoy's life and work in this period with St. Petersburg—even though he did not live there much of the time—because it was there that he met the writers with whom he had most to do and who represented literature to him: Turgenev, Botkin, Annenkov, Druzhinin, Nekrasov, and Panaev. Moreover, a central focus of Tolstoy's interest in this period was what we can call "consciousness," and St. Petersburg was a city of consciousness. Unlike Moscow, it was a thoroughly modern city, which made its inhabitants aware of how modern institutions were changing their lives and their feelings; and the writers of Russia embodied that consciousness in literature.

In the second half of the nineteenth century St. Petersburg was a big city by European standards; the population jumped from half a million in 1850 to a million in 1890, and doubled again by 1914. From 1850 on, industrialization and urbanization shaped and colored the city's life: "Labour unrest, political intrigue, massive demonstrations, and ultimately bloody revolutions were all nurtured by the poverty and despair which were as much a part of industrialization as the factories themselves."[1] Industrialization, James T. Baker says, meant "regularity of habit among the work-force; it changed the conditions of employment from the close personal relationships, good or bad, in the workshop, to the impersonal bureaucratic ones on the factory floor, thereby creating a void between owner and employee; it required new financial structures; it brought new pressures to the urban land market; it required more transport facilities, if not new ones. . . ."[2] Every summer, huge contingents of manpower came to work in building and manufactures, but only transient residence was provided for peasants; long after the emancipation of 1861, social and political regulations continued to be feudal. In addition, the death rate was much higher than in other European capitals.

Above all—for our purposes—St. Petersburg was the city of the *intelligentsia*. This characteristic Russian word means primarily those who live by their minds—by making use of their intellects; but this also necessarily implies those who are alienated from the social faith in Orthodoxy, Autocracy, and Nationalism. (Of course there were exceptions to this—*intelligenti* like Dostoevsky, who declared his faith in those doctrines—but they were conscious always of swimming against the tide.) The intelligentsia overlap with another characteristic Russian group, the *raznochintsy*, those who did not belong to an estate or caste—amongst whom the most typical were those sons of priests who had refused to stay in the clerical caste. Since the caste system corresponded to the faith in Orthodoxy, Autocracy, and Nationalism, the raznochintsy were almost necessarily intelligentsia. And both groups overlapped largely with the radicals and revolutionaries, in both political and cultural matters. Of course, many individuals were in one group but not in another, but our usage of these terms must necessarily reflect the fact that very often the same individuals were in all of them. The map of tendencies in Tolstoy's Russia was dominated by a polarity between all these groupings at one end and conservative nationalism at the other. And since these groups represented, in various ways, modernity, Tolstoy was opposed to them and tried in the first half of his life to convince himself that his allies were conservative nationalists.

The intelligentsia of the 1860s despised "life values" of the kind Tolstoy celebrated in his novels. Worshipping only science, they despised literature and even philosophy. D. I. Pisarev (1814–68), one of their ablest spokespersons, said: "The popularization of science is the most important world-wide task of our age. A good popularizer, especially in Russia, can be of far greater use to society than the talented researcher."[3] He spoke of "our little Pushkin," and said that writer's place was "not on the desk of the contemporary worker, but in the dust-filled study of the antiquary. . . . " He called him "a frivolous versifier, enmeshed in his petty prejudices."[4] Turning to literature in general, he said: "I am delighted to see the shrivelling away of our imaginative literature as a symptom of the growing maturity of our intellect. . . . I utterly reject the notion of the arts having in any way promoted the intellectual or moral advancement of mankind."[5] Such pronouncements, of course, embodied everything Tolstoy most disliked.

In 1864 Pisarev wrote an essay expounding Darwin, and saying that scientists like Darwin and Lyall were the philosophers, poets, and aestheticians of the age. The best index of progress was the "durable, rational and beneficent" subordination of work to scientific method. (Vengerov, who compiled a biographical dictionary of Russian scientists in 1889, said that many of them owed their vocation to Pisarev's writing.) He urged Saltykov-Shchedrin, the satirist, to give up literature for the popularization of science: "[T]here is only one evil among men—ignorance; against this evil there is only one medicine—learning; but this medicine must be taken not in homeopathic doses, but by the pail and by the 40 pail barrel."[6]

N. G. Chernyshevsky, perhaps Tolstoy's main enemy amongst the intelligentsia, said in his "Anthropological Principle in Philosophy" that no philosophy is sound unless it is embedded in natural science. He claimed that the psychological was so entwined with the physiological in man that the social sciences should follow the methods of natural science. (Here one sees another, more "scientific" application of the idea of the self's triumph over the soul.) Modern Western science, represented by George Henry Lewes' *Physiology of Common Life* (very popular in Russia) was thought to have proved this. These ideas got into fiction, too, and constituted the climate of opinion of the 1860s, against which Tolstoy had to assert himself as an artist.

Bazarov, the hero-villain of Turgenev's novel about the intelligentsia, *Fathers and Sons*, was a preacher of physiology in that sense; he was a medical student, and the dissection of frogs was the activity most associated with him. Pisarev said that Bazarov recognized no authority above himself, no moral law, no principle; Pisarev implicitly admired this—"if bazarovshchina is a sickness, it is the sickness of our age."[7] In fact, "Bazarov" was said to be based on another literary intellectual, N. A. Dobrolyubov, a colleague and an ally of Pisarev. In his brief writing career, Dobrolyubov (1836–61), from the age of twenty-one until his death, established a new standard of harshness in polemic, especially against Turgenev—who called him "the literary Robespierre." And whether or not based on Dobrolyubov, Bazarov represented the same idea and elicited the same anger and enthusiasm. Kliment Timiriazev, the plant physiologist, compared Dobrolyubov with Peter the Great, the most drastic of all Russia's reformers.

The greatest single value that served as a common denominator for all the intelligentsia was "progress," an idea Tolstoy explicitly attacked in his essays on education in the 1860s. Faith in progress was the heart of the social philosophy of scientists like Mendeleev the chemist, Mechnikov the embryologist, Vernadski the mineralogist, and Pavlov the psychologist. In political radicals, this faith in progress was compounded with a seemingly contrary criticism of Western European capitalism and liberalism. This made the old term "Westernizer" inappropriate for the new men, but from Tolstoy's point of view the two groups were aligned in error.

To take an example of this anti-Liberalism almost at random, in September 1861, M. Mikhailov's manifesto "To The Young Generation" appeared. This said:

> They want to turn Russia into an England and to feed us on English maturity. . . . We are a backward people, and in this lies our salvation. . . . If, in order to achieve our ends, to divide the land between the people, we would have to kill 100,000 landowners, even that would not frighten us. Besides, this is really not such a terrible thing.[8]

The first part of that could have been written by Tolstoy, in its dissatisfaction with liberal reform; the second part, of course, declared war on him.

Nineteen-year-old P. Zaichnevsky produced *Young Russia* from jail in May 1862. This document contained a fictitious account of a Central Revolutionary committee, denounced Herzen's *Kolokol* (which had been the trumpet for the radicalism of the preceeding generation— a radicalism Tolstoy had admired), and exulted in the rivers of blood to flow. This announced the most violent strain in Russian revolutionary thought, the strain represented most luridly by Nechaev and called nihilism.

In many ways, therefore, Russia in the 1860s was strikingly like America and most Western countries in the 1960s. The young people directed a general rebellion against church, family, marriage, and clothes; the women wore black dresses, men's boots, and dark glasses, cut their hair short, and smoked; the men let their hair grow and wore red shirts or greasy coveralls. They engaged in all sorts of revolutionary activities, getting their training in circles, communes, and artels. They freed aspiring girls from bourgeois society to join them by means of (amongst other things) fictitious marriages. Chernyshevsky arranged one of the first such, between his doctor and the sister of a writer, and wrote about such a case in his enormously influential novel *What Then Must We Do?* Tolstoy, meanwhile, wrote against such marriages, and against radicalism in general, in plays and stories. But satire and negation went against the grain of his personality as a writer (as a novelist) and he was more effective in his portrayals of happy marriages, such as in *Domestic Happiness*. That title, a phrase he used frequently in those years, was in effect a slogan. It meant that he believed there was such a thing, and that nihilism was a mistake.

In *Tolstoy in the Fifties* Eikhenbaum presents that period in Tolstoy's life as a conflict between the writer (who identified himself with all literature) and the magazine *Sovremennik* (which called on all writers to take up political journalism). The editor was ostensibly Tolstoy's old friend and fellow noble, Nekrasov, but in fact the man in charge was the *raznochinets* Chernyshevsky. By 1855 he was in charge of the literature section of the magazine, and later added the sociopolitical. In *Young Russia* Abbot Gleason says that Chernyshevsky made himself indispensable to Nekrasov by his hard work, reliability, and flattery. He combined arrogance with humility, in priestly fashion.[9] The phrasing is bound to suggest Uriah Heep to us, and the allusion can be taken seriously provided we do not swallow whole all of Dickens' propaganda in that portrait. The allusion is appropriate because Dickens in England was engaged in a dialectic quite like Tolstoy's in Russia— a dialectic in which aristo-military values ("gentleman's" values) were besieged by clerical-bureaucratic values in the society at large and counterattacked in fictional images. Chernyshevsky, who was literally of the clerical-bureaucratic caste, fitted its image. He had a tender heart, scruples, and the courage of his convictions: but he had no aristo-military qualities, no love of nature, little sense of art, and in both physical and sexual terms he lacked dignity. He had no physical splendor or impressiveness, and was made absurd by his wife. Tolstoy said he smelled of bed-bugs, which is what David Copperfield might have said about Uriah Heep, off the page.

Lenin, on the other hand, always spoke of Chernyshevsky with hero-worship: as the great representative of utopian (pre-Marxist) socialism, as the all-Russian revolutionary democrat, and so on. Chernyshevsky, he said, described "what a revolutionary must be like, what his principles must be, how he must approach his aim, and what methods he must use to achieve it."[10]

Political radicalism, then, found a hero in Chernyshevsky. The sort of thing Lenin (and Marx) admired in him was the ruthless logic with which in 1861 he decided that "the worst was the best"; that is, the best form that emancipation could take, from a long-term point of view, would be the worst form (the peasants being freed but given no land), because then dissatisfaction would mount faster and revolution would come sooner. This is typical of a series of moral paradoxes entailed by the creed of revolution, which Tolstoy hated.

We can, as he did, associate all the things Tolstoy hated in the climate of his time with the city of St. Petersburg, and we can set the self-consciousness of that city in opposition to the unconsciousness that he encouraged through his novels and associated with living and working in the country. This "unconscious consciousness" was an important part of what Tolstoy offered his readers as an alternative to modern values—it was part of his ideology.

To explain this, let us begin with the other great Russian novelist of the day, who was equally concerned with these matters. In Dostoevsky's *Notes From Underground* we read: "For man's everyday needs, it would have been quite enough to have the ordinary human consciousness, that is, a half to a quarter of the amount which falls to the lot of the cultivated man of our unhappy 19th century, especially one who has the fatal luck to inhabit Petersburg, the most theoretical and intentional city on the whole terrestrial globe."[11] Nineteenth-century Russians were all conscious of having a good deal more on their minds than their fathers had had, and they were by no means sure that this was a good thing. They saw their literature as beginning with Pushkin, and this gave Russian consciousness a peculiarly compressed and concentrated history, a foreshortened and dramatic development. And they often associated this with St. Petersburg. From Pushkin and Gogol through Dostoevsky to Andrei Bely, early twentieth-century Russian literature offers a series of nightmare fantasies about that city and the statue of Peter the Great that dominates it. Both in a feuilleton of 1861 and in *The Adolescent*, Dostoevsky describes someone (obviously himself) having a vision of the statue as suddenly vanishing, and the hot rush of blood to his heart as it went. It was the incarnation of everything modern; Mandelshtam called it "typographical" because of its straight lines, its clear message, and its character of being an utterance.

The kind of consciousness in which Tolstoy was interested was unlike Dostoevsky's, and was not related in any obvious way to St. Petersburg. Implicitly, however, it *was* so related—by negation. It offered a way for people, even living in the industrialized nineteenth century, to root themselves in nature and in personal relations—in the private life—and so to achieve spiritual health in despite of the public life.

The characteristic Tolstoyan moment in the development of a story's themes and values comes when a leading character becomes so totally aware of something outside himself or herself that he or she stops being his ordinary self and in a sense becomes that other thing; the excitement of thus losing himself, however, evolves naturally into a reinforced sense of his own vitality, so that he regains a stronger self. A straightforward case of this is the early work, *The Cossacks*, in which the hero, Olenin, becomes thus aware of the Caucasian mountains, the Cossack way of life, Eroshka, Maryanka, and so on, one after another, and by virtue of his susceptibility to these impressions becomes our hero. (Susceptibility is the point: his fellow officers are less excited by these things, and that is why they are not our heroes; but when Olenin tries to go beyond susceptibility and literally become a Cossack, that attempt is shown as unavailing and improper.)

It is inexact to say "something outside himself," though, for the expanded consciousness may be of something inside the subject but outside his conscious ego. For instance, we realize that Olenin is to be our hero when we accompany him as he leaves Moscow at the story's beginning, and see how he delights in the chaos of his own mind. This chaos derives from commonplace causes like drink and fatigue, but to know it, to delight in knowing that this is his self, makes Olenin a hero of Tolstoyan consciousness. Perhaps the most typical case is that Tolstoy's representative becomes abnormally aware of his *bodily* experience, especially at moments when that overwhelms ordinary moral and rational categories. In *Anna Karenina* Anna can see her own eyes glittering in the dark as she lies in bed;[12] and Levin delights in the unconsciousness that overcomes his consciousness as he mows.[13] In *War and Peace* Natasha is our heroine because of her mind's susceptibility to nonrational stimuli as various as sexual excitement and music, both of which overcome her self-control; when she sings, an impersonal unconscious self takes over her voice, and we are told that that voice itself has "a virginal freshness, an unconsciousness of its own powers. . . ."[14]

Consciousness is therefore a somewhat misleading name for this phenomenon, since unconsciousness is also in question; but some kind of paradox is acceptable in the term because it is inherent in the phenomenon. Tolstoy describes again and again the indescribable, the unknowable experience, dying, delirium, merging with Nature— transformed consciousness of almost any kind; his heroes are those who are exceptionally susceptible to such transformation; his art aspires to bring such experience to the verge of consciousness, and yet leave it substantially outside: still mysterious, still other, still "unconscious."

And Tolstoy not only describes those half-conscious states of being brilliantly, he also convincingly ascribes to them an extraordinary significance. As he describes them, they become (potentially, tentatively) spiritual adventures. When Natasha goes to her first ball, her excitement is not presented as Jane Austen presents Lydia Bennet's, or even Elizabeth Bennet's. Natasha's excitement is just as "worldly" and egotistic, but it is not merely worldly; we see it, because of the way it is presented to us, as an ecstasy, as something comparable, in psychological terms, with religious rapture. And again it is bodily experience that is the archetype; Natasha's excitement, though social in its occasion, is somatic at its source; the body means both nature and unconscious life—in other words, a part of the divine that the mind can glimpse though never possess.

The Tolstoyan hero's consciousness of the mountains, or of the peasants' mowing, reinforces our sense of health and of the positive values of health. The body consciousness of, for instance, Oblonsky and Anna, Levin and Kitty, is primarily a conscious intelligence's delight in physically delightful sensations; the consciousness both is transparent to the somatic sensation and reinforces it. By this means these people make life attractive to others, and those who meet them (including the readers of the novel) feel their own possibilities enhanced. In other words, Tolstoy's mode of consciousness is in the service of life values.

Life values were an alternative to those values expressed in Dostoevsky's consciousness, and in those of the radical intelligentsia, both of which we can associate with St. Petersburg and with anger. In his speech to the Lovers of Russian Literature, on 4 February 1859 (he was accepting membership in their society, announcing a policy as a writer), Tolstoy asked for writers to create a "full, many-sided consciousness," as opposed to the narrow denunciation of social evil. He wrote to Nekrasov in 1856:

> There is a firmly established opinion, not only in our criticism, but in our literature, and even in our society, that it is very nice to be *angry, irritable*, and *malicious*. . . . But I find all this nasty, because an irritable and malicious man is not in a normal state. . . . And bitterness is terribly fashionable with us. People praise you and say: he's an embittered man. . . .[15]

In opposition to anger, Tolstoy set love, and this was a part of his aesthetic. In one of his notebooks for 1860, he wrote: "The first condition of an author's popularity, the means of making himself beloved, is the love he bears to all of his created characters."[16] And this connection between love and artistic truth was felt by Tolstoy's readers. Nekrasov wrote to him: "Truth—in the form you have introduced it into our literature—is something entirely new among us. I do not know another writer of today who so compels the reader to love him and sympathize heartily with him. . . . "[17] And in a note introducing "Sebastopol in December" to his magazine's readers, Nekrasov said essentially the same to them.

What this love meant in terms of art was a heightened susceptibility, an excited responsiveness, a readiness to be carried away by anything good or beautiful. And we can trace the inner discipline this imposed clearly enough in Tolstoy's diary. On 8 December 1850 he wrote: "Only it seems to me that I am already growing cold. Only rarely, especially when I go to sleep, do moments come to me when feeling wants to burst forth; also in moments of drunkenness; but I have promised myself *not to get drunk*."[18] And in the short story "Lucerne" we see that even generous anger can have the same function, if it carries one away: "I was infuriated with that boiling rage of indignation, which I love and even fan in myself whenever it besets me, because it acts soothingly upon me, and gives me, at least for a short time, a certain extraordinary pliability, energy, and power of all physical and moral faculties."[19] As for love in the more ordinary sense, though that was exalted, it too was disciplined, for it had to be spontaneous and unconscious. In his diary for 8 June 1851 he recorded: "It seems to me that that unknowingness [unawareness of even being in love] is the principal mark of love, and constitutes all its charm."[20]

Although this attention to consciousness (pride in it and anxiety about it) was of St. Petersburg, the values expressed in Tolstoy's kind of consciousness were of Yasnaya Polyana and *not* of St. Petersburg. One can say that because of Dostoevsky and the other St. Petersburg writers, because of the radical intelligentsia with whom Dostoevsky had (paradoxically) so much in common, but also because of the city itself.

Eikhenbaum says that in the 1860s Tolstoy made a strategic retreat outside literature to issue his pedagogical journal and to form a separate, domestic, literary counterculture on his estate at Yasnaya Polyana. Thus, his marriage in 1862 had a more than ordinary meaning; "it was the act of breaking off diplomatic relations with the literary world and of a departure into 'domesticity.' "[21] This move carried with it new experiments in literary and stylistic matters: "Oriented towards the sincere expression of intimate personal feelings, writing was used by Tolstoy and his wife to explore their feelings about their marriage, their family life."[22] This was the way Tolstoy prepared himself—in quite a literary-technical way—to present personal relations and especially dialogue in *War and Peace*.

By the end of this period, Tolstoy was ready to begin his great achievement as a novelist; this occurred within and by means of the contemporary phase of novel-writing, and yet proceeded by creating an old-fashioned mode of consciousness that had been proscribed by the leaders of thought and conscience in his country for over a decade. He set himself against the best that was being thought and said in his place and time.

Turning to Gandhi and politics, then, the city to put in parallel with Tolstoy's St. Petersburg is Johannesburg, the capital of the Transvaal Republic, a city of gold mines and diamond mines, of enormous fortunes and unscrupulous exploitation, of adventurers from all over Europe seeking their fortunes. Gandhi called the Transvaal the El Dorado of the Western world, and Johannesburg "the golden city of South Africa. Only fifty years ago, the site on which it now stands was desolate and covered with dry grass."[23] It was another transparent vision, another utterance of the human will. Both cities' names announce their connection—indirect but not insignificant—with Dutch imperialism. Johannesburg was equally characteristic as a modern-system city, but it was of an opposite type to St. Petersburg, adventurers replacing bureaucrats.

The first biography of Gandhi (published in 1909) evokes Johannesburg as his natural backdrop. The biographer, Joseph Doke, describes the city while he sits in a park thinking about Gandhi:

> But even now the roar of the batteries along the reef, like the roar of surf breaking on a distant shore, attracts the ear. At night it comes nearer. On some cold nights, when the wind blows from the mines, the sound is like the roll of thunder, as though the rocks and sands and surf were battling with each other for victory down there on 'the Wanderers.' That roar never ceases. On calm, hot, sunny days it almost dies; it sinks away into a lazy hum like the drone of bees in the clover. But it is always there. The batteries of the reef are never still. Night and day, and every night and every day, without rest, the crushing of the great machinery goes

on, and the rocks and stones and sand yield their golden treasure in response.[24]

And a 1940 *History of South Africa* gives the same picture:

Upon those parts of the town that are within earshot of the roar of the crushing mills, the sudden winds of August drop their charge of fine white dust, carried from the dumps. The dumps are the physical sign of the Witwatersrand's great dependence upon the gold which makes men live constantly in the present, with their eyes constantly on monthly statements of gold production, their fingers on the pulse of the stock exchanges, and their ears cocked for news of international happenings. . . . [25]

In Australia and New Zealand the industrial system based on gold gradually gave way to one based on wool and mutton, and in Canada to one based on wheat; but South Africa continued to rely on gold— and on slave labor. Gold and slaves went together. Chinese indentured labor came in 1904 and 1906, which, as DeKiewiet says, was socially "most unwise."

Diamonds were first found at Kimberley in the Orange Free State in 1870; the Cape Province claimed the relevant land and gave the Boers £90,000 in compensation. Gold was first found in 1867, but because of the Boers' fear of gold-fever, the finder was sworn to secrecy, and the rush only began in 1884. By 1890 the easily workable veins were exhausted, but just in time the cyanide process was invented: this process, which had an extraction value of ninety percent as against sixty percent, made lower-grade ore workable and was declared "not dangerous to natives." With this, mining became more scientific and mechanical.

The history of South Africa is, of course, one of imperialist expansion—of the English against the Dutch, most apparently. The Cape of Good Hope was originally a Dutch colony, first occupied by British forces in 1795, when the white settlers already numbered 16,000. In 1815 the Congress of Vienna gave the colony to Britain, as part of the spoils of the war against Napoleon; and in 1820 the British settlers began to arrive. As a result of the imposition of unwelcome British regulations, including one for the abolition of slavery in 1834, the Boers began in 1836 a Great Trek north in quest of freedom, seeing themselves as the new Children of Israel. They founded a republic in Natal in 1838, but in 1843 that country, too, was annexed by England. In 1857 the Orange Free State and the Transvaal became independent Boer republics, but in 1877 the Transvaal was annexed. In 1879 Boer leader Paul Kruger went to London to present his countrymen's case to the British government, but the Transvaal was granted only the status of a Crown Colony, which led to a war of independence in 1880–81. This record could be read in the 1890s— was read by Gandhi—to the credit of the modern system. The Boers had shown their sturdy independence, and the British had shown their fitness to rule, their magnanimity, and the wars between them had been kept within bounds. The Boers were something of a model for Gandhi to hold up to the Indians in their dealings with imperial England.

The aggressions of both northwest European peoples against the native Africans is recorded only in subordinate ways in their chronicles, and even in those by Indian chroniclers of the history of Indians in South Africa. In 1870 Basutoland was partitioned between the Crown and the Free State; in 1885 the British Protectorate of Bechuanaland was proclaimed; in 1895 Pondoland was annexed to the Cape, and Swaziland was put under the control of the South African Republic; and so on.

Between 1836 and 1840, 6,000 Boers left the Cape Colony on the Great Trek; amongst them was the future president of the Transvaal, Kruger, who was ten years old when he started. In the course of the long trek the Boers shot 6,000 lions, 200 of which were killed by Kruger personally; thus, he was in those days a white hunter (one of the legendary figures of white empire), but he became also a man of God and a political leader (a legendary figure in the style of the seventeenth rather than the nineteenth century). Gandhi greatly admired him.

South Africa was also a vivid example of the profitability of colonies, of their "windfall" aspect. In a colony, for example, railways were calculated to give a profit of ten to twenty percent, while in France the profits were only two to three percent. And the connection of these profits to ostensibly independent considerations of clothing and decency is made clear in a speech by Henry Stanley to the Manchester Chamber of Commerce, in which he said that if the natives of the Congo learned to dress decently even only on Sundays, that would mean a sale of 320 million yards of Manchester cloth, and if they wore them on weekdays, the profit would be £26 million a year.

There are forty millions of people beyond the gateway of the Congo, and the cotton spinners of Manchester are waiting to clothe them. Birmingham foundries are glowing with the red metal that will presently be made into iron work for them and the trinkets that shall adorn those dusky bosoms, and the ministers of Christ are zealous to bring them, the poor benighted heathen, into the Christian fold.[26]

In the 1911 *Encyclopaedia Britannica* the area of South Africa was said to be 1,333,000 square miles; the rainfall is slight, and though the temperature is high, the climate in general is dry and bracing. (Gandhi found it delightful.) The exports were listed in order of importance as raw gold, diamonds, wool, and ostrich feathers, though tea and coffee, tobacco, sugar, and rice were cultivated. In such an account, the drama of the Indians in Natal is diminished to invisibility, as is the even greater drama of the black population. The country is presented as being essentially a source of raw materials for Europeans: "The history of South Africa is, almost entirely, that of its colonization by European powers, of their conflicts with, and influence over, its native inhabitants, and of the struggle for supremacy between the British and Dutch settlers."[27]

Such was history in 1911, but Gandhi was involved in one of those series of events that were nonhistorical. The reservation of choice areas of Africa and Asia as "white men's countries" was a dream of the British imperialists at the end of the nineteenth century, which failed because there was no pool of British labor to do the hard work of colonizing; the only supply of cheap labor in the British Isles was Ireland, and the Irish preferred to go to America. The situation Gandhi faced in South Africa was paralleled elsewhere in the empire, for instance in Australia, where the mining entrepreneurs wanted Chinese labor, and the unions opposed it. William Lane's newspapers, *The Boomerang* and the *Australian Worker*, in the 1890s played on the fear of disease, immorality, and dirt associated with the Asiatic.

The great advantage the Indians had over the Chinese was the position of India within the empire. In 1905 Britain's trade with India was larger than that with Australia, Canada, and South Africa combined, which gave the Indian interest great weight in Whitehall. And the official philosophy of the empire was liberal. Gandhi welcomed a definition by Lord Selborne of responsible government (such as Natal and the Transvaal had) as: "absolute local independence so long as that independence does not encroach on the general harmony of the British Empire, or infringe any of those principles on which it is founded, or any of those imperial considerations which bind it together."[28] On 12 August 1905 he quoted Selborne again and said, "these are the words spoken by one who is the ruler of the Transvaal. May His Excellency have sufficient courage and strength to initiate the policy he has thus boldly enunciated!"[29] As this suggests, he continued to proclaim his faith in the empire, but began to suggest doubts about and criticism of its will to keep its promises. In his article "The Bright Side of the Picture" he described South Africa as a "thoroughly active and self-seeking community," and said that colonization could only be made to work by practicers of self-help.[30] Indians should sacrifice more in the common good, as the English do—compare the amenities of Durban with those of Zanzibar, an Asiatic city.[31] And his account of the Mutiny is quite like the British version (and unlike Savarkar's account).

By 1903, however, White Leagues (organized against the Indians) were appearing and the Indians were blamed for the outbreaks of the plague. Commenting on the Immigration Restriction Act, Gandhi wrote: "The Colonies have become very powerful, and are becoming more and more so day by day. The Indian subjects of the King-Emperor, therefore, have to patiently and quietly submit. . . . "[32] And in "A Retrospect" (dated 30 December 1905): "It is for the Indian to toil, suffer and wait, and we cannot report that he has been able, during the past year, to throw off any of his burdens."[33]

Indentured laborers originally came out for five years as serfs and could stay another five as freemen. But by a law of 1894, they had to go home after the first five years, or reindenture, or pay £3 a year tax on each member of their family. Of the free Indians in Natal, only 250 qualified to vote, and all needed a pass to be outdoors after 9 P.M. The vast majority were laborers, most of whom came from the south of India. According to Gandhi, in *Satyagraha in South Africa,* there were perhaps 30 to 40 Parsis there, and about 200 Sindhis (who dealt in fancy goods) when he arrived. The Indians who knew English usually served as clerks or—if they were colonial-born—as interpreters; that is to say, they were not men of professional training, or of any significant degree of education. Before 1893, though the rich traders had resented their position in the colony, they had only prepared petitions and depositions, with the consultation of European barristers. They had had no Indian lawyers to help them, and they had not joined forces with the laborers.

The Transvaal differed from Natal in two important ways: it was a Boer colony and gold had been discovered there. The Boers struck Gandhi as the epitome of the modern empire-makers, or as an extreme, cruder than the British (their "cousins") and the very opposite to the Indians. Every Boer is a good fighter, he says in *Satyagraha in South Africa*;[34] he does not need elaborate drilling. When the Boer War broke out, "amongst the Boers, the entire male population joined the war. Lawyers gave up their practise, farmers their farms, traders their trade, and servants left their service."[35] The British also largely joined up, and the Indians were called money-grubbers because they stayed at home to make money. "Like worms which settle inside wood and eat it up hollow, the Indians were in South Africa only to fatten themselves upon them (the British)."[36] The Boers knew by heart the Old Testament descriptions of battles, Gandhi said, but they did not know the New Testament. (England knew it but did not believe in it, he added.) President Kruger told the Indians: "You are the descendants of Ishmael and therefore from your very birth bound to slave for the descendants of Esau."[37] This, then, was the environment Johannesburg gave Gandhi. But he remained, of course, an Indian, and as aware of events in India as Tolstoy was of events in Russia.

An equivalent in India for the intelligentsia in Russia was the revolutionary movement that developed there in the last quarter of the nineteenth century, in some ways inspired by the example of the Russian revolutionaries. This movement expressed itself to some degree in the press and in Congress, but, to see its extremist fringe, we can concentrate on the Bengalese and the figure of Arabindo Ghose, which will be an equivalent for the Russian Nihilists and the figure of Pisarev. The years 1860 to 1875 were notable for the Indian press, which functioned as an opposition party; it told readers to imitate the American model of revolution, and it denounced the faith in education and gradualism which the government tried to create: education, it said, produced only clerks and writers—that is, men fit to serve. About Indian acts of terrorism, it refused to take a moral line. "Surely to poison an obscure Colonel was a far lighter crime [than] . . . to emasculate a nation."[38]

Englishmen of good will, like Allan Hume and William Wedderburn, began to fear another mutiny. Hume spoke in 1888 of the Indian intelligentsia aspiring to new institutions. He founded an Indian National Union, which endorsed the connection of India to England but called for some political activity on the part of Indians. Lord Dufferin, who arrived as viceroy in 1884, liked the idea of an association but advised Hume to make it still more political; he suggested an annual congress and a president who had nothing to do with the government. The 1888 meeting was presided over by George Yule, a Scots merchant of Calcutta, who pointed out that democratic institutions had preceded universal literacy in England, so that there was no justice in England's refusing self-government to India on educational grounds.[39]

Congress, however, was still perceptibly British sponsored, even when not ruler sponsored, and there were Indians, especially in Bengal, who were impatient for other more national and more radical institutions. Bengalis were usually considered more intellectual, more individualistic, and more emotionally volatile than other Indians. The ideas of the French Revolution had been discussed and approved in Calcutta soon after they were known in London.

Both urban and rural areas in Bengal were ruled by the Bhadralok. There was a movement to revive classical Brahminism—including a cult of Sakta (or Shakta), the Mother Goddess of strength—for the decline of Brahminism was attributed to the quietism of the Buddhists and to the gentle Bhakti (devotion) of the Vaishnavites. (The cult of Vishnu was lower caste in Bengal.) This cult of Sakta was the equivalent of the cult of Shivaji in Maharashtra, and developed into revolutionary action.

Arabindo Ghose, born in 1872, had a career in some ways parallel with Gandhi's, inasmuch as it was split between Indian national politics and religion. He was the son of a Bengali who married with Brahmo Samaj rites in 1864 and then went to Scotland to be trained as a doctor from 1869 to 1871, from which he returned anglicized and atheist and alienated from his wife. His sons were sent to a European school in Darjeeling, and then in 1880 to Manchester. (Anglicized doctors—and lawyers—were often agents of cultural alienation in India, and appear frequently as fathers or brothers to Gandhi's followers; this explains something in Gandhi's attitude toward medicine and law.) Arabindo's elder brother became a friend of Oscar Wilde and other poets; Arabindo went to Cambridge and France, and passed the examinations for the Indian Civil Service, but returned to India in 1893. (This was the year Annie Besant went to India, Gandhi to South Africa, Vivekananda to America; it was also the year Tilak organized the Ganapati Festivals.)

Arabindo went to teach in the State of Baroda, whose ruler was interested in education. He lived as a Brahmacharin and sought spiritual inspiration, but disagreed with the moderates and the congressional policy of prayer and petition. In 1902 he initiated his brother Barin into revolutionary action, making him a gift of the *Bhagavad Gita* but also of an unsheathed sword. He himself learned to shoot. From the *Gita* he (and the Bengali revolutionaries) took Krishna's exhortation to Arjuna to do battle. They also passed among themselves *Chandi*, a book about Durga (the same divinity as Kali and Sakta), who destroyed the demon Chanda. The implicitly revolutionary legend was that when the thirty-three crores of gods were driven from their kingdom by the demons, or Daityas, they created Durga, Adya Sakti, primordial power, to defend them; and so she might defend them against England in modern times.

In this period Bankim Chandra Chatterji (1838–94), the Bengali novelist, provided revolutionary images through his novels about the conflicts of the Moguls and the Pathans. The most famous of these was *Anandamath* (1880), which contained the song that became the national anthem, "Bande Mataram." It is about a band of sanyasis dedicated to the service of Durga, their Mother Country, by all means, including violence. This novel became a bible for secret societies, and its hero, Satyananda, became their model.[40]

The story of *Anandamath* is based on the rebellion of sanyasis against the East India Company in 1772 to 1774. One band of sanyasis is called Santan, the Children; a new recruit to them, Mahendra, is inducted by a venerable ascetic, Satyananda, who takes him to various temples and shows him the various faces of Durga: the Mother as She Was (to be revered), the Mother as She Is (something fearful), and the Mother as She would Be (more glorious than Lakshmi or Saraswati, Wealth and Learning). Chatterji said the Mother as She Is was the symbol of India's degradation—black because of her misery, naked because of her poverty, garlanded with skulls because of her deaths, and trampling Siva under her feet because of her will to self-destruction. Mahendra takes the vow of the Children to renounce the family and riches, to conquer all passions and never even to share a seat with a woman, to fight for the true religion, and to give up caste. (The Anushilan Samiti actually administered a very similar oath.) This novel had the place among the Bengali revolutionaries that Chernyshevsky's *What Then Must We Do?* held among the Russians.

The revolutionaries took sanyasi names out of *Anandamath* and sang "Bande Mataram," which Arabindo translated thus:

I bow to thee, Mother
Richly watered, richly fruited
Cool with the winds of the south
Dark with the crops of harvest
The mother . . .
Terrible is the clamorous shout of seventy million hands
Who sayeth to thee, that thou art weak:
. . . for thou art Durga holding her ten weapons of war
Kamala at play in the lotuses
And Speech, the goddess, giver of all love,
To Thee I bow.[41]

Rajnarain Bose (1826–99), Arabindo Ghose's grandfather, had been a social reformer in the Brahmo Samaj tradition. But he had made the national movement more defiant; he established a secret society that was dedicated to destroying by force the enemies of India, which was joined by Rabindranath Tagore. (Such societies were for the Bhadralok and included no Muslims.)

In 1906 a new weekly called *Yugantar* was founded, which "breathed bombs in every line." It contained, for example, on 20 May 1902, an article entitled "The Bengali's Bomb." This weekly was banned in 1907, but there were Yugantar groups, which rivaled the Anusilan (culture) groups founded by those inspired by *Anandamath*. From the beginning, *Yugantar* asked its readers to show themselves men in the way they died, if they could not do so in the way they lived.[42] This was as alien to Gandhi's political temperament as the nihilism in Russia was to Tolstoy.

Another book much read by the Bengal revolutionaries was Arabindo's *Bhabhani Mandir*, published (without his name) in 1905. Bhabhani was the tutelary goddess of Shivaji, who named his sword after her, and another manifestation of Durga. Sakta/Shakta is the more abstract and conceptual form of this female power. The book proposes that a temple be erected to her in the hills. She is the Infinite Energy that sets the Wheel of the Eternal to work; she differs in form in each age, appearing sometimes as Renunciation, sometimes as Pity, sometimes as Durga. In our age she has been Lakshmi (Wealth) the mother of Durga:

> Wherever we turn our gaze, huge masses of strength rise before our vision, tremendous, swift, and inexorable forces, gigantic figures of energy, terrible sweeping columns of force. All is growing large and strong. The Shakta of war, the Shakta of wealth, the Shakta of science, are ten-fold more mighty and colossal, a hundred-fold more prolific in resources, weapons and instruments than ever before in recorded history. Everywhere the Mother is at work; from her mighty and shaping hands enormous forms of Rakshasas, Asuras, and Devas are leaping forth into the arena of the world. We have seen the swift, irrestible and impetuous bounding into life of Japan.[43]

Some Shaktis are black, with Tamas qualities, some are blood-red, with Rajasic qualities, and some are white and pure, but all are Mother in her new phase. According to *Bhabhani Mandir*, India is presently weighted down with the inertia and impotence of tamas. Science is but Bhima's mace, a dead weight, without Shakti; and without Shakti, bhakti is but weak and fitful. "Rushing and billowing streams of energy must be poured into her [India], her soul must become, as it was in the old times, like the surges, vast, puissant, calm and turbulent at will, an ocean of action or of force."[44] A nation must spring into existence, as Bhabhani, Durga, Adya Shakti did. That energy can be acquired by adoring the Mother of Strength, as the Japanese have done, for even the gods cannot give strength unless they are asked for it. India must create the new religion for the world. And the book proposes a new order of Brahmacharins, to serve this purpose.

Bartaman Rananiti (1907), the "Modern Art of War," was the main revolutionary textbook. It was published by a friend of Arabindo's and began with an article taken from *Yugantar*, in October 1906, which said that destruction was another form of creation. (Bakunin developed the same idea for the Russians.) It described guerilla violence as the natural way to cut out society's gangrene, and cited Japan's rise to power through war. It used the image of Time, pointing to the English rifle and saying, "See, the warlike spirit is the artificer of the European palace; acquire the warlike spirit."[45]

Mukti Kan Pathe? (Which Way Lies Salvation?), another collection of articles from *Yugantar*, recommended to revolutionaries the use of Maxim guns and the imitation of secret societies as in Russia and in *Anandamath*. The money for revolution must be procured, if necessary by dacoities (robberies). Meanwhile, *Sanhya* (Twilight) in 1908 promised bombs that anyone could use—"Kali Mais Bomba," Mother Kali's Bomb. It asked every family to send one son out as a Kshattriya revolutionary.

The agitation against the partition of Bengal succeeded in that the two parts were reunited in 1912, when the English moved their capital to Delhi. As we have seen, though, the movement had not been entirely successful for the Bhadralok, and the would-be revolutionaries retreated to other fields of activity. During his jail sentence in 1908, Arabindo underwent a change of heart, and came to believe in purely spiritual energy. When he was freed he left British India for Pondicherry, one of the tiny remnants of French territory in India, and set up an ashram there, outside the arena of political action. He practiced a quietistic meditation of a fairly traditional kind, though his philosophy remained in some ways Western—it can remind one of Teilhard de Chardin. Disciples soon gathered round him, and there was a certain circulation of devotees between Gandhi and him (and between Gandhi and Ramana Maharishi, an orthodox guru and saint). People who did not find with Gandhi the purely spiritual reward they were seeking sometimes went to the other two men. But the spirit of revolution did not die, and it was an important presence on the scene which Gandhi watched from South Africa and prepared himself to enter.

By the end of this period, 1862 for Tolstoy and 1906 for Gandhi, these two men had established themselves in the fields of Russian literature and Indian politics (although Gandhi's activity had been restricted to South Africa, he was a leader there and was known to observers in India). But they were only on the verge of their great achievements—the writing of *War and Peace* and the organization of *satyagraha*. And those achievements, though still full of a general faith in modern life, and far from expressing the two men's final attitudes, were great milestones on their ways towards that final goal.

VI
Domestic Fiction and Dominion Status: 1855–62 and 1894–1906

In their youth Tolstoy and Gandhi were still concerned about other things besides literature and politics, and were still in some sense contemplating other careers. Tolstoy was tempted to invest his major energies in education and agriculture, and even in a military or political career; Gandhi, on the other hand, was drawn to religion, to the simplification of life, and to a legal career in India. But these other attractions and alternatives gradually lost power over them during this period, and by the time each was forty, they were concentrating, respectively, on the fiction of domestic happiness—a bourgeois and British literary genre—and on the politics of nation-building within the British Empire.

Tolstoy and Writing

When Tolstoy got out of the army in 1855, he went to St. Petersburg and made his friends among men of letters. It may seem a mere pun on "nonviolence" to say that in leaving the army for literature, Tolstoy was choosing a nonviolent way of life; but in the final analysis the arts and humanities do constitute culture's established alternative to those life-forms which deal directly in violence. Of course, insofar as its works of art constitute one of the glories of any civilization, art lives in silent partnership and complicity with the armed forces of the state; but the individual writer is living by the pen and not the sword. Certainly Tolstoy had not "chosen nonviolence" in the sense that Gandhi was soon to do (in *this* period, however, Gandhi, too, was living in complicity with an army—that is why he gave active support to the British Army in both the Boer War and the Zulu War). But it is not false or meaningless to say that Tolstoy chose nonviolence already in 1855.

Two of the closest of his new friends were I. S. Turgenev and A. V. Druzhinin. In the early 1850s, the latter was acknowledged as a leading literary critic in Russia, and Turgenev was a leading fiction writer, according to B. Eikhenbaum.[1] Both advocated "light literature"—that is, modest, short, and reflective works of semifiction, which eschewed the plot conventions of romance. The novel proper was no longer a favored form. It was therefore not surprising that these men should welcome Tolstoy as one of themselves, for his early "fiction" (notably *Childhood, Boyhood, Youth*) was shaped by just that taste.

But some of his literary projects represent a degree of ambition in him which removed him from full fellowship with those friends. On 14 June 1856 he declared that he loved epic and legend, and wanted to make poetry out of the songs of the Cossacks.[2] And on 31 May he had decided to write a story from a horse's point of view.[3] In this story, in *The Cossacks*, and in his reading of the time, we can see Tolstoy attracted to "the primitive." On 7 June he recorded reading Pushkin and finding most of the poetry rubbish, no doubt because of Pushkin's often frank artificiality.[4] Such tastes suggest Tolstoy's assumption of the identity of Romantic genius.

However, when Druzhinin suggested his friends found a new journal, to be devoted to pure literature, and therefore hostile to political commitment, Tolstoy responded enthusiastically. Amongst the others, Goncharov, Annenkov, and Maykov were already committed to the idea, and Tolstoy wrote to Botkin on 4 January 1858:

> As far as the public is concerned there's positively no place now for belles lettres. But don't think that this prevents me from loving it now more than ever before. I've grown tired of talk, arguments, speeches, etc. . . . What would you say at the present time when the sordid stream of politics is seeking to engulf everything and, if not to destroy art, at least to sully it—what would you say about those people who, because of their belief in the independence and eternity of art, were to join forces and by word (criticism) and deed (i.e. the art of the written word) try to demonstrate this truth and save what is eternal and independent from fortuitous, one-sided, and grasping political influence? Couldn't *we* be those people? i.e., Turgenev, you, Fet, myself, and everyone who shared

and *will continue* to share our convictions. . . . The journal will have one aim: artistic enjoyment—tears and laughter. Its one criterion will be educated taste.[5]

And earlier he had written: "I understand moral laws, the laws of morality and religion, which are not binding, but which lead people forward and promise a harmonious future; and I sense the laws of art which always bring happiness; but the laws of politics are such terrible lies for me that I can't see in them a better or a worse."[6] But the laws of art had to be understood as broadly inclusive themselves before Tolstoy could submit himself to them. Art had to include religion, and philosophy, and ethics, and aesthetics, and go beyond them all. The novel had to be the "bright book of life" itself, as D. H. Lawrence was to put it when he was making exactly the same choices as Tolstoy. This was the idea that was to drive them both towards what Tolstoy called "domestic happiness."

Thus, hand-in-hand with his exaltation of art went his exaltation of Nature and of man's participation in Nature. This was the crucial feature of Tolstoy's aestheticism, as it was of Lawrence's and Keats'. This is, in fact, the true aestheticism of Western high culture, different though it is from all the minor and negative forms that have usurped the name of aestheticism. A typical entry in Tolstoy's diary is this, for 1857: "I love nature when it surrounds me on all sides, spreading out as far as I can see, when the same warm breeze that caresses me goes rolling off and is lost on the horizon; when the blades of grass I flattened as I sat down accumulate into the endless green of prairies. . . . "[7]

I mention Keats because he understood "sensibility" in a way very like Tolstoy's and can help us understand the latter. What Keats celebrated as "negative capability"—when a person "is capable of being in uncertainties, mysteries, doubts, without any irritable reaching after fact and reason"[8]—is just the quality Tolstoy points to in his heroes Pierre and Levin (and Kutuzov and Karataev) as their saving grace, their supreme gift, their essence. While in opposition to "public figures" like Napoleon (both writers treated him the same way), Keats set others who, however famous they might become by accident, belonged essentially to private life and were therefore invisible to the public eye. And he connected them with Shakespeare and poetry. "Shakespeare led a life of Allegory; his works are the comments on it."[9] Keats himself meant to live such a life.

When Tolstoy returned to Yasnaya Polyana in 1856, after his first visit to Western Europe, he devoted himself to writing and designed his life around it in just this spirit. He was, at this point in his career, committed to "pure art." And he drew the same connections between pure art and private life as Keats did: his letters to his cousin Alexandra are explicit about that. Thus, like Keats (and unlike some other enthusiasts for pure art), Tolstoy saw erotic marriage as the central pivot of this life-scheme: a highly principled eroticism, a marriage charged with mutual challenge, the relationship treated as moral and spiritual adventure. Keats, of course, never achieved this, but Tolstoy did build a writing career around that pivot. The year after his wedding he wrote to his cousin that he was now at last "a writer with *all* the strength of my soul, and I write and I think as I have never thought or written before."[10]

He began *War and Peace* forthwith, letting other and more public concerns, like his school, lapse. Moreover, his wife contributed largely to that novel, and to *Anna Karenina*, not only with practical help and appreciative encouragement, but also with crucial material, like *being* the characters of Natasha and Kitty. His marriage and his novel-writing were mutually supportive and mutually dependent. When the latter stopped, the former also failed. It was Tolstoy's "artistic suicide," his wife said more than once, which she minded most, which she could never forgive.

Of course Tolstoy was interested in other things besides art in his youth, notably the politics of emancipation. Part of the structure of the Russian empire was about to be dismantled, and there was anxiety, even amongst those who sympathized with the measure, lest the whole fabric might collapse in the process.

Tolstoy tried to emancipate his own serfs privately, in 1856, but they did not trust the terms he offered them. In 1858 he and Turgenev attended the meeting of the nobility of the Tula district, and signed liberal declarations there. But Tolstoy was always uncomfortable with political issues and decisions, which raised in him feelings of confusion and guilt. He soon broke off his engagement with them, and turned to education and travel.

In 1861 emancipation was finally proclaimed. Tolstoy was in London then, and though he left on the day of the proclamation, he did not hurry home; he went to visit Proudhon in Belgium and Auerbach in Germany before returning to Russia. Once in Yasnaya Polyana, he found he had been elected an arbiter of the peace in his district, and so had to stand between his fellow noblemen and the peasants in deciding issues raised by emancipation. His decisions were in favor of the peasants, and thus unpopular with his fellow nobles. His life was threatened. His judgments were often reversed by the Assembly of Nobles, though usually upheld by the next higher court of appeals.

But he was not convinced of the importance of what he was doing. He soon resigned the post.

Moreover, the Russia he returned to had been intellectually radicalized; the liberalism of Turgenev and his friends was now scorned by idealistic youth, some of whom called themselves Nihilists. We may say that Tolstoy's writing during the 1860s and 1870s was directed against this nihilism. His fiction was a major effort at reconstruction, representing Russian society—its marriages, education, landscape, and songs—as something worthy of love and reverence. This was, after all, the social function of domestic fiction in England, too. And the writers of that fiction, like George Eliot and Charlotte Brontë, made art a twin sister to education, as Tolstoy was also to do.

For besides art and politics, education took up a lot of his energies. It consumed a lot of the total of Russia's intellectual energy at that time. The radicals wanted to arouse the people by educating them; the liberals wanted to save Russia by modernizing it; the conservatives had to engage in education to save Russia from the radicals; and so on. No doubt the most important, for Tolstoy as for everyone else, were the famous Sunday Schools, of which there were 274 by 1862. These voluntary and idealistic efforts by the educated intended to lift other people up to their level.

Tolstoy himself opened a school at Yasnaya Polyana in the fall of 1859, which lasted—with the interruption of his journey abroad—until 1862, when he married. This found literary expression in his education journal, *Yasnaya Polyana*, begun in the spring of 1861. (He got the advice and help of two schoolteachers from Tula—this is one of the rare occasions when the town contributed something to his activities.) Between 1869 and 1872 he ran a second school, which found literary expression in his ABC textbooks. Actually, he had first opened a school as early as 1849, and had tried again in 1857. And in 1872 he opened a smaller school, in which his children taught. Indeed, up until the time of his death there was usually some sort of teaching being done, or being planned, at Yasnaya Polyana. His wife, and later his daughters, were as interested in education as he was. In the long run, Tolstoy was quite successful in affecting the way teaching was done in Russia. If one extends the term *education* to cover the making of books for the barely literate, one may say that teaching was, after literature proper, Tolstoy's major field of action.

All this teaching was done at Yasnaya Polyana or nearby (at one point there were several schools at neighboring villages). One can see in this and other biographical information the very intimate connection between education and domesticity (and art) in his life. These three activities went together, in opposition to the worlds of politics, high society, and administrative power, and also, of course, to that of dandyism, the gypsies, and aestheticism. His educational ideas laid their primary stress on freedom and creativity, and were derived from Rousseau, Pestalozzi, and Fichte—transmitted to Tolstoy, in part, through the German novelist, Auerbach. Tolstoy's schools were, amongst other things, an agency for reclaiming or rehabilitating the young teachers he employed, who were often ex-student radicals. It was partly because one of them, Sokolov, was under police surveillance that Yasnaya Polyana was searched by the police in 1862; they were looking for a printing press on which they thought subversive pamphlets were being printed. But Tolstoy boasted to his cousin Alexandrine that though his teachers arrived all afire with revolution, within a few weeks they were teaching the Bible and destroying their incendiary manuscripts.

On the other hand, his work in education could be, in purely practical terms, an alternative to its two allies, literature and domesticity. He turned from one to the other. Before his marriage, Tolstoy wrote to Druzhinin that it had been hard for him to break the tie to literature, but now that he had done so and was teaching, he found everything about him clearer, simpler, closer. And when he had been teaching peasant children, he had been writing peasant idylls and sleeping with a peasant woman. He was then out of sympathy with pure art—art as represented by Pushkin. Contrariwise, when he got married, he turned around completely; he even stopped teaching and closed the schools, and began to write *War and Peace*. But if he turned from one to another of those three activities, he never turned to the opposite alternatives—a career in politics or business, administration or high society.

Tolstoy's educational intentions were politically conservative. But he was primarily concerned with cultural health and aesthetic play, and with the way school education promotes these values or spoils them. His arguments bring him to the conclusion that "we are fond of Pushkin and Beethoven not because they embody absolute beauty but because we are as spoiled as Pushkin and Beethoven, because Pushkin and Beethoven flatter both our monstrous irritability and our weakness."[11] Pushkin and Beethoven, and high art of their kind (not "domestic" in the sense we are giving that term) were false icons of Tolstoy's religion of culture; they exaggerated and caricatured his aesthetic values. Before his marriage he was able to serve that religion better while teaching than while writing.

His great success was with a peasant boy called Fedka, to whom he taught the pleasure of art, the pleasure of creativity. Tolstoy

described in his journal how a group of his pupils at first cooperated
to invent and tell a story, and how Fedka grew tyrannical over the
others, rejecting their suggestions, as the aesthetic passion possessed
him. The excitement was physiological; the boy turned pale, and for
a long time that night could not get to sleep. But even more striking
for us is Tolstoy's excitement over Fedka's excitement.

> I cannot communicate that feeling of agitation, joy, terror,
> and near remorse that I felt in the course of that evening. I
> felt that from that day forward a new world of joy and suf-
> fering had opened up for Fedka—the world of art. It seemed
> to me that I was spying on what no one ever has the right
> to see—the birth of the secret flower of poetry. For me it was
> both frightening and joyous, as for the seeker of a buried
> treasure who might see the flower of a fern. . . . *There was no
> mistaking it. This was not fortuitous; it [the boy's art] was conscious
> creation.*[12]

That creation was Tolstoy's religion in those days. In part, he felt
guilty: "If you teach a boy to enter the world of art, he will no longer
breathe with full lungs and it will be painful and injurious for him to
breathe fresh air."[13] This was because art brought Fedka "a whole
world of desires which stood in no relation to the surroundings of
the pupils."[14] But Tolstoy's guilt and joy were more than matters of
social responsibility; they were matters of religion. He tells us he felt
it sacrilege to watch Fedka undergoing this change; he felt like a
debauchee corrupting a child; only two or three times in his life had
he experienced such a powerful emotion. "I dimly felt that I had
criminally looked through a glass hive at the work of the bees, concealed from the gaze of mortal man; it seemed to me that I had
debauched the pure, primitive soul of a peasant boy."[15] Clearly, he
felt some revulsion, some seed of what he said in *What is Art?* in 1898;
but in 1862, that revulsion was subsumed as part of the excitement
of the sacred. Art values were life values, and life values were sacred.
Education was important to Tolstoy above all (though not only) because
it included such transactions.

In March 1860 he proposed (via E. P. Kovalevski, an old military
comrade of his and brother to the minister) the founding of a Society
for National Education, which would take the task of education out
of the government's hands. This was another move in the direction
of imitating England, where private agencies did so much that in
Russia was done by the state. Nothing came of the proposal, however,

and in July he went abroad, with his sister Masha and her children. Soon after he came back, he married Sonia Bers and devoted himself to "domestic happiness" in life and art.

Gandhi and Nation-Building

While Tolstoy was becoming increasingly enmeshed in education issues, but gradually involving himself more and more deeply with literature, and with one particular kind of fiction, Gandhi was, in the corresponding phase of his life, moving into politics and towards one particular kind, nation-building within the British Empire. He undertook to raise the consciousness, and then the activity, of the Indians of South Africa, to the level at which they would deserve recognition as political adults. The natural extension of this, in the next period of his life, would be to raise the whole Indian nation's consciousness to a level at which it would deserve independence.

This first version of Gandhian politics had a complete scenario in contemporary histories of English democracy, with a happy ending in which India would become a dominion like Canada. Canada had been granted this status in 1867, and the two countries had had a somewhat parallel history in relation to England; the battle of Montreal, in which Canada was won for England, was fought only two years after that of Plassey. In 1849, the year the Punjab fell into British hands, the Canadian colonists were given responsible self-government. But there was a crucial difference, because the Canadians were white. The French Canadians were, like the Boers of South Africa, "cousins" to the British themselves, and so soon deemed ready for self-government.

The contrast between the two countries, and the destiny this implied for India, was much discussed at the time. In 1898 the *Toronto Globe* said: "Our conception of the growth of Empire is not that Canada should become more like India, but that India should become more like Canada; the ideal being not a group of dependencies governed from one central point but a league of self-governing communities."[16]

Australia formed a federation and became a dominion in 1901, and South Africa did the same in 1910. A dominion was internationally recognized as a separate state, with an ambassador and with treaties of its own. Britain provided naval defense, investments and markets, and powers of veto, but this amounted to very little. In 1907 a dominions division was set up in the British Colonial Office, and an Imperial Conference was held regularly. During the Great War there was an Imperial Cabinet, in which the dominions were represented. In 1919 some of them were given mandates, and in 1926 the Imperial Conference defined the dominion status as meaning autonomy.

This was a peculiarly British form of nation-building, with an elaborate machinery of liberation and a rhetoric of liberalism. As befitted the professed guardian of the modern-system conscience, England had accepted the crucial moral challenge—to achieve greatness without empire. This was a challenge no other country had met. For whereas the nation-building of nineteenth-century Europe was all a matter of helping other white nations towards autonomy, the British Empire included nonwhite races. Would England in fact liberate them, too? Would she recognize their forms of political life as being mature in the relevant sense? It was above all India which presented that challenge, where the whites could never be anything but an insignificant minority. Thus, "dominion status" represented a form of politics as distinctively English as the form "domestic happiness" represented in the realm of literature.

Because this was a British scenario, Gandhi appealed to the British as well as to the Indians in his campaigns. He worked on their conscience by holding up to their eyes a mirror in which they saw their own behavior. "I think it will be readily granted that the Indian is bitterly hated in the Colony. The man in the street hates him, curses him, spits upon him, and often pushes him off the sidewalk."[17] He described the laws that keep them off trams and out of most railway carriages.

Gandhi received many commendations and corroborations from London, from sources that were also harsh on the colonists. The *Times* said the question was whether "Indian traders and workers are or are not to have the same status before the law as all other British subjects enjoy . . . [The Indian] is the same useful, well-doing man, law-abiding under whatever form of Government he may find himself, frugal in his wants and industrious in his habits."[18] The man who wrote that saw the situation in exactly the same terms as Gandhi did.

When Gandhi presented the black side of the picture of empire, moreover, he cited British or white authorities. His pamphlet on the South African treatment of Indians quoted the *Cape Times* as saying (5 July 1891): "Imagination can only picture the commercial paralysis which would inevitably attend the withdrawal of the Indian population from that Colony."[19] Even the *Natal Advertiser*, Gandhi said, had pointed out the need for coolies on farms and railways, and the fact that they "raised the white man one stratum higher": except for them, the white boss would have been one of his own laborers. But, Gandhi said, the Europeans wanted to degrade the Indians in South Africa, to the level of mere labor.

In turn, he was determined to make the Indians seem as progressive—he was determined to make them *be* as progressive—as Robinson Crusoe and all the real-life British adventurers, from Drake to Cook to Livingstone, and all the British heroes of modern-system politics, like Pym and Hampden, Wat Tyler and Oliver Cromwell.

Gandhi still believed in the Protestant ideology of an earlier England, when commerce and Christianity together characterized colonial activity. That idea was not entirely dead at the end of the nineteenth century—both Livingstone and Stanley had appealed to it—but by then most people in government knew (Kipling had taught them) that war-making and a Roman paganism were more truly characteristic of the British empire-builders.

Of course, the contrast between the new and the old ideas of England was not as sharp as black and white. The old idea had included military energy, and Gandhi included military energy among the traditional British qualities he commended to his compatriots. In a speech in Calcutta in 1902 he said:

> As a Hindu, I do not believe in war, but if anything can even partially reconcile me to it, it was the rich experience we gained at the front [in the Boer War]. It was certainly not the thirst for blood that took thousands of men to the battlefield. If I may use a most holy name without doing any violence to our feelings, like Arjun they went to the battlefield, because it was their duty. And how many proud, rude, savage spirits has it not broken into gentle creatures of God?[20]

There is thus a complex idea of "character" at the root of Gandhi's idea of nation-building. The Indians must learn their self-respect from Western as well as indigenous sources, and it will derive from military service and Western political institutions as well as from the love of dharma and the *Bhavagad Gita*.

Tolstoy's Teachers

We can also compare the men who functioned as important teachers of Tolstoy with the equivalent figures in Gandhi's life. These teachers guided the two men towards domestic fiction and dominion status, respectively; or, more exactly, Tolstoy and Gandhi derived that guidance from these teachers. The first of these for Tolstoy was Alexander Herzen, whom he met in London in the spring of 1861.

Alexander Herzen (1812–70), the only son (though illegitimate) and heir of a wealthy father, became a radical through reading the German philosophers, especially Hegel and Schelling, and the French social theorists, especially Saint-Simon, in his youth. But the great determining event of his early years was the nobles' Decembrist Revolt of 1825 and its suppression by Nicholas I, who became a personal enemy of Herzen's. Thus, his political inspiration was aristocratic-romantic. He and his young friend, Ogarev, took an oath on the Sparrow Hills, overlooking Moscow, to preserve the memory and carry through the purposes of the Decembrists. In the 1840s he went into permanent exile, and edited from London a Russian journal that bitterly attacked the tsarist regime.

Herzen's importance was to an unusual degree a matter of personality (as distinct from theoretical system or practical effectiveness)—of the attractive way he embodied brilliant intelligence and generous emotions. And to Tolstoy of all people, personality and embodiment were extremely important. According to P. Sergeenko, Tolstoy told him in 1908 how struck he had been by the inner electricity of the thick-set man who came bounding down the stairs in London in 1861 to greet him. He found Herzen enchanting. "I have never met a more attractive man. He stood head and shoulders above all the politicians of his own and our time. He was a rare combination of scintillating brilliance and depth."[21] There was some expectation among Tolstoy's friends (for instance, his cousin Alexandrine) that Lev himself might follow a career like Herzen's. But Tolstoy had a fundamentally different cast of mind—more religious, less political, than Herzen's.

Herzen had begun his career as an editor in 1849, in France, when he became collaborator with and financial supporter to Pierre-Joseph Proudhon in his *La Voix Du Peuple*. Proudhon was a leader of radical anarchism in France (and, to some degree, was outside it), and his theory and praxis differed from Marx's in many of the same ways as Tolstoy's did. A printer by trade, he was primarily a writer on political topics, not a politician, but he was often in trouble with the government and had to leave France.

Unlike Herzen, Proudhon identified himself with the peasants of his native country, as did Tolstoy (and Gandhi). "My ancestors on both sides were free peasants, exempt from feudal servitude from time immemorial. . . . " He described his mother as "noted for her virtues and for her republican ideas";[22] her father (who was also an influence on the young boy) had defied the local squire. The young

Proudhon lived and worked with peasants (in the countryside outside Besançon) and shared "their landhunger; their rigid views of right living; their deep conservatism; all combined with their passion for equality; their class-consciousness; and their savage resolution to be each master of his own fields and his own household"[23]—so says a critic who is sceptical of the peasant virtues and of Proudhon's devotion to them. This marks Proudhon off from Tolstoy and Gandhi, as being less the man of religious aspiration; they were more spiritual-ascetic.

Proudhon always believed in the Great Revolution and in justice. He attacked the Christian church for offering charity and for putting justice off until the next world. Tolstoy and Gandhi were essentially opposed to revolution, and were not ready to dismiss charity. But Proudhon's politics were very attractive to Tolstoy because of their integrity and their personal character—their freedom from party doctrine and party tactics.

In 1860 and 1861, however, Tolstoy was primarily an educationist. He wrote his article "Popular Education" while in Hyères, and on 6 December 1860 wrote his cousin Alexandrine that his educational work was the only interest still linking him to life, since his brother Nikolai's death.

The other important contact he made during that trip was with the German educationist and novelist Berthold Auerbach. In 1898 Tolstoy told Eugene Schuyler that he had gone to Germany "in the spirit of a sincere disciple of Auerbach, of his village tales, and in particular of his novel, *New Life*. . . . It was to that writer that I owe the fact that I opened a school for my serfs and interested myself in popular education."[24] His enthusiasm for Auerbach brings out clearly the contrast, in Tolstoy's mind, between education-art-marriage and politics-revolution-adventure.

We know that Tolstoy was reading Auerbach as early as 1856, and Eikhenbaum says Auerbach replaced Benjamin Franklin as Tolstoy's lawgiver. He finally met Auerbach on 22 April 1861, and put fifteen exclamation points after the name in his diary, saying that he had admired him from afar for five years. And his enthusiasm persisted, or was never repudiated. The twenty-volume *Collected Edition* of Auerbach's works stood in Tolstoy's study to the end of his life, next to the collected Rousseau.

Auerbach had some direct influence on Tolstoy as a writer; Eikhenbaum says that Tolstoy's unpublished "idylls" of peasant life were written in the "skaz" form as a result of Auerbach's influence.[25] But Auerbach's ideas about education, and the relation of education to art and politics, were even more important to Tolstoy. Both men tried to make the village school into an extension of, an educational form of, village life; they wanted to provide in printed form an equivalent for the old preliterate culture. And both men brought out annual calendars for the people that incorporated a lot of information, about, for instance, scientific agriculture, and a lot of moral precept. (Auerbach's almanac began to appear in 1845.)

It is best to consider Auerbach as a part of that movement of German populism which was generally important to Tolstoy. Wilhelm Riehl, the theorist of the movement, reintroduced the "estate" idea into Western political discourse, making a virtue out of social stasis and class differentiation. Tolstoy saluted him as a reformer in political thought, a thinker as important in its history as Luther was in the history of Christianity. Riehl's work (from a Marxist point of view, reactionary) was inspired by opposition to the rise of Prussia within Germany and to the increasing organization of state power there. Since Russia—at least the tsars' and the bureaucrats' Russia—was just a larger and less efficient Prussia, it was natural for Tolstoy and the Slavophiles to find Riehl's philosophy of resistance exactly right.

But who was this Auerbach who was so important to Tolstoy? First of all, he was Jewish—his real name was Moses Baruch—and his early work was a good deal concerned with Jewish themes. His first novel was a biography of Spinoza, whose works he also translated. He was one of those German Jewish intellectuals who escaped from the ghetto via high culture, like Moses Mendelssohn, and who were the heroes of the peace-loving bourgeoisie, as we see in George Eliot's *Daniel Deronda*. In social origin (and to some extent in political message) he was a typical Jewish *intelligent*, and it is of interest that men of this type should have been important to both Tolstoy and Gandhi at crucial formative stages of their lives.

Auerbach was also politically active in his early years, was arrested for such activities in 1835, and was active again in the 1848 revolution. (He was known to Marx's circle, and it was to Auerbach that Moses Hess wrote one of the most vivid early descriptions of Marx.) But the book that especially influenced Tolstoy was published in 1851, and is in some sense a recantation of his political activism. Its effect upon Tolstoy was to confirm his own inactivism.

This novel, *New Life*, begins in the Bergwald in 1849. A refugee rebel of the 1848 revolution, who is also an aristocrat and a soldier, exchanges identities with a young schoolteacher, Eugen Baumann, who was on his way to a new village where no one knows him. While the old Baumann is thus enabled to fulfill his dream of going to America, the new Baumann takes his place in the village of Erlenmoos.

He decides to build a new Germany from within, by means of education, and thus gives up politics, soldiering, and his identity as a noble. He chooses to stay with the people and the land, the folk culture and the agriculture, drawing new forms of strength from those sources. Like Riehl (and Tolstoy), Auerbach wanted peasants to stay peasants, and to be proud of belonging to that estate. Again like Tolstoy, Auerbach preferred educational to purely aesthetic values, and various debates in the novel show clearly that a choice has to be made between the two.

Morally speaking, therefore, the story is severe and even radical. Politically speaking, however, it proposes a transition to a conservative quietism. And if he is a hero of education, Eugen is also a hero of marriage: everyone in the novel wants him as a husband, for themselves or for a friend. He has been, before 1848, a military and political man, but now he becomes a typical hero of the nineteenth-century domestic novel—a George Eliot or Charlotte Brontë hero.

It is clear why Tolstoy would be able to identify with such a character, and he did so strongly. When he found Auerbach's house, he sent up his name as "Eugen Baumann"—he *was* this young man; he was living out Auerbach's idea. Being a schoolmaster, in the story, means ceasing to be a nobleman. For example, Baumann chooses to marry a village girl instead of a noblewoman; and this change of caste is further brought out by several scenes and turns of plot. Tolstoy was at that time strongly tempted to do something similar.

Thus, the sequence of instructors he sought out—Herzen, Proudhon, Auerbach—show Tolstoy turning from political engagement, to theoretical anarchism, to education-art-marriage. The final option he would commit his life to in the immediate future, and this would command his major energies in the period I have called his manhood.

Gandhi's Teachers

In 1896 Gandhi paid a visit to India which we can see as like Tolstoy's visit to Europe, in that it brought him into contact with important older men who became to some degree his teachers. In Poona, for instance, he met Gokhale, Tilak, and Justice Ranade, hoping to win for his efforts in South Africa the stamp of approval of these nationalist leaders of Maharashtra.

Of these three leaders of Indian national sentiment, the most important to Gandhi was Gokhale. Gandhi noted that when he saw

Gokhale, he said to himself, "You are my man." He addressed him (and him alone) as "Mahatma." Tilak he compared to the ocean, the black water, on which one could not easily launch, but Gokhale was the Ganges, which invites one onto its bosom. The "soft expression" on his "lotus-like" face made Gandhi recognize him immediately as "dharma incarnate."[26]

To the modern Western reader this self-identification as weak is no doubt disconcerting. Gandhi saw Tilak as too vigorous; he preferred Gokhale because he was soft. When Tilak asked why he had not applied himself to political questions in India, Gandhi replied humbly: "I thought it was beyond my capacity."[27] Gokhale, he says, was a mother to him, concerned about the way Gandhi walked, spoke, and dressed. The relationship between them is very important to understanding Gandhi.

In February 1902 Gandhi attended the Congress session at Calcutta, and again failed to do himself justice as a speaker. But he was invited to stay with Gokhale, which amounted to a public recognition of his work. Gokhale said that Gandhi was the stuff of which heroes and martyrs were made, and, though he always advised against things like traveling third class, he admired Gandhi for it.

Tilak and Gokhale were both Chitpavan Brahmins from near Poona. Both were from families who were khots, tax-collectors, and they were born only fifty miles and ten years apart, Tilak in 1856 and Gokhale in 1866. (Thus, Gandhi was only three years younger than the man he called master and Mahatma; but in terms of experience in Indian politics, he was very much the junior.) Though Gokhale had gone to join Tilak at his school in 1883 and stayed there five years, he had made not Tilak but Justice Ranade his guru, in 1887. Mahadev Govind Ranade, born twenty-four years earlier than Gokhale, was a man of similar temperament to himself, mild and gentle, though obstinate and severe with those who offered to serve him. A man of very hard work, a master of statistics and arguments, self-subordinated to his work, he had adapted the traditional Brahmin temperament to the purposes of the modern reformer. This was the line to which Gandhi affiliated himself, though his own range was greater than Ranade's or Gokhale's. In 1904 Gandhi's office in Johannesburg held portraits of Gokhale and Ranade, Christ and Tolstoy.

Gokhale wore Western dress, plus a scarf, glasses, and longer hair. Tilak was shorter, darker, tougher. With a shaven head and a big moustache, the emblem of virility for Indians, he always wore traditional dress, the sadra, dhoti, and chappals. For five years they taught together, for Gokhale began as an admirer of Tilak and his patriotism, but Tilak was known as a vigorous and inspiring, though loud-voiced and careless teacher, harsh and turbulent and determined to lead; Gokhale was soft-spoken, mild, sensitive, remote from crowds, afraid he wasn't liked.

Gokhale was elected to the Bombay Legislative Council in 1899, and sponsored drainage and anti-plague-vaccine measures; he also worked for rural reform, low-interest loans to peasants, well irrigation, and land reclamation. In 1901 he succeeded Pherozeshah Mehta as Bombay's representative to the government in Calcutta. He there pressed for government protection for Indian industry.

His institution was the Servants of India Society, which he founded in 1905. This was an attempt to spiritualize public life in India, to spiritualize nation-building, by training a very small number of public workers (there were only twenty by 1909). They took seven vows, of poverty, obedience, truthfulness, and so on, and for their first five years were under the control of the First Member (Gokhale). They did not support themselves, but took a stipend from the Society (the Aga Khan and the Parsi industrialists, the Tatas, contributed to its funds.) Their political objective was to win for India, by peaceful means, the same dominion status within the empire that had been granted to Canada.

Gandhi's Visit to London

The main equivalent in Gandhi's life for the influence of German populism in Tolstoy's—a support from a distance and an inspiration—was a revival of British Liberalism, which was also a revival of Nonconformist Christianity, at the end of this period. We could compare Tolstoy's visit to Europe in 1861, and his meeting with Auerbach, with Gandhi's visit to London in 1906. There he negotiated on behalf of the South African Indians with the Liberal Party, which was newly returned to power with a large majority and many new Members of Parliament. Most strikingly, it is said that for many of them, as for Gandhi, Ruskin's *Unto This Last* had been formative reading. The election results seemed to promise that an old Tory order had been defeated, and that the New Age that Gandhi had heard discussed in London in the 1880s was about to begin. In *Indian Opinion* on 24 February 1906 he says that never before had a king's speech been so looked forward to by Indians as this one had.

It was, moreover, a Liberal Party heavily influenced by Nonconformist Christianity. As the prime minister Campbell-Bannerman said: "We have been put into power by the Nonconformists."[28] This was a new force in English politics. Between 1653 and 1852, it is calculated, there were probably never thirty Nonconformist M. P.s in the House at any one time (in 1906 about two hundred were elected), and there was never a Nonconformist cabinet minister before John Bright in Gladstone's first cabinet, in 1868. But the franchise reforms of 1867 and 1884 had given the Nonconformists a place in political society commensurate with their numbers and their economic strength.[29]

They had always been resisters. The Dissenter, said Macaulay, "prostrated himself in the dust before his Maker, but he set his foot on the neck of his king."[30] And Watts says: "A consistent thread nevertheless links the Tudor Anabaptist with the 20th century Free Churchman, a refusal to accept the dictates of the state in matters of conscience. The refusal to render to Caesar the things that are God's is of the very essence of Dissent"[31]—and, we might add, of the essence of Gandhism.

Above all, perhaps, the Nonconformists were the natural heirs of seventeenth-century Puritanism, partly just by having been kept outside the mainstream of politics. (As late as 1868 there were fewer Wesleyans than Jews in the House of Commons.) They had not changed caste, as the rest of England had, because they had had no responsibility for the administration of empire. They were still close in feeling to old ideals like Free Trade and to old myths like *Robinson Crusoe*. And the 1906 election was their great triumph. They had raised money for it, their Whitefield's Mission was a virtual campaign headquarters for the Liberals, and they informed the debates with moral fervor on issues like indentured Chinese labor in South Africa ("an affront to God") and the Education Act. They felt the Liberals' triumph to be their own. In fact, among the 200 Nonconformists elected were fifteen passive resisters, thirty Free Churchmen, and eighty-three members of the Liberation Society—altogether, more religious radicals than to any Parliament since Cromwell's.[32]

The election results of 1906 could be read as a rebirth of the England of Bunyan and Defoe, that late seventeenth-century England Gandhi especially admired. The Act of Conformity of 1661, which thrust a variety of Nonconformist sects outside the Church of England, had created a caste split in English society; the banias had their own system of schools, for instance, and maintained close links with the American colonists, especially the New Englanders—the nonconformists were Americans within England, New Englanders in another sense. They were more or less excluded from Parliament, the Church, and the universities, and so were innocent of politics and administration.

Thus, the elections of 1906 promised a new hegemony of the bania, who had no hereditary commitments to the British Empire or to the feudal or pseudofeudal trappings of empire. Instead of those commitments, these men were committed to the Protestant ethic and the spirit of capitalism—in their purest and most ideal forms.

Their campaign of passive resistance to the Education Act of 1902, still ongoing in 1906, was both a demonstration of the conscientiousness of their politics and an important link between them and Gandhi. They would not pay rates that supported a school system linked to the state church; their leader, the Baptist minister Clifford, appeared before magistrates forty-two times between 1906 and 1914, and Gandhi made him judge of an essay competition on the subject of passive resistance that he had organized.

The Liberal-Nonconformist attitude to empire can be compared with the German Populist attitude to literature. The first promised a turn from aggressive imperialism (the acquisition of new territories) to devolution; as soon as one of the colonies showed its political maturity, it would be given independence. The second advocated a turn from revolution and the literature of ideology to marriage and the literature of village life. These two bodies of doctrine influenced the two men in comparable ways, and that influence is clearly demonstrated in their characteristic achievements in manhood. Domestic fiction and dominion status named ideas which were given to them from outside of their own countries, but which they were to put into practice more magnificently than those who had originated them.

VII
Marx and Lenin

We are now halfway through this account of how Tolstoy and Gandhi developed into the leaders of modern nonviolence. From this point on, they cease to be liberals; they become radicals and differentiate themselves more and more clearly from the other writers and politicians that until now they could be compared with. They become revolutionaries. So it is appropriate to juxtapose here the other great revolutionaries of their time, the men of violent revolution.

Of all Tolstoy and Gandhi's contemporaries, the most significant, as giving us a contrastive context in which to understand them, must be Marx and Lenin. As Vinoba Bhave has said: "If the last century were boiled down, the residue would be Marx (in whom Lenin is ingested) and Gandhi (over whom the shadow of Tolstoy spreads). . . ."[1]

We can see some of the origins of nonviolence in the psychic economy of Tolstoy and Gandhi when that is contrasted with the psychic economy of Marx and Lenin. For the first two, violence was always problematic, always forbidden; Tolstoy chose a military career in his youth only to repudiate all war later. Even the implication of violence in the other appetites, notably in sex and eating (above all, in carnivorousness) made all those appetites problematic for them. Thus, power itself, though they sought it in order to make their truth prevail, was for them dangerous, monstrous, always on the verge of sacrilege.

Marx and Lenin seem to have been as free as any men ever are from such difficulties (from such humanity). They were not "violent men"—a label which might indeed imply some emotional feeling about violence; they merely integrated it into their psychic, and political, economy as an element of efficiency and effectiveness, and so had no problems with their appetites or with power itself. At certain points in the making of revolution one will probably engage in terrorism, as in the administration of justice one will of course punish, probably execute, perhaps hundreds of thousands of people, and in negotiating foreign relations one will of course make war and will naturally employ the most efficient killing machines. This does indeed make sense—is common sense, while what Tolstoy and Gandhi offer makes only uncommon sense.

We see here the relation of politics and religion to what is usually called "personal temperament." From this point of view, Tolstoy and Gandhi shared a "hypersensitive" temperament that put them at odds with Marx and Lenin. From another point of view, of course, they were unlike each other; the young Tolstoy had a very different temperament from the young Gandhi. The former assumed—with some difficulty—the ardent and expansive style proper to a young soldier and noble; the latter presented himself as meek, timid, diligent, anxious. But they changed. Around 1881 we see Tolstoy admiring the meek and passionless temperament of his son's tutor, Alekseev, and trying to be like that himself. In Gandhi's case, after 1900 we see him engaging in leadership, in acts of physical courage, in rebuilding his body by means of Nature Cure methods. And this reminds us that personal temperament is not merely a matter of endowment; it is partly a matter of choice and will—we choose to be a type of person. That is why the sources of nonviolence in psychic economy or personal temperament are profitable to study.

Tolstoy and Marx

Tolstoy was born ten years after Marx (he was exactly the same age as Marx's great rival, Lassalle) and their family circumstances were quite different. Karl Marx was an oldest child, of ebullient energies and striking talents, who dominated those around him. His father early spoke in alarm of "a certain demonic egotism, which might unfit him for intimate human relations, and the best sort of happiness."[2] Heinrich Marx seems to have ceased exerting authority over Karl while he was quite young. In 1837 he wrote to his son: "and since [your] heart is obviously animated by a demon not granted to all men, is that demon heavenly or Faustian? Will you ever—and this is not the least painful doubt of my heart—will you ever be capable of truly human, domestic happiness?"[3] (Perhaps Tolstoy and not Marx should have been this man's son, for this was the value to which Tolstoy was to devote his art and his life up to 1881, domestic happiness.)

Even in those of Karl Marx's relations that were happy, there was the hint of a conquest, shown in his early years by meeting his elders as their equal or superior. Ludwig von Westphalen (who became his father-in-law) won his friendship because, as one biographer says, Marx "had been treated by a man much older than himself on terms of equality."[4] His friends when he was a doctoral student in Berlin were nine or ten years older than he; while Jenny von Westphalen, the girl he married, was four years older (which made a big difference when he was in his teens) and she broke an engagement to another man for him.

All this is very unlike Tolstoy, who was younger than his brothers, did not dominate others until late in life, and married a girl only half his age. Older men with whom he entered into a significant relationship were the American Tolstoy and the Epishka/Eroshka of *The Cossacks*; and in those relationships his part was rapt fascination. He presented himself to others as younger than he was, not older, and did not negotiate for terms of equality. In his youth he seems to have known few older men, just his brothers and friends, and older women who offered no direct erotic challenge. In Gandhi, on the other hand, we do detect an effort to treat with older men (notably his father) but through serving and nursing, through a humble and in some sense feminine activity which never attracted Marx.

Tolstoy's best energy was taken up in introspection, as we have seen. Marx, Isaiah Berlin says, "was by nature not introspective, and took little interest in persons, or states of mind or soul. . . . He detested romanticism, emotionalism, and humanitarian appeals of every kind. . . . Like Lenin after him he seemed to have nothing but contempt for those who, during the heat of the battle, while the enemy gained one position after another, were preoccupied with the state of their souls."[5] At the same time, Marx was remarkably theoretical and remote from things like the factory work he discussed so knowledgably; he confessed to Engels: "I understand the mathematical laws, but the simplest technical reality, where observation is necessary, is as difficult for me as for the greatest ignoramus."[6] Whereas Tolstoy had to do or at least to see everything for himself—the ploughing and the scything, the doss-houses and the prisons.

And then of course we must remember that Marx was a Jew. Heinrich Marx was named Hirschel at birth, and his brother and father were the rabbis of Trier. (He converted to Christianity at the age of forty-two, but continued to act legally for the Jewish community there. His mind was formed by eighteenth-century rationalism and reformism, but he particularly admired—as the promoter of that philosophy—Frederick the Great and his kingdom of Prussia.) It may be important that he expressed liberal sentiments at a banquet in 1834, but retracted them under pressure. His son, Karl, would be sixteen then, and he was not a boy to forgive weakness.

Karl was nearly always perceived by others in terms of power. Thus, Mevissen described him in 1842: "Karl Marx from Trier was a powerful man of 24 whose thick black hair sprung from his cheeks, arms, nose, and ears. He was domineering, impetuous, passionate, full of boundless self-confidence, but at the same time deeply earnest and learned."[7] Annenkov wrote about Marx four years later: "Marx belonged to the type of men who are all energy, force of will, and unshakable conviction. With a thick black mop of hair on his head, with hairy hands and a crookedly buttoned frock coat, he had the air of a man used to commanding the respect of others. His movements were clumsy but self-assured. His manners defied the accepted conventions of social intercourse and were haughty and almost contemptuous. His voice was disagreeably harsh and he spoke of men and things in the tone of one who would tolerate no contradiction."[8] And Frederick Lessner wrote about him in 1848: "His forehead was high and finely shaped, his hair thick and pitch-black, his gaze piercing. His mouth already had the sarcastic curl that his opponents feared so much. . . . He never said a superfluous word; every sentence contained an idea and every idea was an essential link in the chain of his argument. . . . Marx represented the manhood of socialist thought."[9]

This is a man who, very unlike Tolstoy, entered early into full command of his masculine powers, including the power to dominate others. Engels said Marx was a dictator pure and simple, over the *Neue Rheinische Zeitung.* Berlin says that Marx became, in Brussels in 1834, "the organizer and leader of an active and expanding revolutionary party."[10]

All this activity of course did not lie within Tolstoy's scope. What makes the two comparable is that both nevertheless began their thinking with the concerns that Rousseau and Hegel had bequeathed to the world—the development of consciousness in the individual and in world history. In Marx's essays for his Abitur from school in 1835, we can see the same ideas as we saw in Tolstoy's diary in 1847.

It is hardly surprising that Marx and Tolstoy should share some of the same ideas, since they belonged to the same generation and had some of the same interests and acquaintances—for instance, Annenkov and Herzen, Proudhon and Auerbach. Both were life-long students and polymath scholars, struggling to encompass the whole world with their minds and thus master it. The two were, of course, very different in their spheres of activity and in the values they affirmed. The point of focusing upon the ideas they had in common and the context they shared is just to bring out more clearly within their divergence its character of deliberate and conscious option. They were close enough to each other that if Marx turned left and Tolstoy turned right, the road each took was visible to the other. (After 1881, Tolstoy's direction may be said to have aspired to the vertical plane.)

Tolstoy, as we can see in his diary, feared his own powers of scepticism, criticism, and satire, and tried to diminish them. Marx identified himself with those powers in himself. When the *Neue Rhein-ische Zeitung* folded in 1843, he wrote an article about himself which he arranged to have printed anonymously in a Mannheim paper, saying that "the faculty of criticism has seldom been seen in such destructive virtuosity [as in Marx]."[11]

He was criticism incarnate. His polemical style was recklessly personal, to both his victim and himself, recklessly abusive, and frequently fecal in its metaphors. Around 1860 he spent eighteen months writing such a piece, entitled "Herr Vogt," devoting all his powers to destroying what other people thought an insignificant enemy.

Marx chose to build up a formidable body of theory, economic and political, which promised to be an armory for a political party. He wedded the intellect to the pursuit of power just when (after Hegel) the two seemed to be far separate; in a sense he sacrificed philosophy proper, and the philosophies of politics and economics, to praxis—except that he made praxis seem impossible to understand without theory. And he did this not only by means of pure thought but also by means of conflicts with others and by establishing a sort of dictatorship of Socialist thought. This policy can be seen as a translation into other terms of that cult of power so notable in his personality and even in his physique from his earliest years.

Tolstoy chose instead to write novels—to charm, move, and entertain the world. The result of that choice was that he worked for and in a sense through women, as we shall see. He lived in the country, where his parents had lived, and not in exile or in the modern metropolis, as Marx did. In the middle period of his life Tolstoy did not challenge his government. He turned his back on politics, a gesture which was in itself a statement that in politics the best was not that much better than the worst. And when he turned again towards politics, in his final phase, he challenged not only his government but every government. This option, or series of options, expresses his anxious search for an alternative to power.

Gandhi and Lenin

The parallel between Gandhi and Lenin is easy to draw. Lenin was born in 1870, only one year after Gandhi, and in the 1920s they were the world's two most prominent leaders of revolution. As early as 1927 this parallel attracted the attention of René Fülöp-Miller, who in the introduction to his *Lenin and Gandhi* points out that both men "undertook the heroic . . . experiment of putting into practise the long cherished dreams of humanity, . . . upheld by the emotion of an ecstatic faith, the faith that their country was called to redeem humanity."[12] Each appropriated, to Russia or to India, the role of demonstrating a new truth that was to supersede the old ones, a truth that was to come out of the East and redeem the world by displacing the wisdom of the West. (This is the wisdom we have been calling the "ideology of the modern system.") Both had the fascination, but also the disturbing and repelling arrogance, of a prophet, Fülöp-Miller says. The difference between them was that Lenin believed in an unlimited, though temporary, use of violence.

As the phrasing of those quotations will indicate, Fülöp-Miller maintained a critical reserve as part of his response to the moral claims of both men, a reserve which expressed his own identification with Europe and its high culture—with the modern world system. "Thus Europe," he says, "will listen to both accusers, but will be able consciously to oppose to this damning verdict the defense of a rich and manifold culture based on the moral freedom of personality."[13] And the defense he offers is in fact the one we still rely on, however much more battered we may feel our moral record to have become since 1927. " . . . a rich and manifold culture based on the moral freedom of personality . . . " Is this not what most of us feel is too valuable to be traded in, even for what communism or Gandhism can plausibly offer in exchange?

Lenin (Vladimir Ilych Ulyanov) was born in Simbirsk, a provincial city in Eastern Russia, in a family with a high sense of cultural responsibility, as was Gandhi's. His father was an inspector of schools, and devoted to his work, who had owed his own chance of an education entirely to the self-sacrifice of an elder brother. The mother was a well-educated woman, brought up in the modern German tradition, who had incorporated the values it taught, like frugality, cleanliness, punctuality, efficiency, as well as interests in literature, chess, classical music. The household was dedicated to education and to intellectual skills, which were fostered by all sorts of family competitions.

Simbirsk, when Vladimir Ulyanov was born there, contained about

30,000 people, and had a certain reputation as an embodiment of sleepy provinciality. It was where Goncharov had begun his life, and we can associate it with *Oblomov's* description of rural mindlessness and unchangingness. The Ulyanov family were the opposite of mindless and sleepy, and represented the future in Simbirsk; they were all keen and go-ahead, sharp-witted and hard-working, in the realm of education. But politically the father was completely orthodox.

Vladimir himself (called Volodya) was the noisiest and naughtiest of the children. Rough, aggressive (he broke his toys), and full of mockery (like Marx), he particularly rivaled and challenged his older brother, Alexander (Sasha), who was a quieter, more conscientious and industrious character. Even when Sasha became convinced that the political structure of Russia was corrupt and must be changed, and that violent means were the only ones available, he did not breathe a word of such matters to Volodya.

In 1882 Sasha went to St. Petersburg University to study chemistry. In 1886 their father died, and with the removal of the disciplinary restraint, Volodya grew ruder and harsher-mannered at home, for instance to their mother. In January 1887 Sasha became a member of a group that had vowed to assassinate the tsar on 1 March, for which purpose Sasha constructed the bomb. They were detected and arrested before the attempt could be made. Sasha took full responsibility for the plan, and made an extraordinary speech from the dock, full of the most high-pitched but clear-sighted idealism about the political situation; he saw that terrorism was self-defeating, but he believed it was the only thing anyone could do, and so he sacrificed himself in a useless but necessary cause. Thus, he established himself as a sort of saint of terrorism, and the effect of his execution was very powerful on many people.

It seems likely that this event was of the greatest importance in understanding the development of his brother who was to become Lenin. (It corresponds, in Gandhi's life, to his father's death, an event which traumatized his feelings about sex.) Volodya had always been more brilliant at his schoolwork than Sasha; the younger brother spent less time on his lessons, for he understood everything at a glance. He was a hero of self-assertion, while Sasha was a hero of hard work and self-submission; and there had been a contest and conflict between them, in which the younger seemed to be telling the other that he was more of a man, more of a force, more of a natural genius. It was then revealed, however, that the elder was a hero of revolution, a man who dealt in death, a leader and a saint; and he had kept that part of his life a secret from his younger brother, in order to protect him. It seems likely that this was a great shock to Volodya; after this he dedicated himself to self-discipline with a ferocity that provoked the astonishment of all who knew him. He did not want to be a saint of self-sacrifice himself, but he was determined never again to be found inferior in the power of silent work, self-control, and indifference to applause.

When he was first arrested and asked what he thought he would do when released, he replied: "What is there to think? My path has been blazed by my older brother. . . . "[14] And it seems to have been Sasha's influence that delayed his full conversion to Marxism—which came a little later than other members of his generation of revolutionaries. He spent the early years of his apprenticeship in Narodnaya Volya circles in Kazan and Samara, which he associated with Sasha.

It is notable that immediately after Sasha's death Volodya re-read Chernyshevsky's *What Then Must We Do?* which presents a revolutionary hero as a model for readers to imitate, and which has been (partly because of Lenin's endorsement) a scripture of the Russian Communist movement. He was so moved by it that it became the most important book of his life—yet he had read it three years before that and had felt no response. In 1887, however, he knew that the book had "fascinated and captivated my elder brother," and so he read it again. "It ploughed me over again completely." He took notes and made summaries of it. "After the execution of my brother . . . I began what was a real reading and pored over the book, not [for] several days, but several weeks. Only then did I understand its full depth."[15] He read it five times over in the summer of 1888, and in 1904 he said that this novel had been the main influence on him before he read Marx-Engels, and Plekhanov, their principal Russian interpreter.

In January 1889 Lenin became a theoretical Marxist, which meant that he joined the wing of the radical movement in Russia most opposed to the Populists and the Tolstoyans. (Tolstoy is not usually counted a Populist because he stood outside politics altogether; but of all the varieties of Russian radicalism, it was the Populists he was closest to.) And there are many striking resemblances between Russian populism and Gandhi's movement in India. The Populists wanted to defend the people of the villages against the cities, and thus to revive, restore, and strengthen the old culture against the modern world system. Plekhanov, the Marxist theorist and Volodya's first master, demolished the Populist case for the Russian peasant in a series of works between 1883 and 1895. Lenin went even further, declaring that Populist agrarianism would mean small-scale capitalism, and that only the rural proletariat was a revolutionary force.

In May 1889 Volodya and his mother and sisters moved to Samara, at just about the same time as Gandhi went to London. Both men studied law and both took their degrees in 1891, though, being political idealists, they used their skills only in good causes. Their early practice taught them both to hate other lawyers and the system, and to look for other modes of action.

At the London Conference of 1903, both Plekhanov and Lenin declared that ruthlessness was necessary in the cause of revolution, and that democratic institutions like universal suffrage could be dispensed with. Later, Plekhanov repented these declarations, but Lenin did not, and this had something to do with his winning control of the revolutionary movement away from the other man. He was the tougher, in every way. A good deal of the Bolshevik funds were supplied by armed robbery (for instance, one in Tiflis in 1907 procured them Rs 300,000), and there was a scandal involving counterfeit money in Germany, which aroused the indignation of the German Socialists. The Bolsheviks were also willing to play the game of double agents with the State Secret Service, dangerous as that game was to their own morality. Gandhi refused to let his followers do such things.

Like Marx, Lenin needed to be the master, the elder, the adult in any group, and to come of age before his time. He was known as "the old man" at twenty-four. He needed to challenge older men for recognition as their equal in force—something Tolstoy and Gandhi did not do—and in his case the encounter we know most about, with Plekhanov, was very painful. His relations with Plekhanov were highly emotional, and included a quarrel in 1900 over the editing of *Iskra*, the revolutionary journal which they, Martov, and Axelrod edited in Munich. Both men were of despotic personal character; Plekhanov was more the brilliant conversationalist and humanist scholar, while Lenin limited himself to being a "professional revolutionary." When Plekhanov demanded a double vote on the editorial board, a bitter quarrel ensued, which Lenin described in a confidential report, "How the *Spark* [*Iskra*] was Nearly Extinguished" (this takes up fifteen pages of volume 4 of his *Collected Works*). B. D. Wolfe says that no other document is so psychologically revealing about Lenin:

> My "infatuation" with Plekhanov disappeared as if by magic. . . . Never, never in my life have I regarded any man with . . . such "humility" as I stood before him, and never before have I been so brutally "spurned" . . . he is a bad man, yes a bad man, inspired by petty motives of personal vanity and conceit—an insincere man . . . both of us [Lenin and

Potresov] had been enamoured with Plekhanov, and, as we do with our beloved, we forgave him everything, closed our eyes to his shortcomings. . . . Our indignation knew no bounds. Our ideal was destroyed; gloatingly we trampled it under our feet. . . . Young comrades "court" an old comrade out of the great love they bear for him—and suddenly, he injects into this love an atmosphere of intrigue. . . . An enamored youth receives from the object of his love a bitter lesson; to regard all persons "without sentiment"; to keep a stone in one's sling. . . . [16]

And, in fact, for the rest of his life, Lenin was notably impersonal.

Thus, we see in Lenin, as in Marx, a man very early in command of his forces—much earlier than Gandhi, who in 1891 and 1892 was still fumbling at his identity, still finding it hard even to be a decent lawyer, and who could dominate no circle of admirers or disciples. Like Tolstoy at twenty-two or twenty-three, Gandhi was still a divided personality, purposeful and indeed powerful at the core but soft, malleable, overly impressionable in many areas more visible to the world and even to those close to him.

Marx's Work and Marriage

The other great book of the 1860s about history and the unconscious forces that drive men, besides *War and Peace* and *Crime and Punishment*, was Marx's *Capital*. The struggle to write it was even more prolonged than Tolstoy's to write *War and Peace*. Marx worked eighteen years altogether on *Capital*, and finished only the first volume. *War and Peace*, too, represents only a fraction of the subject Tolstoy wanted to write, and was never finished, in the sense that in subsequent editions Tolstoy made substantial changes. Marx was constantly urged on by Engels, but kept making delays (excused by sickness) and detours (excused as strategic). Jenny said he kept adding historical materials "since nowadays Germans only believe in voluminous books."[17] But there is reason to believe that the causes for his not finishing were inside him. Marx felt compelled to rewrite anything that had been written four weeks before. Tolstoy had a similar compulsion, and in both men we are bound to connect it with their inordinate pride and ambition. Some of this pride was consciously self-destructive. Marx wrote to Engels in 1868: "I am a machine condemned to devour books and then throw them up in different form onto the dung heap of history."[18] But whereas Tolstoy forswore his voluminousness when he turned to religion, Marx bequeathed his method to his movement. As Isaiah Berlin says, "No social or political movement has laid such emphasis on research and erudition."[19]

Marx married, in 1843, at the age of twenty-five, significantly younger than Tolstoy. He had gone to live in Paris (and then Brussels), where he met revolutionary leaders from other countries, like Bakunin and Proudhon. By 1845, it is generally agreed, he had stopped seeking or even responding to new ideas, and was identified with the role of master and judge, teacher and guardian of the truth. So secure was he in that role that he felt able to leave to others, notably to his wife and his friend, Engels, the ordinary moral respectability of providing his family with what they needed. Tolstoy did not leave so much to Sonia (though he left a great deal), and the prestige of art, which exempted him from ordinary duties, Tolstoy shared with Sonia. Marx and Jenny shared the misery; Tolstoy and Sonia shared the creativity.

Another difference is that Marx and Engels were always deeply involved in struggles for power, amongst the various Socialists-in-exile groups. The years 1858 to 1864 was the period of Marx's intense and ugly competition with Lassalle for leadership of the German Socialist movement. (In their correspondence, Marx and Engels showered racist abuse on Lassalle, as a "Jew" and a "nigger.") Later came the struggle against Bakunin. The nearest thing to an equivalent for this in Tolstoy's life, his quarrels with Turgenev and his insults to Chernyshevsky, are on an altogether smaller and milder scale.

The style of *Capital* is brilliant and impressive, at least in climactic moments. "Modern society, which, when still in its infancy, pulled Pluto by the hair of his head out of the bowels of the earth, acclaims gold, its Holy Grail, as the glittering incarnation of its inmost vital principle."[20] Or a description of machinery reads: "a mechanical monster, whose body fills whole factories, and whose demonic power, at first hidden by the slow and measured motions of its gigantic members, finally bursts forth in the fast and feverish whirl of its countless working organs."[21] This brilliant and impressive literary style was the natural counterpart of his social personality. In London in 1852 he issued a challenge to a duel, and in 1858 he assured Lassalle that dueling was acceptable, as a protest against bourgeois culture. When a hostess told him she couldn't imagine him living in an egalitarian society, he replied: "Neither can I; those times must come, but we must be gone by then."[22]

Marx and Engels despised the Slavs, as Herzen and Bakunin despised the Germans. "The bloody mire of Mongol history, not the rude glory of the Norman epoch, forms the cradle of Muscovy," said Marx. "It is in the terrible and abject school of Mongolian slavery that Muscovy was nursed and grew up."[23] This is because Marx and Engels believed essentially in the modern world system, once it had been transformed. They were scornful of other modes of civilization. Writing about the Schleswig-Holstein question, Engels said that Scandinavian nationalism was "enthusiasm for a brutal, dirty, piratical, Old-Nordic nationality which is incapable of expressing its profound thoughts and feelings in words, but certainly can in deeds, namely in brutality towards women, perpetual drunkenness, and alternate tear-sodden sentimentality and berserk fury."[24] He branded the whole Slavic people as reactionary and "without history"—"all these small pig-headed nations will be annihilated."[25] Marx called Kossuth the representative of "an obscure and semi-barbarous people still stuck in the semi-civilization of the 16th century."[26]

The contrast is striking between this cultural chauvinism and Tolstoy and Gandhi's Orientalism. And Marx and Engels were even more scornful of non-European civilizations, such as India's. In the nineteenth century, of course, most Europeans saw all Asian societies as being versions of Oriental Despotism, which knew no change, no development, no freedom of trade, and so on. Marx got the idea from the Mills and Richard Jones, and it answered well enough to the facts of the stagnant Mughal Empire in India. He saw China as a "giant empire, containing almost one-third of the human race, vegetating in the teeth of time."[27] He saw Mexico and Peru, North Africa, the Middle East, and Central Asia in these terms. When he talks about world history, he means Greece, Rome, and what comes after in that line, culminating in nineteenth-century England.

Marx's early and late dream was (like the capitalists of his time) "to liberate industrial enterprise from the impediments of feudal and military privilege, but at the very same moment to subject that enterprise to social discipline."[28] The club he joined in Cologne included financiers, industrialists, and future prime ministers of Prussia. His *Rheinische Zeitung* had as a subheading: "For Politics, Commerce, and Industry." Its declared object was to defend the interest of the Rhenish middle class and expand railways, postal service, cheap custom dues, and so on. This is even the message of the Communist Manifesto, as far as previous events go. Those who have driven the nobles and clergy from the seats of power (the merchants) have taken over, and deserve our applause. The bourgeoisie "has accomplished wonders far surpassing Egyptian pyramids, Roman aqueducts, and Gothic cathedrals; it has conducted expeditions that put in the shade all former Exoduses of nations and crusades."

The crucial difference between Marx's humanism and Tolstoy's can be defined in terms of two kinds of cynicism-and-idealism. Tolstoy and Gandhi were cynics in that they denied the reality of most forms of human power and splendor, including art and heroism. But this led them to disengage from most forms of power and splendor. The cynicism of Marx and Lenin led them to engage all the more stren-uously in the pursuit of power, since they saw through the pretended detachment or innocence of other people.

If we compare Marx's situation in writing *Capital* with Tolstoy's in writing *War and Peace*, we find striking similarities but also striking contrasts. Jenny did a lot of work for Marx: she wrote almost all his correspondence and transcribed all his manuscripts; she begged the money from friends and relations that kept them going, attended meetings for him, picked out articles for him to read, kept records, and looked after everything to do with his work while he was away. And this was the best part of her life: "The memory of the days I spent in his little study copying his scrawled articles is amongst the happiest of my life."[29] But one can see no sense in which *Capital* expressed Jenny's personality, experience, or relationship to Marx.

Like Sonia, Jenny was a lively and ambitious personality mated to someone more dominant, and she became hysterical; *mercurial* is a word often applied to her. In 1854 Marx wrote: "For years now my wife has totally lost her good humour—understandable in the cir-cumstances, but no more agreeable for that; she plagues the children to death with her complaining, irritability, and bad humour."[30] And she spoke frequently of death, as Sonia was to do later. In 1862 he wrote: "My wife tells me every day that she wishes she were in the grave with the children and I really cannot blame her."[31]

Engels explicitly disbelieved in "family happiness"; Marx seems to have been ambivalent about that ideal, but it was never the object of his devoted effort, as it was of Tolstoy's. Circumstantially, the parallels between the two family situations are striking. Like Tolstoy, Marx had an illegitimate son—by the family servant—who grew up nearby but unacknowledged. He was born in 1852, and Tolstoy's son must have arrived about 1861, exactly the same point in his life, chronologically. In Marx's case, the child was born some time *after* his marriage, however.

The Marxes' circumstances were of course sordid in the 1850s, the period of their lives which corresponded to the 1860s in the

Tolstoy's lives. They lived in some of the worst sections of the huge metropolis of London, in acute discomfort and social shame, plagued by creditors and having to move often. Marx swore that the bourgeoisie would one day pay dearly for each one of the carbuncles he suffered (and which he treated by characteristically violent means—with arsenic, opium, and creosote.) But in some ways he was a typical big-city Bohemian intellectual, who created disorder around him everywhere. In Paris in 1845 he habitually sat up in cafes until 3 A.M. and rose at noon; he was, Raddatz says, the *only* émigré who made no effort to earn a living.

It is revealing that Balzac was so much his favorite novelist; Balzac's vision of the modern state replaced Hegel's as an influence on Marx, according to C. J. S. Sprigge. Balzac depicted a Paris made up primarily of huge fortunes, sudden bankruptcies, and secret scandals in high places. Marx loved to spread scandals, even of such absurd kinds as that Lord Palmerston, the English prime minister, was in Russian pay. (Marx worked with a crazy Tory called David Urquhart to propagate this story.) He suffered—and Tolstoy did not—from what in modern radicals we call "conspiracy-mania."

Lenin's Work and Marriage

It was in the life period we have called youth that Lenin met Nadezhda Krupskaya, soon after he moved to St. Petersburg in August 1893, and joined a Social Democratic circle to which she belonged. He was already a sardonic and masterful presence; he urged her group to give up propaganda seminars and move on to mass agitation. He soon wielded authority among them. His 1894 attack on the Populists, "What Are the Friends of the People?" was passed around in the circle under the name of the Little Yellow Notebooks.

Two years older than Lenin, Krupskaya was the daughter of impoverished nobles, but had long been involved in radical or revolutionary causes. She had done some work for Tolstoy's enterprise of publishing literature for the people (she translated and abridged a Dumas novel for *Posrednik*) but in 1891 was converted to Marxism. Lenin was arrested in 1895, she in 1896, and she asked to be sent to his place of exile in Siberia, where they were married in 1898.

They were comrades. They immediately began to translate Sydney and Beatrice Webb's *Industrial Democracy* together. But they were not equals. She sank her claims and her personality almost completely in his, serving as his personal secretary and representing his interests in all the ostensibly independent roles she filled. It was a marriage half-way in style between Tolstoy's and Gandhi's, in that Krupskaya had a fully awakened mind, and yet she subordinated her personality completely to her husband's purposes. Lenin was leader and teacher as well as husband to her.

In exile they trained themselves in various kinds of disguise, deceit, and revolutionary adventure. Lenin was now head of the League for the Liberation of Labour, and he wrote pamphlets in invisible ink and became a master of many forms of illegality. He was opposed to making individual terrorism the major form of revolutionary activity, but not to using it on occasion.

In 1901 Krupskaya rejoined him in Munich (her sentence having run out later) where he was editing *Iskra* and was engaged in his bitter struggle against Plekhanov for its control. In 1902 he wrote *What Then Must We Do?* using the same title as Tolstoy and Chernyshevsky. This tract holds the same place in Lenin's thinking as *Hind Swaraj* does in Gandhi's; it draws the blueprint of party structure that was to be realized and finally to triumph in 1917.

At the Second Congress, held in 1903 in Brussels and then in London, the same questions were at issue: who was to be eligible for membership? And how was party discipline to be administered? Lenin and the Bolsheviks (who at this Congress emerged as a group, with their opponents, the Mensheviks) declared the need for a hard core of professional revolutionaries, with a tight control over a larger, looser body.

Seen in the widest perspective, Lenin's life in this period was marked by two large events, the Russian Revolution of 1905 and the outbreak of war in 1914. In Switzerland when the revolution began, in January 1905, he did not return to Russia until November of that year. When the revolution was defeated, Lenin went into exile again, until 1917.

During those years, the Russian government's combination of modest reform with repression drained away the membership of the RSDWP (the Revolutionary Social Democratic Workers Party), which was split anyway between the Bolsheviks and the Mensheviks, a split which Lenin insisted on maintaining. His uncompromising and aggressive policy seemed politically suicidal, but it triumphed, partly because it built up his formidable personal image. One opponent said: "There is no other man who is absorbed by the revolution twenty-four hours a day, who has no other thoughts but the thought of revolution; and who even when he sleeps, dreams of nothing but revolution."[32] One can imagine that Smuts might have said something like that about Gandhi. Moreover, there is the further likeness that in both Lenin and Gandhi the powers of feeling and of will were all translated into reason, into explanations, into step-by-step plans of action. They were the least flamboyant and romantic figures amongst their rivals, allies, and enemies.

When the war broke out in 1914, and the Western Socialist parties made declarations of patriotism, Lenin denounced them all, proclaimed the Second International dead, and appealed for the formation of a Third that would turn this imperialist war into a civil war—would turn the soldiers' guns upon their commanders and rulers. This idea, too, was in the short run quite unsuccessful. He was again living in Switzerland, where he attended Socialist- and Communist-held conferences, but he quite failed to get general support for his policy, even among antiwar Socialists. He devoted himself to the writing of *Imperialism: The Highest Stage of Capitalism* (1917), in which he focused on the same topics as Gandhi's *Hind Swaraj*. He blamed the war on imperialism, and blamed that on a handful of banks, which possessed enormous surplus capital and needed colonies for investment purposes. The war, he said, was the result of conflicts over the possession of lands still virgin to investment. Thus, Lenin's intellectual interests were turning at this point in the same direction as Gandhi's, and though the Russian Revolution of 1917 was to plunge him into national affairs, he remained concerned with the Comintern and with the fate of Europe's colonies throughout his life.

⸢*The Last Years*⸣

It was in the last period of Tolstoy's life, in 1883, that Marx died. In both cases there were intrigues and quarrels between family members and disciples over the use of the literary property—the actual manuscripts and the right to dispose of these and to speak as the great man's heir. (Gandhi, for instance, was solicited to support Tolstoy's disciple, Chertkov, against Sonia in one of the quarrels over the Tolstoy manuscripts.)

But in their last years, despite such parallels, the gulf separating Marx on one side of the revolutionary movement from Tolstoy and the anarchists on the other grew deeper and wider. Tolstoy himself read Marx in the last period of his life. In his 1898 preface to Edward Carpenter's essay on science, he said: "The most widely disseminated political economy [that of Marx] . . . demands the intensification of the cruelty of the existing order, in order that there may be a realization of those more than doubtful predictions."[33]

Something similar could be said about the gulf between Gandhi and the Marxists who followed Lenin. The latter developed ever more strongly their faith in violent revolution and in the rapid industrialization of Russia—and of India—while Gandhi preached and practiced the opposite.

Lenin had not foreseen the revolution of 1917. He arrived in St. Petersburg only in April, a month after the deposition of the tsar, and came into immediate conflict with the Kerensky government. Lenin said the Soviets should sue for peace, confiscate estates without compensation, nationalize the land, and divide it among the peasants. Kerensky said reform must wait upon the restoration of order. Lenin went underground in July.

In October he reappeared—entering the country in disguise—and in a ten-hour debate at the Bolshevik Central Committee, persuaded it to make an armed take-over. On 7–8 November the provisional government was arrested. In January the Constituent Assembly met, but was dispersed because it was hostile to sovietism. In March Lenin accepted bad peace terms from Germany, and forced them through by the threat of resignation. For the next four years he was engaged in civil war, against former military leaders, who were well supplied by the Western powers. The military caste of Russia was defeated by revolutionary theoreticians. In this, the Russian revolution ran parallel to Gandhi's: the military caste, and even the army itself, turned out to be safely treatable as a minor factor. Lenin insisted on rights of self-determination, even of secession, for the non-Russian nationalities within the Russian empire, and called for rebellion by subject nationalities in other European empires. He made the industrial workers the new privileged class of Russia. The peasants were made to yield all their grain surpluses; on the other hand, however, they saw their major enemies, the landlords, totally dispossessed. And in 1921 the New Economic Policy ended such requisitioning and allowed open-market selling of grains.

During this period Lenin was in constant danger, from others (he got two bullets from an assassin in August 1918) and from his own health, which was sacrificed to his work. In 1922 he suffered partial paralysis; in March 1923, a stroke; and another, final one in January 1924.

The fate of Tolstoy's reputation in Russia looks very unlike Gandhi's in India. Lenin declared that Tolstoy's late development was a great misfortune for his country, not only in its intrinsic foolishness but in the way it distracted him from his true calling—to write fiction. He attacked Tolstoy in, for instance, *Proletar* in 1908, thus: "As a prophet who has discovered new receipts for the salvation of humanity, Tolstoy is ridiculous. . . . On the one hand, we have an author of genius . . . on the other hand we have the landowner and fool in Christ."[34]

Thus, Tolstoyism was repudiated in Russia after 1917, while in India after 1947, Gandhism was—officially—Holy Writ. But in unofficial fact, the contrast is more blurred. The official father of the free Indian nation was Gandhi, but the unofficial father may have been Lenin, insofar as Nehru represented the country. His enthusiasm for Lenin in *Glimpses of World History* was more ideological and discipular, less sentimental and whimsical, than his affection for Gandhi. Lenin was a mastermind and a genius in revolution. "There was no doubt or vagueness in Lenin's mind. His were the penetrating eyes which detected the moods of the masses; the clear head which could apply and adapt well-thought-out principles to changing situations; the inflexible will which held on to the course he had mapped out, regardless of immediate consequences. . . . His speech was an electric charge which pained but at the same time vivified."[35] And he attributes to Marxism as a whole the same clarity and energy and modernity. Marx's *Capital* is a purely scientific work, avoiding all vagueness and idealism. It sees history as "a dynamic conception. And it marched inevitably on, whatever might happen. . . . It was man's destiny, according to Marx, to help in this grand historical process of development."[36]

This philosophy is the very opposite of Gandhism. Nehru evokes Lenin: "So, calmly but inexorably, like some agent of an inevitable fate, this lump of ice covering a blazing fire within went ahead to its appointed goal."[37] By contrast, Gandhi was a pathetic pilgrim, in Nehru's eyes, trying to lead men backwards. His sentiment was for Gandhi, his enthusiasm for Lenin.

VIII
The Return to the Sources

During the first half of the lives of Tolstoy and Gandhi, Russia and India, respectively, remained outside the modern world system of culture. Even in the 1880s Tolstoy's friend V. V. Stasov, a music critic, wrote:

> Who in the 19th century knows and listens to French, German, Italian and English folk-songs? They existed, of course, and once upon a time they were in vogue, but upon them has descended the levelling scythe of European culture, so hostile to the ordinary native elements. . . . In our fatherland, things are completely different. The folk song is still heard everywhere. Every peasant, carpenter, stone-mason, yard-keeper, coachman, old woman, laundress, and cook, every nurse and wet-nurse, brings it along to St. Petersburg, to Moscow. . . . [1]

And in 1913 T. G. Masaryk wrote: "Russia has preserved the childhood of Europe; in the overwhelming mass of its peasant population it represents Christian medievalism, and, in particular, Byzantine medievalism."[2] England and America had held no surprises for him when he visited them, being developments of something he was familiar with at home; but Russia was what Europe had been long, long before. (He said, "I owe to Tolstoy my introduction to the Old Believer wonderland."[3])

Lanza del Vasto's *Le Pélerinage aux Sources* (from which I take the title of this chapter) is a brilliant demonstration of how India could be just the same thing, for a European visitor in the twentieth century, as Russia was at the end of the nineteenth. Lanza del Vasto went to India in 1936, primarily to see Gandhi, but instead of taking part in Gandhi's social and political movements, he immersed himself in Hindu religion, making a pilgrimage on foot to the source of the Ganges in the Himalayas, in the manner of a fakir. His comments on the religious people he met (monks, pilgrims, anchorites, devotees, disciples, holy fools) and on their powers, superstitions, austerities, and penances, take the reader back to pre-Renaissance Christendom. When he returned to Europe, he founded an Order on the periphery of the Catholic church, which was dedicated to the Gandhian Revolution but also to renewing in Christianity that more ancient sense of the sacred.

Thus, Tolstoy and Gandhi were born in countries with cultural-spiritual traditions and social-historical circumstances that were immensely to the advantage of antimodern reformers. They found to hand strong traditions of a cultural life quite unlike that emanating from England, and including forms of literal nonviolence. They were born into spiritual treasure houses, or better, into houses with attics full of such treasure, into which they had to find their ways.

For Tolstoy and Gandhi the source was of course more specific than "Russia" or "India"; if they turned toward certain elements in their national heritage, from others they turned away, as exaggerations of what they disliked in modern Europe. (Gandhi called Indian cities blotting paper copies of English cities.) Roughly speaking, they went back to the culture of their childhood, or something earlier.

As a child, for instance, Tolstoy in some sense knew a religious piety in illiterate peasants that he himself aspired to at the end of his life. Thus, his aunt Aline gave orders to look after a crazy pilgrim named Marya Gerasimovna, who dressed as a monk and called herself "Ivanushka"—a figure who may be recognized by readers of *War and Peace*. Tolstoy's father, like Prince Andrei in that novel, made fun of this religiosity; he embodied modern scepticism. But Tolstoy's mother was religious, and Marya Gerasimovna was made godmother to Tolstoy's sister, Masha—which shows how close the Europeanized nobility could come to the un-Westernized peasantry. Tolstoy said in his *Reminiscences*: "I was lucky enough to learn, as a child, and unconsciously, to see the greatness of their spiritual heroism. They did what Marcus Aurelius calls the greatest thing—endure the scorn poured on one for being virtuous."[4] Some of them, like the Yasnaya Polyana peasant, Evdokimushka, deliberately provoked such scorn.

As an adolescent, moreover, Tolstoy, while in hospital in Kazan (recovering from his first attack of gonorrhea) conversed with a Tatar lama, who was there because he had been beaten up and robbed; the man said he had suffered the attack without self-defence or escape attempt, closing his eyes and offering up this suffering to God. Tolstoy was very struck by this; it could hardly enter into the complex of habits and values he was building up for his own use, but it stayed in his mind as a sign of the other, the non-European, the Eastern, mode of being.

Among Tolstoy's brothers, however, Dmitri (also called Mitenka), while at Kazan University, was beginning to turn to a Christian equivalent of the lama's values. When Tolstoy has described his own infatuation with dandyism, he adds, "There was not a trace of anything of the kind in Mitenka."[5] Dmitri began to attend services in the chapel of Kazan prison, and carried candles for the convicts there. He dressed badly and was mocked by his brothers' friends with biblical nicknames like Noah and David. He read Gogol's ascetic and mystical book, *Selected Passages from a Correspondence with Friends* (1846), and wrote out, on the model Gogol supplied, his own views of a serf owner's responsibilities to his serfs.

Gogol's book was an occasion of scandal and ridicule to the progressive and modernizing liberals of Russia. The literary critic Belinsky wrote a famous letter to Gogol denouncing it, and the book more or less vanished from consciousness during the 1850s. And, as one would expect, Lev Tolstoy, too, was at that period attracted to an opposite philosophy, of life values, of vitality, of growth, of strength. But in his final phase he read *Selected Passages* again and found it to be a work of genius.

In his youth, the Church was there but not there, for Tolstoy. It seems fair to say, summarily, that in his youth he knew Christianity as a religion for women and children—and servants—not for men. This does not mean that religion made no impact on him. As we have seen, he responded to many of its aspects, some merely picturesque, others genuinely impressive. The road that ran along the boundaries of the Tolstoy estate was walked by many poor pilgrims, on their way to visit holy shrines; he knew of remarkable feats of asceticism, in the tradition of the Russian Orthodox Church; and members of his family, including his sister Masha, ended their days in monasteries.

Despite all that, the ethic and life-style of the men of his own caste were quite un-Christian—were worldly, sensual, pagan, chivalric, military. Tolstoy was born, as he often said, into the military caste in Russia. This meant more than that they were huntsmen and warriors. Sexually, for instance, the ethic of that caste took no more stock in the virtue of chastity *in men* than it did in the meekness and nonviolence recommended in the Sermon on the Mount. Tolstoy's brothers inducted him into sexuality with a prostitute, in early adolescence, and he began a career of quite animal sexuality, feeling scarcely any moral conflict, any sense of sin. After all, Christianity had never been for him an articulated ethical code—as it was, for instance, for George Eliot in her early days.

Politically speaking, Tolstoy's family and caste tradition did offer him a model of rebellion—against the autocracy and the state it represented. The nobles of Russia had staged several such revolts, often on liberal principles. The most famous, that of the Decembrists, occurred only three years before Tolstoy's birth and involved close friends of his father. This tradition, strengthened by the caste hostility between the nobles and the bureaucrats who served the state, was indeed important to Tolstoy through much of his life; the radicalism of his late years was, however, something different. Aristocratic liberalism then seemed quite un-Christian to him; it was for him tainted with that cool removal of a boy from all religious influences as he entered puberty, which he himself had suffered.

Something like this happened in every Christian country, but in Russia it was, we gather, more clearcut. In England, for instance, the nobles and the clergy belonged to the same families, went to the same schools, intermarried, and interdined; and Protestant piety was strongly echoed in secular writings like Carlyle's and George Eliot's. (Tolstoy was very struck by England's advantage in this matter.) In Russia, priests and nobles were entirely separate castes, with very different educations, houses, and reading and living habits. Such few aristocrats, of birth or mind, as there were among the priesthood would be found among the black clergy, the monks, not among the white clergy, the parish priests, who ranked very low by cultural standards. The Church was humble, before the State and before the nobility, in Russia: it did not raise its voice to make imperious claims or deliver dreadful warnings. Thus, Christianity, in its Eastern Orthodox form, was picturesquely present to Tolstoy—in, for instance, the dawn mass on Easter morning—but ethically it was so obvious, so formularized, so merely pious, as to be effectively absent. This indeed was true of that Church in general: its church services were aesthetically splendid, its inmost life of prayer was impressively ascetic and mystical: but in between those two extremes, as a moral and an institutional presence, it was negligible or contemptible.

It is, however, worth noting something of that religion which Tolstoy did not then see but rediscovered later. This is the very ascetic, self-annihilating, unworldly, and antiworldly character of its spirituality. G. P. Fedotov says that the first and greatest of Russian saints were kenotic (the word I used about Tolstoy's late prayers); he mentions the princes Boris and Gleb, and Saint Theodosius.[6] Boris and Gleb are saints because of the way they accepted death, and Theodosius, the founder of the Kiev Monastery, because he always wore patched and uncouth garb, worked in the fields, and generally impoverished himself, as his way to love Christ. At night he spun wool and sang psalms. Invited to a prince's banquet, he protested against the musicians, who distracted men from duty with pleasure, and instructed his monks to keep always working for the poor.

Eastern asceticism, Fedotov tells us, did not inflict dramatic tortures on the flesh, but dried up the blood and its appetites, and all the other bodily secretions, save tears. The praise of tears is a major theme for Abraham of Smolensk and others; tears, repentance, and alms are to Russian devotion what purity and justice are to Anglo-Saxon. A saint is a starets, which means an old man, because the withering or drying up of the flesh is the necessary condition of sanctity.

We know much less about Gandhi's immediate environment. This is because he was not a writer, much less a novelist, much less a great autobiographical novelist, like Tolstoy. But we do know that the conduct of the Gandhi household (like every good Hindu household) was heavily ritualized by caste and other prescriptions. Cooking was elaborate and time-consuming, and cleanliness was religious in its implications. The Russians, or more exactly the Muscovites of old Russia, had a phrase, *bitovoye blagochestie*, meaning household honor, or honor or piety embodied in life-style: this term they used to describe the way of life that preserved old values, in defiance of the new. Nikolai Zernov says, "the ritual art of living is widespread among most Asiatic peoples. China, India and Japan have developed it, each in their own way, but Russia was the only Christian country in which it reached a high level of perfection, and retained it till the 20th century."[7] It is something that is important in most traditional societies, and less so in those that live in expectation of the new and the changing. It was strongest, therefore, among the peasant classes in Russia. And the Hindus had something similar, and much more widely prevalent, in Gandhi's youth, though it was under attack even then from "reformers."

In his *Autobiography* Gandhi tells us that "A wave of 'reform' was sweeping across Rajkot at the time . . . [Sheikh Mehtab] informed me that many of our teachers were secretly taking meat and wine." Thus, reform for Hindus meant essentially expanding the self and developing appetites, in imitation of the English. Gandhi regretted that this involved deceiving his parents. "But my mind was bent on the 'reform.' "[8]

As for religion, the Gandhis were devoted to Krishna, one of the twelve avatars of Vishnu, the preserver. Vaishnavism, the cult of Vishnu, is one of the two great devotional religions of Hinduism, and the Gandhis took it seriously. Family prayers at the Gandhis' lasted from six to eight A.M., with a Brahmin coming to lead a prayer at the end; and twenty to thirty people came daily for alms or a cup of whey.

Kaba, Gandhi's father, sat and peeled vegetables in the temple as he listened to his petitioners. Prabudas Gandhi says that "a kind of ashram had also come into being during Kaba Kaka's lifetime,"[9] even in the family home. Thus, we see the seeds of some of Gandhi's enterprises even in his childhood, embodied in his parents—as we can see Tolstoy's mature idea of Yasnaya Polyana as a family home as inspired by memories of his parents.

There was nothing in Gandhi's family heritage quite like the Decembrist revolt in Tolstoy's, but there were traditions of nonviolent resistance and of saints offering political advice, in his native region of Kathiawar, which were alive in his boyhood, nourishing his imagination in the way the Decembrists did Tolstoy's. There was, for instance, a sequence of Jain Acharyas, who wrung from the rulers they advised many economic, religious, and political concessions. These acharyas practiced the *pada yatra*, the walking tour, as Gandhi and his disciple, Vinoba Bhave, were to do. One of them, Vijaya Dharma Suri (born a Shrimali Bania in 1868, the year before Gandhi was born) became the Jain Acharya in 1893, and went everywhere barefoot and with a begging bowl.

And there were political traditions of resistance, specific to Kathiawar, which Gandhi was able to adapt to his own purposes. Kathiawaris used fasting and passive resistance and guerilla warfare as political leverage by and against the government—for example, in Surat in 1878 there was a five-day hartal against a new license-law—traditions known to India as a whole but kept alive longer than usual in Kathiawar.[10]

The people of India haunted Gandhi's imagination just as the Russian people haunted Tolstoy's. The images they give us differ, as much as the snow and ice of the Russian winter, the stove and the tightly sealed *izba*, differ from the torrid heat and the monsoon of the Indian summer, the palm-leaf fan and the lattice walls. The differences, however, are less important than the similarity. Three aspects of Gandhi's image stand out: malnutrition or sheer starvation—rows of men dying with their bones sticking out through their skin; enforced idleness—months of the year when agriculture is impossible, and there is nothing else to do; and complete inertia—the men of remote villages who gaped at him with dull, uncomprehending, incurious eyes. That was something he often referred to: he wanted to put luster back into Indian eyes. He engaged in politics in order to do that, following the modern Western prescription. But he also employed religion, following what he felt to be the Eastern and older truth. By engaging them in political action, he hoped to give the Indians pride; by reviving their religious piety, he wanted to give them pity.

But Tolstoy's and Gandhi's religion, while on the one hand traditional, was on the other modern, in the sense that it was not theological but existential. Their sense of God was notably moral and psychological, as opposed to ontological. When his nephew Jamnadas consulted him about religion in May 1913, Gandhi wrote: "There is no need . . . to deny the existence of God. We may try to define God in accordance with the limits of our knowledge. . . . God is no dispenser of rewards and punishments, nor is he an active agent. . . . [He] is pure consciousness. . . ."[11] And again on July 2: "God exists, and yet does not. He does not, in any literal sense. The atman that has attained moksha is God."[12]

Tolstoy's doctrine was very similar. It is perhaps misleading to call such religious thinking "modernist," since it has precedents far back in religious history. But it always has an innovative character within each church because it dissolves away the theology that the priests preserve.

From the moral point of view, Gandhi says, "The greater the scope for compassion in a way of life, the more of religion it has."[13] The status of pity is a crucial characterization of world-views; rather generally exalted in eighteenth- and nineteenth-century Europe, it was attacked implicitly by Marx and explicitly by Nietzsche, and in the twentieth century ranks low; that Tolstoy and Gandhi are exceptions in this is one of the marks of their profound originality.

However, the most important social idea on which Tolstoy and Gandhi drew in their resistance to the modern world was that of "caste." They condemned caste, in its sense of sectarian pride and superiority, but they also found something else in it to value. Above all, they found a truth in caste-thinking that modern social thought missed. Their modernizing opponents, meanwhile, condemned caste for being out of date as an idea as well as a fact; so we find Tolstoy, often, returning the charge, and finding the worst aspects of caste pride in the modern world, and especially amongst intellectuals; while Gandhi we sometimes find defending the idea.

We must begin with some definitions. The Hindus' use of the term *caste* distinguishes two main meanings. According to the first, it means varna; and there are four great varnas: the brahmin, or priest; the kshattriya, or warrior; the bania, or merchant; and the shudra, or agriculturist. Used in this sense, caste is primarily a framework of thought—designed by the top caste, the brahmins—which puts together a wide range of human activities and helps the Hindu to understand and accept the relations between society's different parts and seemingly centrifugal activities. (Our modern idea of society does not help us to understand such differences, in the sense of accepting them emotionally—it emphasizes a single intercompetitive upward striving on the part of everyone.)

According to its second sense, caste means jati; there are at least three thousand of these group-types in India, and many are quite narrowly limited, geographically as well as socially. Each one is a hereditary contractual group that prescribes for its members (not that they obey all the prescriptions) a wide range of duties and prohibitions and mutual dependencies—social, marital, religious, and mensal. Caste in the first meaning is a contract between jatis, distributing the different possibilities of human temperament and achievement; in the second meaning, it is a contract between the different members of one jati—though it includes, among its prescriptions, the relations of those members to other jatis.

Jati has been explained in Western terms by J. M. Hutton in *Caste in India*. He makes it plausible as a social form that combines the functions of the Trade Union, the benefit society, and the orphanage; it is a conservative force socially and economically a stabilizer. But he admits that jati prevents India from making that transition from a status society to a contract society which Maine said was necessary to political progress—to the sequence of political forms. Gandhi did not believe in political progress, but he did not therefore defend jati. In fact, he condemned it as a social evil. But he did defend varna, as a political ideal, very strongly, and we must try to understand his reasons.

Our own historical memory of course carries no trace of varna in the literal sense, but it carries powerful traces of the feudal classification of all the members of society into nobles, priests, merchants, and serfs, as mutually supportive classes. This is essentially the same thing as varna, and its memory lingers on in us as a disused alternative— one which, though officially disused, is always being revived for various fanciful, humorous, or radical purposes. In the late nineteenth century, Ruskin used that scheme as a criterion by which to measure and condemn British capitalism. (It was partly this caste-quality that made Ruskin's thought attractive to Gandhi and enabled the powerful inspiration Gandhi drew from him.)

On the whole, though, a powerful inhibition suppresses in us any serious attraction to that scheme of ideas. However hostile we may otherwise feel about modern society, we are glad that it stands for dynamic self-determination in politics and economics, in religion and personality—for "equality of opportunity." (We know inequality exists in our society, but we fight it as a flaw, deplore it as a relic, or excuse it as the expression of equal opportunity for unequally gifted individuals.) These are our determining political passions, and caste-thinking stands opposed to all of them. Max Weber, surveying the social systems of the world, declared caste the one most completely opposed to that of modern Europe.

Tolstoy, as we have seen, used the term *military caste* to describe the nobility he was born into, and Russians in general used caste for other large groups in their society; very notably the clergy, quite often the merchants, and sometimes the Cossacks and the military, were described as castes. These callings were hereditary; they carried with them a corpus of educational, religious, work, and behavior practices; and they cut their members off from the members of other castes. Until late in the nineteenth century, Russia was in these ways more like medieval Europe than like the modern-system countries. This is not to say that Russia stood still while Western Europe developed; some of these features—for instance, the caste position of the clergy— developed largely in eighteenth-century Russia. But the antithesis between Russia and the West in this matter was *felt* very strongly, and was felt as an opposition of old to new. Caste groups belonged to the past, and even to use caste-terms, except with explicit irony or condemnation, was to betray the modern values of democracy and progress.

Gregory Freeze says that the transformation of medieval *chiny* into *soslovia*, estates, was a "process unique to Imperial Russia; while other European countries were beginning to break apart the traditional structure, Russia began to build just such an order of closed social estates. . . . The nobility was created from the various service people of Moscow. . . . "[14] In the mid-seventeenth century, the merchants of the *posad* were "turned by the state into a closed caste, and were burdened with heavy governmental taxes."[15] (The merchants' and the peasants' communes rendered communal service to the state by paying taxes, while the gentry rendered personal service—as civil and military officers—and this was a crucial distinction.) And the clergy were quite habitually described as a caste in the 1860s. This "caste-like structure," says Freeze, "first arose in the 18th century, as medieval Muscovy became modern Imperial Russia."[16] The Russian clergy married—in fact, they had to marry; it was their sons who went to seminary, where their education cut them off from the rest of the world; and their daughters and widows often carried a benefice with them—that is, a bishop would appoint to a parish whichever priest married the daughter or widow of the previous incumbent. But the clerical caste included also deacons, sacristans, psalmodists, watchmen, bell-ringers, wafermakers, and their wives and children. (It is characteristic of caste-thinking that wives and children are identified by the men they belong to.) The government drew on this caste for new bureaucrats and professional men, taking the cleverest students from the seminaries; and in times of crisis would take them for army conscripts, peasants, or factory workers. This caste had in some ways the lowest prestige of all the Russian castes.

An especially sharp dislike ran between the clergy and the nobles. (Also a sharp separation: it is said that Pushkin, the darling of the nobility, and St. Seraphim of Sarov, famous within the Church, both lived out their lives without ever hearing each other's names, though their dates were 1799–1837 and 1759–1833, respectively.) We come across this dislike in Tolstoy's life and work, but Belinsky also used "seminarian" as a term of abuse, and Herzen hated the "Christian humility" of the priests' sons he met at Moscow University. Furthermore, Turgenev said, "never has Russian literature, prior to the invasion of the seminarians, pandered to whipper-snappers with the object of gaining popularity. All who love Russian literature and cherish its honour should do everything possible to deliver it from these vandal parsonets."[17]

Thus caste was a large fact; but it was referred to mostly for purposes of "humor," however angry and passionate. To take it seriously was to betray modern values. I use caste terms in this book, not merely as the language of Hindu or Russian culture, and not merely as Tolstoy's and Gandhi's language, but as the best one for understanding the process of history in which they found themselves. It is so largely because of the connection between this set of sociological terms and some of Tolstoy and Gandhi's ultimate values—which were hostile to the values of the modern world system, embodied in modern sociology.

They themselves were quite aware of this connection. "I have not hesitated . . . to consider [*varnashrama*] as a gift of Hinduism to mankind. Acceptance of that *dharma* is, so far as I have been able to see it, a condition of spiritual growth," said Gandhi.[18] He developed this idea: "Today nations are living in ignorance and breach of that law and they are suffering for it. The so-called civilized nations have by no means reached a state which they can at all regard with equanimity and satisfaction."[19] If varna is not followed, there will be civil war. "As millions of people awaken, they will all want to become rich, they will all want to attain greatness, no one will want to take up professions which are regarded as low and class feeling will intensify."[20] In 1934, when all his writings on this topic were collected under the title *Varnavyavastha* (caste-division), he said, "Hinduism is but another and imperfect name for *varnashramadharma*."[21] And he claimed this to be true socialism, because the shudra, the member of the lowest Indian varna, was, as the servant of all, also the lord of all—which could by no means be said of the envious proletarian. "All that comes from the West on this subject is tarred with the brush of violence. I object to it because I have seen the violence that lies at the end of this road."[22]

In "Class vs. Caste," written at the end of 1920, he noted that "we in India have evolved caste: They in Europe have organized class."[23] Both conserve the social virtues, but the beauty of caste is that it is not based on distinctions of wealth, but is an extension of the family principle. A caste is a group of families who follow the same route of self-perfection. Gandhi was ready to accept birth as the mechanism by which one was first selected for one caste rather than another, though he insisted that the individual had to ratify his selection by working at his vocation. (This goes against the West's insistence that milieu is more important than heredity, he points out.) The spirit of caste is not arrogant superiority but "the classification of different systems of self-culture. It is the best possible adjustment of social stability and progress."[24]

Looking now at the Russian equivalent, we cannot quote from Tolstoy directly, but we can quote from an author whom he admired and endorsed:

> the life of society can be improved only when each individual person and whole classes acquire the ability to limit themselves, to not exceed their proper spheres. Let the man of the middle class again desire to be a man of the middle class, the landholder to be a landholder, and may the aristocrat not consider himself a privileged person, born to rule over other. Let each person proudly and joyfully acknowledge his membership in the social circle to which he belongs by birth, upbringing, education, and calling . . .[25]

So said Wilhelm Riehl (1823–97), the professor of cultural history at the University of Munich from 1859 and a leader of German populism. Tolstoy read his four-volume *Natural History of the People as the Foundation of German Social Politics* (published 1857–65) with enthusiasm. This work was very popular in Russia in the late 1850s, and remained so until the 1880s, according to Eikhenbaum.[26] Tolstoy's diary for 8 February 1860 said Riehl was to politics what Luther was to religion and Bacon to science.[27] Tolstoy was then very impressed by all the German Populists. And Riehl's tendency was widely recognized—by its opponents—to be antimodernizing and "Oriental."

Between 1857 and 1859 the political journalism of Katkov's *Russian Herald*, about class matters, was based on Riehl, who was expounded by V. Bezobrazov. The key idea was that only peasants and aristocrats constitute the stable elements in society. The other classes, notably the middle class and the proletariat, constitute "forces" or "movements." Thus, big cities are dangerous, villages admirable. When the Westernizer, S. M. Solovev, attacked these doctrines in his "Historical Letters" to the *Russian Herald* in March 1858, he called this "political Buddhism."[28] "In Riehl's book we often confront our familiar old Buddhism . . . the Buddhist protest against progress." Thinking of the Slavophiles, he said: "The new Buddhists usually complain that civilization, in encouraging relations between nations, smoothes over national traits." And Iuri Samarin, a Slavophile friend of Tolstoy's, described Riehl (and de Tocqueville in France) as "western Slavophiles." He thus accepted Riehl's social theories as part of his own Slavophile faith.

For us, it is also important to see how closely related this German caste theory was to asceticism and religion (as was Slavophilia itself). In a preface to his sixth edition of *Bourgeois Society*, in 1866, Riehl wrote, "in this sense my book expresses an ascetic philosophy; but for the individual person as for social groups, this higher principle of self-limitation is also a Christian principle."[29] And from this point of view, Christianity and Buddhism were very close; indeed, Gandhi's and Tolstoy's late philosophy has generally been described as Christo-Buddhist.

That is why, if we consult political radicals of even a mild temperament or, indeed, liberal humanists, we find something like a consensus of opinion against Tolstoy and Gandhi. These two stand outside the main tradition of left-wing thought, and left-wing sensibility. How then can we define the tradition to which they do belong? Primarily, of course, by the phrase "religious radicalism" and by the precedents they themselves point to. Anyone who believes the Sermon on the Mount, or the equivalent Buddhist documents, seriously, cannot but end up in Tolstoy's or Gandhi's position. And all through history people have: in Russia, some of the saints of the fourteenth century and some of the schismatic sects that separated off from the Orthodox church; in Europe, the extreme sects of the Reformation, like the Anabaptists and the Quakers; in India, some sects of the Jains, the Vaishnavites and the Shaivites. It makes perfect sense, as an "explanation" of Tolstoy and Gandhi, to say that they allied the spirit of this religious radicalism to modern political and social concerns, and to some of the rational and moral methods of modern high culture.

There are, however, other ways of explaining them, other lines of descent behind them, other spiritual forebears for them. An important concept to begin with is cynicism, the philosophy of Diogenes of Sinope, the man who lived in a tub and went looking for an honest man with a lantern by daylight. In his *History of Cynicism* Donald R. Dudley relates Diogenes to Socrates and Plato. In the classical tradition of Greece, as Dudley points out, cynicism was made to seem a rudimentary and debased version of Socrates' ethics. Plato is alleged to have said about Diogenes: "That man is Socrates gone mad." The remark acknowledged a strain of cynicism in Socrates, but excised it. Thus, Platonism both exiled Diogenes and redeemed (or emasculated) Socrates in the name of classical humanism.

But in fact cynicism was more than a debased echo of Socrates' excesses; Dudley says it was "the most characteristically Greek expression of the world-view of Vanity Fair," which rejected civilized values and reverted to a life based on a minimum of demands.[30] (And note that Vanity Fair is a Puritan Christian slogan.) What Diogenes said was that men had lost the secret of living well because of their need for honeyed cakes, and unguents, and statues. He was attacking the elaborateness of his civilization, just as Tolstoy and Gandhi were to attack their own. Just like them, he scourned science, philosophy, and all knowledge. And the connection with Socrates is in itself a clue, for they both took a special interest in that great predecessor; Tolstoy prepared a life of Socrates for his series of popular books, and Gandhi adapted it for Indian readers.

Like Tolstoy and Gandhi, the Cynics were anarchists; they were not revolutionaries, but culturally their rebelliousness went further. The rumors about them said they ate, slept, and fornicated in public, shamelessly, like dogs (hence their name). These were of course rumors, promoted partly in defense of classical humanism. In fact, says Dudley, there were three aspects to the Cynic life: the homeless wandering from place to place, the scornful analysis of established values, and satirical writing. He mentions Syrian satirists because Syria was a homeland of cynicism. This combination of satire, homelessness, and personal abjection will remind us of our modern Cynics of the arts, like Antonin Artaud.

Syria was also the origin of the most savage Christian asceticism, and there were many links between the early Christians and the Cynics. St. Basil admired Diogenes, and St. Gregory Nazianzen showed great sympathy for cynicism. What the two movements had in common was scorn for the luxurious late-Roman civilization of the upper classes around them. Christian preachers sometimes in those centuries presented the Lazarus of the Gospels in sermons as a beggar-philosopher of the Cynic type. And if the Cynics of Alexandria encouraged anti-Roman feeling among the lower classes, stressing the irremediable squalor of the human condition and unmasking the polite lies of civility, the early Christians were equally severe critics of worldly society. For St. John Chrysostom (very popular in medieval Russia), prosperity was a cause for concern, not congratulation. Christians were all called upon to renounce all possessions—which are goods stolen from the poor. Christian poverty meant need and suffering and pain, and Christ could be found only among the poor. Holiness could be won in homeless wandering, or in a solitary cell, far from civilization.

Anchoritism reached the West from the Middle East about 400 A.D., and ever since then this kind of "anti-social" behavior, expressing this view of the world, has persisted on the fringe of the Christian church. Father Florovsky says in "Antinomies of Christian History: Empire and Desert" that the organized monasticism of later times was an attempt to evade the question of whether the Caesars could accept Christ and vice versa. Those early anchorites who fled into the wilderness to live alone clearly had no faith in the christened empire.[31] They chose Christ and denied the emperor. The empire immediately recognized the monks' movement into the desert as a threat to its own claims and its own existence, and therefore persecuted them. The monasteries, by organizing the monks, reclaimed them to some degree for civilization. Even so, to become a monastic novice one had to disown the world and become a foreigner—at least theoretically—in all earthly cities. "As in the pagan Empire, the Church itself was a kind of 'Resistance Movement,' *Monasticism was a permanent 'Resistance Movement'* in the Christian Society."[32] That is exactly what Tolstoy and Gandhi founded within modern culture—a resistance movement.

Something similar is still seen in India, says Dudley; "the naked philosophers are as conspicuous in India today as when Onesicratus [a Greek Cynic] saw them on the banks of the Ganges."[33] Perhaps he was thinking of Gandhi in his loincloth. But one thinks also of the Jains; both the Cynics and the Jains are said to have ended their lives by committing suicide either by starving or by holding one's breath. Moreover, there is the Cynical Hindu anti-institution of becoming a saddhu, which means moving outside family and civil society entirely, becoming an outcaste, and practicing asceticism of every kind.

But of course there was an important difference between cynicism and religious radicalism, allies though the two were against high culture. Cynicism was destructive, not reconstructive. Diogenes, Dudley tells us, refused all respect to marriage, encouraged stealing from the temples, and even defended cannibalism. That marks a decisive difference between him and Gandhi, between cynicism and radical religion. Both were radical criticisms of civilization, but they were not equally destructive. Perhaps the best way to understand how widespread this conflict is, and to see both the alliance and the difference between these two criticisms, is through the thesis of M. Detienne's *Dionysos Slain*. This is a structural-anthropological study of Greek myth (especially that of the Titans tearing the god Dionysus apart, to devour him) in its relation to city life and civilization. The Greek city constituted itself philosophically upon the basis of the eating of cooked meat, a form of alimentation half way between the divine and the animal. Eating meat was a proof of wealth, cooking it a proof of civilization; and so the right way to cook it and the alternatives to cooking it (one of which is portrayed in the myth of Dionysus slain) were fraught with significance and emotion. From that basis arose the superstructure of city culture, in which work and domesticity, peace and agriculture, were the civilized norms, and hunting and sexuality were liminal spaces, where the norms could be transgressed.

This idea of a civilized humanism was attacked in various ways: from above by the Pythagoreans and Orphics, who protested against meat-eating as something animalizing and debasing; and from below by Dionysians and Cynics, who protested against the cooking of meat as hypocritical and self-exalting. They recommended that men eat instead raw meat, ripped from an animal they had chased, or even become cannibals. Clearly, Tolstoy and Gandhi can be aligned with the Pythagoreans, modernists like Artaud and Genet with the Cynics.

Detienne's theory also explains those areas of social experience, like eroticism and hunting and war, from which most of our official philosophies avert their eyes, but which are defended vigorously when attacked by men like Tolstoy and Gandhi. These experiences are overtly forbidden, tacitly encouraged. Detienne analyses the hunting myths of Atalanta and Adonis to show how hunting, for instance, takes place in a permissive space where social laws can be flouted.[34] A fundamentally adventurous activity that leads to blood-spilling and meat-eating, it is linked with war, another activity "morally" reproved but imaginatively endorsed by civilized culture. (Both are contrasted with the normative activity of agriculture.) "Situated at the intersection of the powers of life and the forces of death, the hunter's space constitutes at once that which is beyond the farmer's fields and their negation."[35]

Work is the society-constituting activity that forms a dynamic antithesis to violence and eroticism. "The community is made up of those whom the common effort unites; cut off from violence by work, during the hours devoted to work."[36] But though this is the sacred truth, secular wisdom permits many deviations from it. Hunting and wars are permitted desecrations—transgressions of the society-constituting taboo on violence, but consecrated transgressions—which means the military caste is sacred though also sinister. They are priests of blood, their sacred robes stained red. "The act of killing invested the killer, hunter or warrior, with a sacramental character."[37] In the radical social theory of Christianity and Buddhism, says Georges Bataille (and in Tolstoy and Gandhi, we might add), those taboos are reaffirmed. They are reinforced against the relaxations introduced by secular culture, which always aims at inclusiveness, tolerance, and imaginative adventure. (Hinduism is a good example of such a culture, allotting space to kshattriya as well as to brahmin, exhorting Arjuna to do battle even against his kinsmen, and assigning to each individual a period of worldliness before a period of spirituality. Gandhi, incidentally, warned his followers against any such chronological appeasement of the claims of the spirit.)

Cynicism, says Detienne, was a deconstruction of Greek culture, recommending or enacting a return to savagery and a renunciation of fire and technology. We are familiar with such deconstruction, as a range of feeling, in many aspects of modern intellectual culture. What Tolstoy and Gandhi represent is the allied but quite different phenomenon of reconstruction, which corresponds to the Pythagoreans and the Orphics on the Greek scene. The latter refused all meat (or, in the case of some of the more moderate Pythagoreans, refused pig meat and goat meat) and, like the Cynics and Dionysians, constituted an anticity culture upon that refusal. But their dissent lay in the opposite direction from the Cynics', for they identified themselves with the highest demands and the highest aspirations, and refused both tolerance to the lower and respect to the middle or neutral—the neutral here meaning the intellectual and imaginative play of mind within the free leisure spaces won by wealth and power: high culture and art.

Within Christendom it is not so easy as it is within Greek culture to see this neat balance and counterplay among the critics of civilization. One can only suggest that some such balance and counterpoint links the radical religion of Tolstoy and Gandhi (the Orphics and Pythagoreans) with the frenzied modernism of extremist politics and art (the Cynics and Dionysians). Tolstoy and Gandhi are to be understood, I think, as reconstructors, as the thinkers who combine antihumanism with humanism, and save as much as can be saved of the virtues of both.

IX
Some Counterplayers:
1862–70 and 1906–15

In this period of their manhood, Tolstoy married, in 1862, and wrote *War and Peace*, while Gandhi, who broke off sexual relations with his wife in 1906, led the great campaign of nonviolent resistance to the government of South Africa on behalf of the Indians there. These were two great achievements in life-enhancement. From our point of view, however, the two men were not parallel in this period, for Gandhi was already a practitioner of nonviolence, while Tolstoy was still the novelist of *War and Peace* and thus the (tragic) celebrant of war. Symbolically, Gandhi, partway through the period, discarded Western dress for good, taking to prison garb at Tolstoy Farm (his ashram for satyagrahis) and to Hindu penitential garb later, when satyagraha claimed its first martyrs. Tolstoy's change of costume—to peasant dress—was to come later.

Nevertheless, seen in the perspective of his total development, Gandhi as well as Tolstoy had still far to go. For one thing, he still believed in the British Empire; even while he combated the colonial governments of South Africa, he regarded them as defecting from the empire's ideals, to which *he* was loyal. Believing in the empire, he kept a qualified faith in constitutionalism and dominion status. His idea of politics was not as fundamentally religious as it would become in India and was not as categorically a politics of peasants. The full implications of *Hind Swaraj* (his manifesto of 1910) were not yet apparent.

In this period, then, we still need to look at Tolstoy in the context of various literary contemporaries, and Gandhi amongst his political rivals. In Tolstoy's case, we can take Chernyshevsky, an ideological opponent, Strakhov, an ideological ally and warm admirer, and Dostoevsky, his great rival and contrast. Alongside Gandhi we can put

Jinnah, Tagore, Coomaraswamy, Sarojini Naidu, and some of the prominent revolutionaries.

But when we thus put them among their "professional" equals and rivals, we become aware, especially in Gandhi's case, of the radically religious ground to their activities, which was their distinguishing mark. We become aware of their ambivalence about those "professions," an ambivalence that looked like instability to their equals and rivals. Tolstoy and Gandhi were always problematic personalities, and always in growth, as compared with those who settled down to being productive in a well-defined sphere of activity. For that reason, it is appropriate to begin this chapter by defining one or two of each man's important pedagogical friendships.

Friends

In this period of their youth, Tolstoy and Gandhi were still engaged in friendships in which they played the subordinate role, but they were moving towards dominance. This change is more clear-cut in Gandhi, who found his effectiveness in the world of action, whereas Tolstoy's strength as a novelist lay in his sensibility, and so he prized and to some extent fostered his naïveté. But Tolstoy showed himself restive in his relationship with Boris Chicherin, where he was treated as the junior. However, he did form such a friendship with Chicherin when he was nearly thirty, and another such with Fet; while Gandhi's equivalent new relationships were with Henry Polak and Hermann Kallenbach, in which he was in most ways dominant. The drama of dependence for Gandhi occurred in earlier formed friendships, with Sheikh Mehtab, his boyhood friend in Porbandar, and Raychandbhai, the mystic contemplative he met in 1891.

Surprisingly, it was not with any of the Slavophiles that Tolstoy formed an alliance of friendship when he entered the world of political philosophy after 1856; rather, it was with a man who was for the Slavophiles a symbol of doctrinaire detachment from life—a man who in turn accused them of anti-intellectuality. This was the Westernizing liberal Boris Chicherin (1828–1904), a professor of philosophy at Moscow University up to 1868, and an all-round intellectual. Later in life he was a devout member of the Russian church and became a tutor to the royal family, without ceasing to be a liberal. He also served briefly as mayor of Moscow.

To understand this friendship we have to extend, and to some degree alter, the picture of Tolstoy we get from his novels. In *Anna Karenina* the figure of Koznyshev the philosopher is drawn largely from Chicherin, and that is a diagnostic and depreciatory portrait; we see why we should love and admire Levin by seeing how different he is from Koznyshev. But in the novel Koznyshev is the hero's half-brother, and so the reader never raises the question of why these two so different men are so intimately associated. In life the two men chose each other as friends, and we are bound to ask why. The answer to the question is a sympathy, ideological as much as personal, and felt by Tolstoy quite as much as by Chicherin. In other words, Tolstoy was drawn to the liberal position and to the personality that embodied it—he in some sense preferred it to the Slavophile position and personality in the mid-1850s.

It was about 1856 that he began to draw close to Chicherin, and the two became friends in 1858.[1] From the beginning Tolstoy would refer to Chicherin in his diary as an enemy of life and poetry, but he also found him a powerful (though narrow) mind. Chicherin, who was a Hegelian, taught him to place everything in the pattern of history, Tolstoy said. The other significant element in their relationship was Tolstoy's wooing of the other man. It was a function of Tolstoy's deliberate naïveté that he presented himself as younger than those he was interested in, and submitted himself to them—in effect, knelt to drink in their virtue. In the late 1850s, as Eikhenbaum says, Tolstoy was "temporarily in [Chicherin's] power, as had been the case earlier in his friendship with Druzhinin."[2] Chicherin wrote to Tolstoy in the tone of a conqueror of his heart—preceptorially, sentimentally, teasingly. "How difficult it is for you to attain a simple understanding of things! It is no accident that your handwriting looks half-feminine. One must ravish you as one ravishes a woman. . . . "[3] Expectably, Tolstoy rebelled against such a relationship before long, for he was really far from naïve in many areas of knowledge and feeling. (He *knew* Chicherin as Chicherin never knew him.) When Chicherin told him, in late 1859, to go to Italy to learn the secrets of art, Tolstoy (who had studied those secrets with some success) broke off the relationship, telling him that they were too different and had only been playing at friendship.

Chicherin went on to become a close friend of Pobedonostsev, the future procurator of the Holy Synod and persecutor of the late Tolstoy; this friendship, though, was limited to the 1860s and 1870s, when Pobedonostsev was still something of a liberal himself. For Tolstoy, the friendship which succeeded Chicherin's was with Afanasi Fet

(1820–92), who was ideologically something like an opposite to the other man.

Fet was the son of a rich landowner of Mtensk called Shenshin, who had, like Herzen's father, married in Germany without the blessing of the Russian church, so that his sons were illegitimate. The future poet was brought up with his mother's family name, Fet, but he was determined to re-enter his father's caste, and served in the army from 1845 to 1858, as a means to that end (as an officer, he was automatically a noble) while pursuing a legal indemnification. It was not until 1873 that he won his case and became Shenshin; therefore, most of his life was spent in pursuit of his aristocratic identity.

He was always conservative in his ideology, though too sceptical to be a Slavophile. While preparing for the university, he lodged with Pogodin, and as a student spent a lot of time with Apollon Grigoriev, the future critic and theorist of Pochvennost (rootedness). Grigoriev's doctrine was a sort of literary populism, on which both Dostoevsky and Tolstoy drew, and which was susceptible of very liberal interpretation. But Fet was a conservative through and through, in all his personality and his opinions, and a pessimist. His enthusiasm, his susceptibility, his spirituality, went into his poetry and was translated into eroticism (he wrote some passionate love poems at seventy). He wrote mostly short lyrics, very pure in their language and traditional in their form. Heine was his early master.

Fet joined the *Sovremennik* circle about 1850, along with Turgenev and Botkin, but soon felt uneasy with its liberal consensus, just as Tolstoy did. In 1860 he bought a farm, having recently married, and moved out of the city, rarely to return for many years. He was not too far from Yasnaya Polyana, and many visits were exchanged between the two families. He wrote articles on agriculture and country life for conservative magazines. His opinions grew more reactionary as general literary opinion grew more radical, and he gradually stopped writing or publishing his verse. He was generally labelled a *krepostnik*, an advocate of serfdom; and Turgenev called him a deep-rooted and fanatical reactionary. But the real strength of his thought and feeling was turned away from politics into private life. In 1863 he translated Horace—like himself, a poet-farmer who celebrated an epoch of imperialism. We might also compare him with Robert Frost in our own time.

His friendship with Tolstoy began in 1857–58 and lasted until the early 1880s, when Tolstoy changed his life. Tolstoy wrote him more than 160 letters that have survived (as compared with the 33 he wrote Nekrasov, the 9 to Druzhinin, the 16 to Botkin, and the 3 to Herzen[4]). Efim Etkind says that Tolstoy idolized Fet: he quotes Tolstoy's reflections on friendship in "Youth," where he said that one friend is always the lover, the other the beloved; the first kisses, the second presents his cheek. Tolstoy said that his own representative in the story, Irtenev, played the former role, was the one who gave his heart away, and Etkind says that Tolstoy gave his own away to Fet.

Tolstoy associated Fet with his brothers, especially after Nikolai's death. He no doubt saw in Fet a man who boldly and deliberately renewed that aristocratic life-style in which Tolstoy and his brothers had been brought up, and which was now universally condemned by writers. Tolstoy wrote Fet, for instance, "I love you just as my brother loved you and remembered you up to the last minute."[5] (Nikolai Tolstoy wrote to Fet in 1860: "What I love you for, dear Afanasy Afanasievich, is this, that you are all truth; what comes out of you is in you, and is not mere words, as is the case with dear old Ivan Sergeievich [Turgenev]."[6]) And Etkind describes as the central document of their correspondence Tolstoy's letter of 28–29 April 1876, where he said he would send for Fet—and for his brother Sergei— when he was dying; because they had both stood on the limit of life and looked into Nirvana. Fet was frankly un-Christian. In the late 1870s both Tolstoy and Fet were reading Schopenhauer with enthusiasm, and their friendship was based on a shared sense of death and meaninglessness.

In Fet we see in more accentuated form the combination of private life and aestheticism that Tolstoy chose when he married, and the same basis of conservatism and political cynicism beneath it. There was a generosity in Tolstoy's work, and in his mind, which was not there in Fet's; however, Tolstoy came to feel that that generosity was dishonest, was a function or a grace of his deliberate naïveté, his permanent instability and open-ended transitoriness. He admired and was subject to Fet because the latter paid the moral price for his stability. Later, of course, Tolstoy paid a far greater price for *his* *in*stability, redeeming his pledge to sacrifice everything else for the highest good he could see.

The roughly equivalent friendships in Gandhi's life were with Henry Polak and Hermann Kallenbach. We know much less about them than about Chicherin and Fet because they were not writers and they have not been the object of scholarly research. It is nevertheless clear that they represented certain ideas to Gandhi, and constituted significant influences upon him.

One of those ideas was Jewishness. Both Polak and Kallenbach saw the position of the Indians in South Africa as like that of the Jews in Europe, and under their influence Gandhi read Israel Zangwill and learned some of the anecdotes and phrases in which the Jewish sensibility is embodied. He applied to the Indians in South Africa the warning: "When any Jew sins, the whole race sins." He appealed to the rise of Yiddish to the rank of a literary language, as an example to the Indian languages like Gujarati. In general, he saw the way Indians were treated in the British Empire as comparable to the ways Jews had been treated in Christendom; and the religious root of the Jewish identity reinforced his conviction about the importance of religion in politics.

Another of those ideas was Russia. Gandhi got to know a variety of men from Russia or Poland in South Africa, and various editorials in *Indian Opinion* testify to the clarity and the force of the idea of Russia for him. Polak and Kallenbach were the two of those men who were closest to him.

And, by the token of those two ideas, they also represented a third, the specifically modern form of "intelligentsia" insofar as that is to be associated with social and national rootlessness: being *raznochintsy*, to use the Russian term. The men Gandhi had known in London, figures like Edwin Arnold and Edward Carpenter and Henry Salt, unconventional though they were, were one hundred percent English in origin, and their experience (as distinct from their speculation) could be said to be equally limited. Polak and Kallenbach were more like the men Gandhi might have met in contemporary New York or Chicago. They prepared him for the twentieth century— as few other Indian politicians were prepared.

Polak was a stocky, handsome young Englishman, described as "always full of indignation." Only twenty-one when he met Gandhi, he had come to South Africa for his health, and was assistant editor of the *Transvaal Critic*. He had been influenced by the Ethical Culture movement in England, was a vegetarian, and had read Ruskin and Tolstoy before he met Gandhi. It was he who gave Gandhi the copy of *Unto This Last* that produced a fateful effect upon him. He became a leader of the South African Indians in his own right, and he also became Gandhi's closest friend during the latter's stay in their country.

Hermann Kallenbach was a square-headed German Jew from Memel, whose parents were in fact from Russia. He was a successful architect in South Africa, who lived luxuriously. He designed homes for the rich (Johannesburg was a boom town) and his own home was a showplace. According to Gandhi in *Satyagraha in South Africa*, he had been brought up in the lap of luxury, and "indulgence had been his religion."[7] But he was also interested in "experiments in truth." A pugilist and wrestler who had developed his physique by the methods of Sandow, the legendary strong man, he was also interested in Buddhism. After falling under Gandhi's influence, he learned sandal-making from Trappist monks, and then taught that and carpentry to Gandhi.

Of the two, Polak was the more simply, overtly, and gaily resistant to Gandhi, the more assertive of his own temperament, the more challenging and contradictory. He represented the modern world, the world of the post-Victorian young Englishman, to Gandhi. Contact with this was something Gandhi much enjoyed—in other relationships, too—and it was an important part of his education, even though his public pronouncements often seem totally oblivious of it or unsympathetic with it. After Polak he made friends with Reginald Reynolds and Verrier Elwin, for instance, both of whom vividly represented this modern, ironic, socially rebellious, laughingly indignant, young manhood. (Nehru was an Indian equivalent.) This was another version of the New Life, since it broke decisively with the ponderous patriarchalism of pre-1914 England. It was, of course, quite different from Gandhi's New Life, since its general mind-set remained a young man's however old the individual members grew. We might perhaps say that this version of the New Life was destined to hegemony in British high culture in the interwar years. This was in the long run unfortunate for the fate of Gandhism, but at the level of personal relations Gandhi liked young Englishmen of this type.

Kallenbach was more nineteenth century in style, more ponderous, more alternately committed to the world, its wealth, and its luxuries, and then ascetically rebellious against it. It is appropriate that he should be the one to love Tolstoy's *Confession*, for he was cast in that more Victorian mold. He also seems to have been more deeply impressed by Gandhi, more nearly ready to throw in his lot with him (as he did in 1914). Being separated from Gandhi then (by his failure to get a visa for India), Kallenbach relapsed into his old life and became again a rich, self-indulgent South African architect. But he went to India later and lived in the ashram with Gandhi. Polak, on the other hand, quarreled with Gandhi in 1931 during his visit to London, and afterward criticized him severely. He found Gandhi too extravagant in his methods and too religious in his principles. In other words, Polak became a member of the liberal-radical intelligentsia of London in the 1930s.

Tolstoy's Rivals

N. G. Chernyshevsky was born in the same year as Tolstoy but into the priestly caste. He had some of the qualities traditionally associated with that caste, being pre-eminently a theoretician and intellectual, conscientious and hard-working, with a colorless personality and no heart—the way *War and Peace* understands personality and heart. However, Chernyshevsky became not a servant of the Russian government, but its enemy. Having begun as assistant to Nekrasov, as editor of *Sovremennik*, he gradually took over all the work and determined editorial policy in a more radical direction. He attacked Turgenev as too feebly liberal, and quarreled with Herzen (whom he had earlier worshipped) in 1859. These two men we could roughly align with Tolstoy, and with Nekrasov, as repentant nobles, men of broad culture, post-Decembrist radicals. This whole tradition was repudiated in the late 1850s, by Chernyshevsky and his followers, in the name of a new, narrower, angrier, more Puritan radicalism.

Chernyshevsky wrote comprehensive reviews, both summarizing and polemical, of the new scientific knowledge and the political science and sociology of his day in the West. And when imprisoned in 1861 he wrote *What Then Must We Do?* a Tale of the New People, which became immensely popular with young radicals, although artistically very inept. This novel appeared in 1862, the year of Tolstoy's marriage, and since it deals quite largely with marriage, the two events, or the ideas they embody, can be set in antithesis. Like Fet and Katkov, Tolstoy was very indignant about the novel; by August 1863 he had written an article against it, and by November or December he had finished the play *The Infected Family*, with a Chernyshevskian subtitle, "The New People." Chernyshevsky's central character is a woman who escapes from conservative bourgeois parents by making a merely legal marriage to a medical student with radical sympathies. She is then able to devote herself to running a seamstresses' cooperative, and their marriage ripens into comradeship, and on his side, into love. Eventually, however, she falls in love with his best friend, whereupon her husband disappears, faking a suicide, in order to leave her free.

Chernyshevsky used real events and people as his sources, and the reform of marriage and love, and the relations between the sexes which this story recommends, is quite the opposite of Tolstoy's. From a Tolstoyan and a common sense point of view, Chernyshevsky's idea must be called idealistic: it proposes a model of marriage based exclusively on shared ideals. As we have seen, Tolstoy wrote a satirical play (more than one, in fact) against Chernyshevsky's idea, but it is also possible to regard the whole narrative of *War and Peace* as a rebuttal of *What Then Must We Do?*

The great defender of *War and Peace*, and an important friend to Tolstoy in the 1870s and 1880s, Nikolai Strakhov, was also born in 1828, the same year as Tolstoy and Chernyshevsky. And, like Chernyshevsky and the raznochintsy writers, he was born the son of a priest and brought up by his uncle, a seminary rector. His criticism of seminary education was not that it was intellectually oppressive or physically miserable, but that it alienated the boys from life. It made them feel that "The only good is to be cleverer than the others; the only measure of human worth is the intellect; the only passion is egotism."[8] This theme of "alienation from life" runs through much of his self-analysis, and his dealings with Tolstoy and Dostoevsky. (For he was also, and earlier, a close friend to the other great Russian novelist of his time. He saw himself as typically the sober disciple of mad geniuses like Dostoevsky, Grigoriev, and, later, Rozanov.)

Strakhov began by teaching science, between 1852 and 1860, and writing a monthly magazine column on science. Journalism was then almost the only field for intellectuals, for the liberal professions scarcely existed in Russia before 1870. This was the career pattern—seminary, school-teaching, science, journalism—of many of the raznochintsy radicals. But Strakhov became a Hegelian idealist, and joined forces with Dostoevsky and Grigoriev, to defend philosophical idealism against positivist attack.

However, he allied his idealism to an "organic" criticism, which made much of "rootedness" and "the soil"—values very sympathetic to Tolstoy. These were Grigoriev's ideas, and Strakhov's criticism derived from Grigoriev; he treated literature as the nation speaking, a voice emerging from cultural roots. *War and Peace* was therefore for him an almost perfect novel, and its heroes perfect Russians.

In the 1880s Tolstoy was out of sympathy with many of Strakhov's ideas. But the real problem in their relations was that Tolstoy was dissatisfied with his *own* ideas—with the life values he embodied (magnificently, from Strakhov's point of view). For instance, Strakhov sent Tolstoy a self-accusing story fragment (written in 1866) in which the autobiographical hero kept "postponing life." In his reply, Tolstoy claimed to recognize *himself* in that portrait, but to be proud of the resemblance. Such superfluous men were to be understood as a new phenomenon in European life, he said, which European thought was not equipped to understand (and so understood as merely failure) but which Eastern philosophy understood and valued highly.[9] In other words, Tolstoy was ready to respect a rejection of "life" in the name of religion. And in 1879 he more directly upbraided Strakhov for his nostalgia for passion: "You want the good, but regret that there is not more evil in you; that you have no passions. You want the truth, but regret and seem to feel resentful that there is nothing rapacious about you. But what is good and what is bad? You evidently don't know well enough not to be afraid of making a mistake in doing good."[10]

Two hundred and twenty letters from Tolstoy to Strakhov survive, two hundred and thirty-three from Strakhov to Tolstoy. They read Buddhism together, went to Optina Pustyn monastery together, and on occasion Strakhov intervened helpfully between Tolstoy and Sonia in their quarrels. But as time went by, Tolstoy became more radical, politically and religiously, and his relationship with Strakhov, like that with many other friends, withered.

Dostoevsky represented the opposite of Tolstoy in many ways. He wrote to Strakhov in 1871 (May 18/30) that Russian literature had been a landowner's literature, which by now had said all it had to say—"splendidly in Tolstoy." The writers of the future would be different. Tolstoy's pre-eminently aristocratic fiction was the last of its kind.[11] Dostoevsky sometimes called himself a literary proletarian, and, in fact, his landscape was the city and his subject city life, with all its feverish formlessness. (In *The Adolescent* he says that only aristocrats should be written about in novels, because only they achieve form and beauty in their lives.) He followed the French writers (like Gautier and Balzac) who found all of modern life epitomized in the crowded, big city lodging house, and who urged writers to turn away from the adventures of the frontiers to those of the city streets.

This subject was an objective correlative for a sensibility quite the opposite of Tolstoy's, and there was much in Dostoevsky's early circumstances to have started him off in that opposite direction. Though technically a noble, his father was a doctor and his mother belonged to a merchant caste family. The father's temperament was difficult, and especially after the mother's death there were severe stresses in the family relations, which worked upon nervous and epileptic tendencies in the boy. And then the father died tragically in 1839.

The family as a whole was less happy than the Tolstoys, and it belonged to a different part of Russian culture. Dostoevsky says that his family knew the Gospels almost from their cradles. Their mother taught them a kenotic Christianity, using the German primer *104 Sacred Stories*. They observed all the holy days, paid visits to the Kremlin churches, and made a pilgrimage in the spring to the Troitsa-Sergei monastery. His nurse, Alyona Frolovna, who called herself a bride of Christ, was an important figure in the home. But besides this colorful folk Christianity, there was, in the letters between the parents, a blend of sentimental unction and intense practicality that reminds English readers of Defoe and Richardson. In noble families Christianity often seemed to belong to the servants, to be acknowledged by the masters as a social duty, and to be met by the children only in the servants' quarters. There are vivid examples of that in Herzen's *Memoirs* and it is also true of the Tolstoys. But the Dostoevskys were quite different.

Dostoevsky was precocious, both intellectually and as a writer. During his student years at the military engineering academy, he was absorbed in German romanticism and French socialism; and at the age of twenty-six he was saluted by Belinsky, the high priest of Russian criticism, for his first novel, *Poor Folk*. He belonged to an older generation of Russian intellectuals, the idealistic generation of "the forties." Those intellectuals were characterized by an intense excitability by moral ideals like self-sacrifice, a feverish search for them, and a susceptibility to high-wrought rhetoric, in addition to—by extrapolation—a contrary susceptibility to the appalling opposite passions of malice, sneering disbelief, and pettiness. To want one's eyes to be always fixed on the noble and the ideal is to make oneself hypersensitive to the sordid and ridiculous; and such is the temperament of Dostoevsky's heroes and novels.

Dostoevsky was arrested in 1849 as a revolutionary and was condemned to death, but reprieved when he was before the firing squad and sent to Siberia. There he underwent a large change in his political and religious convictions that was almost the reverse of Tolstoy's thirty years later, for Dostoevsky became fervently reactionary.

Thus, before Tolstoy had become known as a writer, Dostoevsky (though only seven years older) had gone through a number of dramas, many played out on the public stage. Comparatively speaking, Tolstoy was a private personality, at least through his career as a novelist. Moreover, Yasnaya Polyana was a retreat, and a modestly imposing one. Dostoevsky, on the other hand, lived an exposed and notorious life.

Gandhi's Rivals

We can select a group of rivals amongst whom to place Gandhi by means of an incident that occurred on his way back to India from South Africa.

Gandhi arrived in London on 4 August 1914, the day war was declared. He left on 18 December, having been sick much of that time and following an unsatisfactory involvement with a volunteer Indian ambulance corps. This time he hated living' in London—the speed, the noise, the size, the ugliness, the artificiality, the excitement—because he had come to hate modern civilization. He felt what Tolstoy felt when he had to live in Moscow again in 1881. Gandhi had come to England on his trip home because Gokhale was there, but the latter was delayed in France, and they did not actually meet until 18 September. On 8 August, however, a reception was given for Gandhi at the Hotel Cecil, and amongst those present were several with whom he was to have significant relationships: Sarojini Naidu, Lala Lajpat Rai, Mohammed Ali Jinnah, and Ananda Coomaraswamy.

Jinnah's career ran curiously parallel to Gandhi's. He was born in 1876 (only seven years younger than Gandhi) of Kathiawari parents, who moved to Karachi only when he was born. His father was a rich merchant who traded in hides and arabic gum. He belonged to the Khoja Moslems (converts who retained their Hindu caste and family classifications), and Jinnah is a Hindu name. Indeed, like Gandhi he spoke Gujarati in his father's house. Like Gandhi again, Jinnah went to England to study law; but he was only sixteen when he arrived, being a more precocious mind and personality.

Like Gandhi, he was married before he went to England in 1893; and like Gandhi, his mother (but in his case also his wife) died before he returned. During his three-year stay in England, he listened to Parliamentary debates often, and admired Gladstone. He also toured in a theatrical company and played Romeo. He was a handsome man—a striking presence—and an effective speaker; because of his theatrical and rhetorical personality—the very opposite of Gandhi—he was a figure Tolstoy might have drawn in the court scenes of *War and Peace*. During those years in London he was taken up by Dadabhai Naoroji, the veteran Indian nationalist who lived there. He helped Naoroji fight his campaign for Parliament. Gandhi revered Naoroji, and visited him, but did not achieve a personal friendship with him.

Back in Bombay, from 1897 to 1900, Jinnah had to start from scratch, as Gandhi had tried to do a little earlier. But Jinnah succeeded; he faced penury at first, but soon he was earning more than any other lawyer in the city. He was very elegantly English in his clothes, wearing a monocle on a grey silk cord, a buttonhole, and a stiff collar, and also in his manners, for he addressed everyone as "My dear boy" and carried a long ivory cigarette-holder. He had something of a mania for cleanliness, avoiding the touch of others and washing his hands every hour. The opposite of Swadeshi as a personality, he never mastered even Urdu, and was almost openly uninterested in the Muslim religion. But he was passionately interested in national politics when played according to Parliamentary rules; in fact, politics were his only hobby, and he was very good at them. He was taken up by Gokhale and Sir Pherozeshah Mehta. He aspired to be "the Muslim Gokhale."

Sarojini Naidu wrote an early book about him, entitled *Mohammed Ali Jinnah: Ambassador of Unity*, and the unity in question is that between Muslims and Hindus, which was then her and Jinnah's cause.

The Muslim League was founded in 1906, but Jinnah stayed aloof until 1913. In 1916 the league and the Congress concluded the Lucknow Pact, which gave the Muslims the principle of separate electorates. These concerns and relationships, together with Jinnah's work for the Transvaal Indians, suggest how very close he was to Gandhi in politics in those years. There were even sympathies of temperament, suggested by both men's extreme fastidiousness—neither was in any sense hearty; both were in some sense frail, psychologically as well as physically. But while Gandhi sought an authenticity by rooting himself in the depths of the human condition, Jinnah defiantly identified himself with the superficies—with current styles of dress, behavior, and action.

At the Nagpur Congress in December 1920, Jinnah told an Indian journalist: "Well, young man, I will have nothing to do with this pseudo-religious approach to politics. I part company with the Congress and Gandhi. I do not believe in working up mob hysteria. Politics is a gentleman's game."[12] This journalist says that Jinnah's skill as a debater was mostly in picking on his opponents' weaknesses; his language was simple but his gestures were dramatic—for instance, he stabbed the air with a forefinger and consulted his notes with his monocle.

Implicitly he denied the possibility of ultimate meanings and meaningfulness for people. Curiously enough, "No" and the other modes of negation were favorites of his; and Nehru—who understood him very well, having a similar elegance though a broader and richer nature—described him as an incarnation of negativism. Agnes Smedley knew him in Berlin in the 1920s and described him as "cold, sleek, cruel-faced."[13] The tragedy of Indian politics was that such a man could be chosen as leader by a whole nation of Muslims—that negativism could be made a political principle, too.

Another curious link between him and Gandhi was Sarojini Naidu herself, for after 1914 she devoted herself to Gandhi's cause, becoming one of the most colorful figures in his entourage; she became attached to him and not to Jinnah. She, Jinnah, and Gokhale (who was for her, too, *the* master of the older generation) were all in London in April and May of 1914, and it seems likely that it was then she accepted the hopelessness of her personal attachment to Jinnah, confiding in and consulting with Gokhale about the matter.

The main evidence for this speculation lies in unpublished letters in the National Archives in Delhi. She wrote to Gokhale during her journey home on 10 October 1914 that the sea voyage would help her meet and conquer her emotional difficulties, in which he advised her. She wrote on 14 October: "Don't think I have forgotten [what?] you have [said?] about remaining impersonal and intellectual. I have forgotten nothing you have told me."[14] And on 16 November she wrote him a detailed description of her house and family, ". . . because I feel that it will give you pleasure—and reassure you wholly—to know about my daily life in the . . . family and friends—and it will answer all your unspoken questions."[15] She uses Noblesse Oblige twice, and connects it with India and service. And in later letters, she often intimates that she has given up the hope of private happiness and devoted herself to "work"—national work. It is generally assumed that the man in question was Jinnah.

Naidu was born in 1879, ten years after Gandhi, into a brahmin family of artists and intellectuals. She composed poetry very early, in a Pre-Raphaelite-ornate style, and she was cursed with that easy fluency against which modern poetic taste has reacted—she may have turned away from poetry and toward politics for that reason. But in politics, too, she seems always to have embodied effusive speech for others.

Involved in politics, then, she first took up women's causes. She became a notable orator, though her speeches had the same weakness as her poems. Gokhale once told her: "You are typically Hindu in spirit. You begin with a ripple and end in eternity."[16] After a speech in 1925, while everyone was applauding wildly, Motilal Nehru asked, "But what did she *say*?"[17] She was above all a colorful presence, dramatic in gesture, impulsive in speech, and dressed in vivid saris, gold bangles, chains and brooches, and twin tiger-claw clasps.

It is therefore interesting that Naidu should have devoted much of her later life to Gandhi (traveling with him, nursing him through the Untouchables' fast, going to jail with him in 1942) while his career gradually came to head-on collision with Jinnah's.

She was surprisingly irreverent about Gandhi, calling him "Mickey Mouse" and refusing to participate in his austerities. But one must suppose that at heart, and in silence, she took him more seriously than she took other people. When he began to fast in the fall of 1932, he wrote her a possible farewell letter, saying: "If I die I shall die in the faith that comrades like you, with whom God has blessed me, will continue the work of the country. . . . I think that I understood you when I first saw you and heard you at the Criterion in 1914."[18] That last sentence sounds like a claim to know the serious person beneath the personality.

Of course, her relationship with Gandhi was nothing like that with Jinnah; it was not in the least erotic—perhaps it was most like the teasing comradeship and enjoyment of oppositeness he had with Sonja Schlesin; nor is there any reason to suppose that she chose the one man to spite the other. If there was a connection in her mind in 1914 between this new loyalty and the old, most likely it was that she chose someone as unlike Jinnah as possible, as an escape from the griefs that relationship brought her. But for Jinnah there was almost certainly—over time—a large emotional significance to this. He was to undergo a series of losses, of fields of action open to him (Congress and the Home Rule League) or of people devoted to him, like Naidu, who turned to Gandhi instead. That experience I think one must connect to the resentful negativism that shows itself in his dealings with Gandhi and the Gandhian cause. In 1942 he told Louis Fischer that both Gandhi and Nehru had begun their careers by working under him in the Home Rule League.

Naidu was one of that group of "Orientalizers," of whom the most famous was, of course, Rabindranagh Tagore. Gandhi differed from the Orientalists by engaging in politics, and within politics, by engaging in direct action. But he also differed from another group of significant contemporaries by refusing to engage in revolution or terrorism. Amongst these the most important was Vir Savarkar, the man responsible for Gandhi's assassination, and his colleagues and converts, like Virendranath Chattopadhyaya and Har Dayal.

Savarkar began as a disciple of Tilak, as we have seen, and developed a philosophy of Hindutva, the renaissance of Hindu nationalism and imperialism. He employed terrorist methods and was self-professedly responsible for the assassination of Sir Curzon Wyllie in London in 1909 (an act Gandhi publicly condemned at the time). He was sent back to India as a prisoner (escaping on the way but being recaptured) and spent many years in custody and exile. Gandhi more than once tried to conciliate him, but his attempts were in vain. Savarkar saw Gandhi as a traitor to Hinduism, and in 1948 it was Savarkar's faithful disciples who assassinated Gandhi.

Virendranath Chattopadhyaya spent his life in exile in Berlin. His companion there from 1919 to 1927 was Agnes Smedley, who had been introduced to the Indian independence movement in New

York, through Lal Rajpat Rai. In *Battle Hymn of China* she says: "Viren-dranath was the epitome of the Indian revolutionary movement, and perhaps its most brilliant protagonist abroad."[19] The Indian students on scholarship in England came to see him during their vacations, and got their true education from him. He sneered at Hinduism as a cow-dung religion and told them that only clerks lived an orderly, respectable life. Smedley speaks of his "cultivated, labyrinthine Brahmin mind" and says: "To me he was not just an individual but a political principle. For me he embodied the tragedy of a whole race."[20] Men like him "hunted British rulers of India and Egypt with pistol, bomb, and knife. Some had been shot, some hanged, others impris-oned for life."[21] Though he was twenty years older than she, and "very little interested in women," she presents him as a figure of erotic glamor: thin and dark, with a mass of black hair, a fierce face, "some-thing like thunder."[22] He "existed like a storm," influencing everyone he met, himself unchanging. Later he joined the Communist party and helped found the League Against Imperialism. After 1923 the couple had to keep moving their lodgings and changing names, and their poverty and instability, and her servitude to him, drove her to the edge of insanity. This story, which prefigures much in Doris Less-ing's autobiographical fiction, retells the main erotic legend of feminist-wing radicalism. No such legends attach to Gandhi.

Nehru was influenced by Virendranath Chattopadhyaya in the 1920s, and felt obliged to explain to him his drift away from socialist towards nationalist politics. In 1929 Virendranath warned him that he was being trapped by the cunning Mahatmaji and that he must split Congress in order to "destroy a patched up unity and clear the way for a solid anti-imperialist movement."[23]

A rather similar figure was "M. N. Roy" (his given name Naren-dranath Bhatacharya), the leader of the Indian Communist party in later years. Born a brahmin in 1887 (or 1893) in Bengal, he became a follower of Arabindo's brother, Barin, in 1904, and in 1906 he took up bomb-making and engaged in acts of terror.

Roy is interesting, too, as a temperament; he can remind one of Virendranath and of the revolutionary figures in Tagore's stories and novels on such themes.

He was an aristocratic brahmin. In his memoirs, he refers to his "Brahmin's tradition of intellectual aristocracy."

> My socialist conscience struggled hard to deny to myself the
> empirical truth that, while I felt at home in the company of
> a feudal aristocrat, the uncouth comrades never ceased to

embarrass me. . . . Concretely, I felt that an aristocratic intellectual, emancipated from the prejudices of his class, might
be a more disinterested and culturally more Dionysian
revolutionary than the most passionately class-conscious
proletarian.[24]

As the word *Dionysian* may suggest, there was something Nietzschean
about Roy; his biographer calls him a restless and ruthless man, and
in his relations with women he was notably exploitive.

Thus, the human context for Gandhi, as for Tolstoy, is something
much closer to our own sense of the politically and intellectually normal than their own writings suggest, at least when those are read in
the context of traditional interpreters. Gandhi's pastoralism and Tolstoy's vitalism can make it seem as if their experience did not include
some of the major features that characterize our own. But Russia in
the 1860s was in fact remarkably like America in the 1960s; and figures
like Jinnah and Roy, and Strakhov and Chernyshevsky, are easy to
find on our own scene. Tolstoy and Gandhi selected from the facts
and forces around them, and made very eccentric selections by the
standards of their contemporaries; in a sense, they invented those
forces they said they represented, since without Tolstoy and Gandhi
those options would have been said not to be there. They forced a
new vision, as well as a new conscience, upon their contemporaries,
and we will not understand what we can make of them unless we
realize how much imaginative force they exerted. They differ from
us not because they grew up in a different world, but because they
created a different world for themselves from among elements that
we would have found very familiar.

X

The Unwilling Subjects of
Empire: 1870–81 and 1915–21

In the period I have labeled "Manhood," Tolstoy and Gandhi achieved deeds that made them world-famous. Tolstoy wrote two great novels—after *War and Peace* followed *Anna Karenina*—and Gandhi led two great political campaigns—after his triumph in South Africa followed his capture of the national leadership in India, which humbled the rulers of the British Empire. Both achievements, disparate though they were, defied imperialism. They were both, in their different ways, triumphs of nonviolence. But their opposition to empire could not be called radical, much less religious. These were liberal and secular protests against imperialism. Tolstoy and Gandhi later felt that there were firm limits to the effectiveness of this liberalism.

It was only in the next period, which I have called "Old Age," that Tolstoy turned away from this social and secular faith, towards something essentially opposite. For Gandhi, the chronological change is not so clear-cut. From early on, Gandhi was trying with his right hand to make religious values prevail in politics, while with his left he advanced the political interests of Indians against those of competing groups. But one can say that it was in old age that he became most aware of the difference between the two activities, especially when he saw his followers take up the work of his left hand and ignore that of his right. He himself shifted to and fro, trying to combine the two. (India was to be a great nation, but one dedicated to more than national values.)

Nevertheless, within the limits of liberal anti-imperialism, Tolstoy and Gandhi's work marked out new areas of freedom and fulfillment, independent (and defiant) of state government and economic privilege, of all wealth and power establishments. Moreover, they themselves extended their experience out towards the limits of civilization.

There were many Russians and many citizens of the British Empire who were in effect outside the empire, and Tolstoy and Gandhi wanted them to stay outside, and yet to be given a voice and a standing, a sense of self-respect. In other words, they wanted to create an arena of human life larger than empire, within which imperial interests would be diminished and overshadowed by others, and a moral perspective created.

The most striking case of this extension of sympathies for Tolstoy was his establishing a second home in the province of Samara, effectively on the eastern frontier of Russian society, where his neighbors were Bashkiri tribesmen. Gandhi's equivalent was his going to live on Tolstoy Farm, where the Indians became pioneers, clearing and digging up virgin land, and building themselves places to live.

Tolstoy bought land in June 1871 while on a trip to Samara with his brother-in-law, Stepan Bers. He bought 3,600 acres with his literary earnings. This land was divided into twelve "fields," two of which were sown with wheat (one a Russian variety, one a Turkish), a third with corn, and the other nine were pasture. (Samara had essentially a single-crop economy.) Oxen pulled the ploughs, but Samara was above all a land of horses. Tolstoy wrote to his wife about the magnificent spectacle of thousands of horses—the mares and foals separate from the stallions—coming down from the mountains to the steppe. He bred Bashkir mares with English and Russian trotters, and by 1877 had 150 horses on his farm. He rode Bashkir style, using Bashkir wooden stirrups.

This was what was called ranching in America, rather than farming, and it had the same element of wildness in Russia. The oldest son, Sergei Tolstoy, tells us he rode semitrained horses across the steppes and watched wild horses being tamed. The herd was guarded by stallions trained to bite and kill horse-thieves. When some Kirghiz stole forty of the Tolstoy horses (planning to drive them into no man's land beyond the Urals, two hundred versts away), the Tolstoys pursued them, and there was a fight with whips. And in 1876 Tolstoy got to know a merchant in Orenburg who traded in tiger-skins with Turkestan, and whose grandfather had lived by selling Russian girls as slaves to Central Asia's bazaars.

The life was primitive. There was no wood on the steppe, and the Tolstoys burned bricks of manure. They ate mutton and drank kumys (fermented mares' milk) almost exclusively. A Muslim Bashkir, Muhammed Shah, brought his tents, his family, and ten milking mares to live beside them, and talked to Tolstoy of the old Bashkir ways. Because serfdom had never been established in Samara, he shook hands with the Tolstoys, free from peasant deference. On the other hand, his wife and daughter-in-law did all the work and took no part in social life; Sonia Tolstoy was indignant on their behalf.

The Tolstoys lived in a felt-covered hemispheric cage of wood. The family went there first in 1873, and Tania records the strangeness of the landscape and the life. There were no woods, ponds, rivers, or mushrooms, as at home; instead, there were eagles, buzzards, tarantulas, wolves. Tolstoy wrote to his wife: "We've just been riding after buzzards, and as always only frightened them off, and then we came on a wolf's litter, and a Bashkir caught a cub there."[1] In these letters he evoked the legend of the Swiss Family Robinson, and, in his diary, said that Part II of his new novel would have a Robinson Crusoe figure, who "starts an entirely new life, made up of only the most indispensable factors of existence."[2]

It is clear that this idea, essentially the same as what excited Gandhi on Tolstoy Farm, stayed with him a long time. In his diary for 19 June 1896 we read: "The picture of life in Samara stands out very clearly before me: the steppes, the fight of the nomadic, patriarchic principle with the agricultural-civilized one. It draws me very much."[3] Sonia, on the other hand, disliked not only the primitive conditions of life in Samara, but the Robinson Crusoe idea itself. On 13 October 1884 she wrote to him from Moscow that she knew he had stayed behind alone in Yasnaya Polyana not to do intellectual work—the most important thing in the world to her—but to play at some Robinson Crusoe game. For her Samara was primarily a business investment, and there were many bitter quarrels between husband and wife over his inefficiency in managing it. (The Samara estate became known as "the Eastern Question" in the family because of these quarrels.)

For Tolstoy, Samara was also a place where he made contact with sectarians—especially the Molokans, with whom he had many discussions—and with other kinds of religion. There was a hermit who lived in a cave and slept in his coffin, near Buzuluk, whom Tolstoy visited. But his interest was in all those who stood outside or against the life of empire, and so it extended out from the specifically religious to the tribesmen. He went to the fair at Buzuluk, which was attended by many different nationalities; and in 1875 he arranged horse races for the Bashkirs, feeding his guests with sheep and a foal, and giving a bull, a gun, a watch, among other things, as prizes. The horses, mounted by ten-year-old boys, had to cover a circle of five versts thirty-two times. It was a patriarchal festivity Tolstoy presided over.

The Bashkirs were one of those tribes known collectively as "Tatars." In 1897 there were two million Transcaucasian Tatars, almost as many Volga or Kazan Tatars, and two hundred thousand Crimean Tatars. But the term was also used to cover all the Muslims in Russia, of whom there were then twelve million. The looseness with which the term was used is like that we find with "Cossack," and the reason is the same in both cases. These terms point outwards, to social groups on the edge of civilized society, and do not discriminate or even fully circumscribe their object; their function is partly to name the difference between all such groups and these others at the center of empire.

The Bashkirs were tribes who had taken part in Pugachev's revolt against Catherine the Great in the eighteenth century, and had been exiled to the Samaran steppe thereafter. As such, they represented large historical forces; Marc Raeff says Pugachev's rebellion was against Peter the Great's modernization of Russia, and was the retarded counterpart of the West European revolts of the sixteenth and seventeenth centuries. Russia was always behind, Peter's work having been done a hundred years after the equivalent in France and Spain, and fifty years after that in Sweden and Prussia.

The Bashkirs hated and raided Russian factories and the city of Orenburg, which represented all Russian cities to them (Tolstoy's property was only 120 versts from Orenburg). But they more obviously represented nonhistorical or prehistorical forces. They led a pastoral nomadic life on land where nothing but silvery feather grass grew for hundreds of miles. There had been regiments of them in the Russian army that Alexander led to Paris, but now those regiments had been disbanded and they were demilitarized. In the winters they lived in primitive villages, but every spring they moved out to wander the steppe. They had passed into that other phase of employment by the dominant culture; no longer soldiers, Cossacks, watchmen, private guards, they were now picturesque survivals or exiles, either as tribes to be visited by tourists or as individual waiters or dancers in the great cities.

Tolstoy's kumys cure meant drinking fermented mare's milk and eating mutton. But it also meant riding a great deal, living in a tent, sleeping on the ground, and generally entering into the Bashkir lifestyle. Tolstoy, for instance, wrestled with them; and no doubt felt their virtue pass into him with their sweat. To take a kumys cure was a Russian institution; it was something both Tolstoy's father and Sergei Aksakov's mother had done; it was one of the ways in which the revolt against civilization could be built into the culture and transformed into a renewal of the civilizing race's vocation. It was allied to, on the one side, the cult of the Caucasus and the Caucasian revolt, and, on the other, the reading of Scott, Cooper, Marlinsky, and Tolstoy's own *Cossacks*.

Tolstoy's buying of land in Samara (later he bought another 4,000 acres) represents yet another mode of interaction between the frontier and the metropolis, one in which the corruptive consequences of this romantic embrace are more obvious. Around 1870 all the tribes' reserve lands in Orenburg were sold off, plus 360,000 desyatinas in Ufa.[4] The best land went for R16.8 per desyatina, but the banks advanced loans with repayments spread out over thirty-seven years because the investment was so good. One million desyatinas were sold and resold in that way, and the Bashkirs lost all their land; they were dispossessed, like the North American Indians, and by Tolstoy amongst others. Raeff says: "The Bashkirs had to yield their land, grazing grounds, and fishing places under duress and at derisive prices, much like the American Indians selling Manhattan Island."[5]

Such buying had been going on for some time. It is described in detail in Sergei Aksakov's *Memoirs of a Russian Family* (1858). Aksakov's father had bought 7,000 desyatinas very cheap from the Bashkirs, thirty versts from Ufa, but the sale was disputed by two villages of squatters and in 1858 was still not settled. It was very difficult to establish title with people who had no notion of surveying or of Western property law, and who had established boundaries by the course of streams and corners by notable trees.

As we know, Aksakov's work has much in common with Tolstoy's early fiction, in its celebration of the Russian landscape and people. When Tolstoy spoke of describing a Russian Robinson Crusoe on the plains near Samara (in the next novel he planned to write after *Anna Karenina*), he could have been recalling Aksakov's portrait of his grandfather, the hero of that work. The grandfather was short but broad, with a frank, open expression. A good land-manager and a source of moral authority for miles around, he is like Tolstoy's Levin or Pierre—minus their Hamletism. At the end of their novel-careers, he is what they will become. He wore homespun, and had two servants who slept on the floor of his room, and whom he would set on to fight each other for his amusement. He was patriarchal.

This man knew how to buy land direct from the Bashkirs at as little as R100 for 20,000 desyatinas: you invited a dozen Bashkir chiefs, provided sheep for them to kill and a bottle of whiskey and a bucket of beer, and entertained them for a week or two. Hating lawsuits, however, he bought his land ("black virgin soil, over two feet in depth," his grandson says) from Russian intermediaries. He bought 12,000 acres for R2,500 and moved his serfs 400 versts east from civilization, to set up a ranch kingdom; he needed elbow room, he said.

"How wonderful in those days was that region, with its wild and virginal freshness!" says Aksakov. "Both steppe and forest were filled beyond belief with wild creatures. In a word, the place was, and still is, a paradise for the sportsman."[6] A Russian sportsman could thus own Nature, though he felt the pathos of his own destructiveness. "But man is the sworn foe of Nature, and she can never withstand his treacherous warfare against her beauty."[7] (The adventure literature of England is also filled with this guilty and erotic pathos.) As in America, some of the Russian settlers imitated the primitive tribes; Aksakov's uncle, Karataev, wandered the steppe with a tribe all through the summers, speaking their language, shooting with bow and arrow, drinking the mead, singing their songs, growing bow-legged from his days in the saddle.

Empires recommend such experiences to their citizens and make them available. It was under the auspices of the British Empire that Gandhi was in South Africa, after all, and the colonial situation made available to him that experience at Tolstoy Farm which was the equivalent of what Tolstoy knew in Samara. In June 1910 his friend Hermann Kallenbach gave his farm at Lawley, near Johannesburg, to the satyagraha cause, and announced its title, in the midst of his and Gandhi's most ardent concern with Tolstoy. Gandhi announced that Kallenbach was going to retire from the practice of architecture, and live in poverty, and in fact he taught carpentry, gardening, and sandal-making on the farm. (His living expenses, according to Gandhi, dropped by ninety percent.) Descriptions in Gandhi's letters of life there are full of zest in the physical work—chopping and sawing wood, fetching water and doing laundry, rolling stones for a foundation. "I for one am a farmer and I wish you all to become farmers," he wrote to Maganlal in August:

> My way of life has completely changed here. The whole day is spent in digging the land and other manual labor instead of in writing and explaining things to people. I prefer this work and consider this alone to be my duty. . . . I regard the Kaffirs, with whom I constantly work these days, as superior to us. What they do in their ignorance we have to do knowingly. In outward appearance we should look just like the Kaffirs. . . . The body is like an ox or donkey and should therefore be made to carry a load.[8]

These are the Robinson Crusoe pleasures, here recaptured. "Having founded a sort of village we needed all manner of things large and small, from benches to boxes, and we made them all ourselves."[9] And as in *Robinson Crusoe*, the reduction to simplicity produced an exaltation of the spirit. The experience was profoundly important to Gandhi. "My faith and courage were at their highest in Tolstoy Farm. I have been praying to God to permit me to re-attain that height. . . ."[10] The difference is that in Defoe's story the hero returns to England to enjoy the fruit of his labors—his exhilaration and exaltation of spirit re-empower his love of his own civilization—whereas in Gandhi something like the reverse happened.

Thoreau's self-simplification, reported in *Walden*, also derives from Crusoe's, but the South African setting makes Gandhi's story especially interesting because it gives the ideas they shared a large and political scope. That interest is also increased by the decline of the *Robinson Crusoe* pleasures, or at least of the virtues among the whites there. (In April 1908 Sir Percy Fitzpatrick of the Progressive party of South Africa called upon the white man to "justify himself" by "out-working the native."[11]) It was the brown-skinned Indians who began to practice those virtues that had been the pride and the moral prerogative of the whites.

In these years, 1910 to 1914, Gandhi in some sense wanted to change his identity for a farmer's. In March 1914 he wrote Chaganlal that the Gandhis had been a famous or notorious family; "that is, we are known to belong to a band of robbers."[12] (In literal fact, they had been administrators.) If their elders had done some good to others, it was incidental. Chaganlal and Maganlal should cease to be Gandhis. "We should become farmers," or else weavers.

In a sense the Indians became Europeans on Tolstoy Farm, only not ruling class Europeans but those outside or against empire. "We had all become laborers and therefore put on laborers' dress but in the European style, viz. workingmen's trousers and shirts, which were imitated from prisoners' uniforms."[13] Making their own wooden spoons there, like Robinson Crusoe himself, Gandhi and his friends were full of faith. "I had in those days as much faith in the nature cure of disease as I had in the innocence of children."[14]

And one can indeed see Gandhi's interest in nature cure, and something in his strictly aesthetic sensibility, as corollaries to this experience. Around this time he wrote a series of essays on health in *Indian Opinion*, which endorsed the simple life and naturalness, even to the point of nudity. On 15 July 1911 he wrote in *Indian Opinion*:

A moment's thought ought to convince our friends that a nation cannot be built out of clerks or even merchants. "Back to the land" is General Botha's advice even to the Europeans who, after all, do follow many useful occupations. The world lives on its farmers and those who are indispensable to farmers, e.g. carpenters. . . . We all live upon the great industry of the Natives and Indians engaged in useful occupations in this country. In this sense they are more civilized than any of us.[15]

In the fifteenth health essay the farmer's life is recommended for health and also for the skills accompanying it. Farmers have to know when seed is to be sown, how to tell direction by the stars, and how to live. "[A farmer] has to feed his children and has, therefore, some idea of the duties of man, and, residing as he does in the vast open spaces of this earth, he naturally becomes aware of the greatness of God. Physically, it goes without saying, he is always sturdy."[16] All men should do eight hours of physical work per day.

As for aesthetic sensibility, Gandhi showed for the rest of his career an intense appreciation for "organic" phenomena, which we are surely justified in connecting with this experience. (Though we might remember that he had before this himself delivered Kasturba of her fourth child—in other words, his sensibility was already unusually oriented towards organic life.) This is a stress of sensibility common enough amongst those who have read D. H. Lawrence or *Anna Karenina*, but not so common amongst those who, like Gandhi, read instead the *Ramayana* and the *Bhagavad Gita*. Here, for instance, is a passage from a letter about unpolished rice. "I opened out one grain from the paddy and showed to those around the full unpolished grain. I had not seen it before. But in a heap of half-polished rice I saw a whole paddy grain. I immediately removed the husk with my finger nails. Out came the beautiful red grain from its husk."[17] It is a moment of birth he is evoking. As Madan C. Gandhi says, Gandhi found a dead polish in the smooth starchy texture of mill cloth. Homespun seemed to him soft, lovely, graceful, its coarseness the very weave of nature. And just so he loved the flour patterns on Indian doorsteps, and the light shed on banana-branch arches by earthen oil lamps.[18]

Clearly, Gandhi's interest in the primitive and the original was not so much as Tolstoy's was an interest in tribal society; that element, however, was not entirely lacking. His taste for the outdoor work at

Tolstoy Farm led him immediately, as we have seen, to an appreciation of the Zulus (the Kaffirs, as he calls them.) And he remained fascinated by the idea of the Pathans, whom he associated with the Zulus, as a martial tribe. In 1934 he wrote: "Personally I would like to bury myself in an Indian village, preferably in a Frontier village. If the Khudai Khitmagars [the followers of Abdul Ghaffar Khan] are truly nonviolent they will contribute the largest share to the promotion of non-violent spirit and of Hindu-Muslim unity. . . . "[19] And later: "The future I do not know except that Utmanzai [Abdul Ghaffar Khan's village] is my Mecca, Jerusalem or Kashi."[20] It was only the viceroy's refusal to let him into that traditionally troubled area which prevented Gandhi from carrying out this plan, which he several times proposed in the 1930s.

Tolstoy and Gandhi had therefore something in common in their interest in primitive life-styles and living conditions. And this derives in part from the historical situations in which they grew up, and what these situations had in common. Doris Lessing writes in *Going Home*: "I am struck continually by the parallels between pre-revolutionary Russia as described by Chekhov, Turgenev, Tolstoy, and Gorki, and that part of Africa I know. An enormous, under-populated, under-developed, unformed country, still agricultural in feeling and resisting industrialization. . . . "[21] But the part of Russia that answers most closely to Africa was not the part described in *Anna Karenina*, but the part Tolstoy would have described in that other novel which he didn't write—Central Asia, the vast expanse of which Samara constituted but one shore. This is essentially one enormous plain that extends from the Ural Mountains and the Caspian Sea all the way to the Chinese borders of Mongolia. Most of this land effectively belonged to the tribes, and Russian power was rarely directly manifested or felt. There was also a succession of north-south mountains, from the Altai down to the Pamirs, east of which the influence of China dominated. To the north the area was bordered by the black earth strip that had attracted Russian settlers from the seventeenth century on, and north of that is the forest belt of taiga, which marked the southern border of Siberia.

By the nineteenth century there were six major ethnic groups in this area, some of them pastoral nomads, others oasis peoples. The last to come under Russian domination were the Turkomans, who were defeated in a series of battles that ended in 1885. Only then was slavery and the slave trade abolished, whereupon the men turned to alcohol and opium, and the women had to work. Until 1910 Russians were allowed to buy only newly irrigated land—the old being reserved for the natives. But in 1884 American cotton was planted successfully, and the area moved towards a one-crop economy. Tolstoy relied on the existence of these expanses, to dwarf cities to manageable size for him.

At the time Doris Lessing wrote *Going Home*, she was a fairly orthodox Communist, and her contempt for Tolstoy's politics as reflected in *Anna Karenina* was complete. She continues her analogy:

> And in the person of Levin [Tolstoy] one finds the decent worried white liberal who is drawn by the reserves of strength, the deep humanity of the African, but yet does not trust him to govern himself. Levin, in Africa, is always dreaming of going native, of escaping from the complexities of modern civilization which he sees as fundamentally evil. He philo- sophizes; goes on long trips into the bush with his African servant to whom he feels himself closer than to any other human being and to whom he tells everything; half believes in God; knows that all governments are bad; and plans one day to buy a crater in the Belgian Congo or an uninhabited island in the Pacific where at last he can live the natural life.[22]

Clearly, this does not try to be fair to Tolstoy—though we may suppose that he, from his post-1880 point of view, would have agreed with Lessing in her severity. But we can defend what he was doing as embracing, and preparing to represent, all those other, disinherited, groups within the Russian empire.

However, Peter the Great had created a genuinely multinational empire, which gave administrative power to non-Russian minorities, like the Baltic Germans. In fact, it was Muscovy, the heartland of Russia, that was often in opposition to the state, especially in religious matters, for there were many Old Believers in Muscovy. Thus, this group, too, should be counted amongst those who were outside or against empire.

As a result of Russia's various annexations of territory, by 1900 9% of Russians were Roman Catholic, 9% Muslim, 5% Protestant, and 3% Jewish. And of the 71% who were counted as Orthodox, it is estimated that perhaps 20,000,000 were really Old Believers. Venturi says that the merchants, artisans, and businessmen of Russia, though separated from each other by distinctions of caste and corporation, were in some ways united by the bond of the Raskol (the Schism that began in the seventeenth century)[23] because so many of them were Old Believers. And both the government and the revolutionaries (and

Tolstoy) looked upon the Raskol as a source of revolutionary potential. Herzen and Ogarev, even in exile in London, hoped to reach the villagers of Russia via the secret network of Old Belief; V. I. Kelsiev had recommended them to study the history of the Schism, and told them that the Nihilists were only the nineteenth-century equivalent of the early schismatics. He brought out four volumes of Raskol documents in 1860–61, and in 1862 a periodical addressed to the Raskolniks began to be published in London.

In the 1860s N. Melkhov, a tsarist official, estimated that a quarter of Great Russians were Old Believers–that is, one out of six members of the Orthodox church. Yet their books remained unprinted because they were not a part of the official culture; for instance, the remarkable autobiography of the sixteenth-century archpriest Avvakum, an important document in Russian literary history, was only published in the 1850s. Even the handwriting of Old Believers was different from that of other people, being still close to that practiced in the seventeenth century. And they had no schools of their own, while the Muslims, who were about the same in number, had 25,000 schools. Even under Alexander II they could not easily get government appointments or educations, and during the war of 1904 their Archbishop of Nizhni-Novgorod was drafted as a private.

Besides the schismatic Old Believers there were the sectarians, most of whom were similar to Protestant sects in the West. The 1860s was the time of greatest conversion of older sects to Stundism, a German movement which in the 1870s merged with the Baptists, becoming more evangelical, less spiritual. These people, too, were "represented" by Tolstoy, even politically; the most famous case was the Dukhobors, a sect who refused military service and who were allowed to emigrate from Russia because of Tolstoy's campaign for them. And his followers, notably Chertkov, compiled an archive on the sectarians in general and took up the cause of defending their interests wherever they were threatened.

But there were even elements within rebellious youth who were in sympathy with part of what Tolstoy stood for. Besides "the superfluous" and "the bilious," there were those who turned to the people, the narodniki, the populists. They were not prepared to rejoice in the pleasures and triumphs of nobles on their estates, as described in *War and Peace* and *Anna Karenina*, but they shared with Tolstoy his interest in the peasants. Like him, they studied the folk songs, tales, proverbs, riddles, and customs, and studied them as ways to identify themselves with the narod, the people.

It is obvious that the British Empire was even more heterogeneous than the Russian. It will be more interesting then, in discussing Gandhi, to focus on the *way* he represented the subordinate elements in the imperial structure. (Such representation was a part of Tolstoy's work, too, and since Gandhi's was the more striking, it can stand for both, just as Russia can stand for both empires in the matter of heterogeneity.)

In Gandhi's South African period he, of course, spoke for a disenfranchised and disinherited section of the British Empire—the Indians in South Africa. To some degree he spoke for, and associated himself with, the Chinese there. He did not—and has often been blamed for this—to any significant degree speak for the Negro population. In his Tolstoy Farm days, however, his imagination was sufficiently engaged by the Zulus to make them his models of manhood.

From his Jewish friends, he learned to think about the problems of the unrepresented of any alien group within the state or empire that has a private culture and whose intellectuals are split in their loyalties, belonging half to their people and half to the modern world—as he himself did. In later years he had to ask himself in what sense he could be said to represent the Untouchables, or the Muslims, and above all the martial races, all of whom had other representatives, often very antagonistic to Gandhi.

He based his claim to leadership upon his claim to represent—which meant his intuitive knowledge of what the masses were feeling. "I have one qualification which many of you do not possess. I can almost instinctively feel what is stirring in the heart of the masses."[24] In 1938, when there was violence between Hindus and Muslims, he wrote that there had undoubtedly been violence on the Hindu side. "I must own that had I been properly attuned to the music of ahimsa, I would have sensed the slightest departure from it, and my sensitiveness would have rebelled against any discord in it. . . ."[25] Or again, "I must undergo personal cleansing. I must become a fitter instrument, able to register the slightest variation in the moral atmosphere about me."[26]

When he fasted, Gandhi usually insisted that he did so for himself alone, although in some more remote sense he certainly "represented," for instance, the Untouchables in 1933. But in a different way he also represented all those who had fasted before him in similar causes, less famously, less publicly. Religious history, he said, does not tell us of "those who silently and heroically perished in the attempt to win the answer from a deaf God. . . . For Him life and death are one, and who is able to deny that all that is pure and good in the world persists because of the silent death of thousands of unknown heroes and heroines?"[27]

He also represented his comrades in the ashram. When Maganlal Gandhi died in 1928, Gandhi wrote: "He was my hands, my feet and my eyes. The world knows so little of how much my so-called greatness depends upon the incessant toil and drudgery of silent, devoted, able and pure workers, men as well as women . . . [Maganlal] . . . who was a personification of industry, who was the watchdog of the Ashram . . . His life is an inspiration for me."[28] Gandhi claimed that he was in some sense taking over Maganlal's identity after his death. He went to live in Maganlal's room, and wrote: "If ever there was a person with whom I identified myself, it was Maganlal. . . . [29] Imperceptibly and involuntarily, a struggle is going on within me. Maganlal's soul rules over my heart."[30]

In a more obvious sense, he represented the Muslims to the Hindus, the Untouchables to the castemen, the villagers to the townsmen, women to men, and the sick and crazy to the healthy.

When he got to India in 1915, Gandhi took up the cause of the Untouchables, the classic case of those outside the system; from 1932 on, this was a major concern of his. But perhaps even more striking—theoretically speaking—is the way in which he approached the Muslims and tried to make them accept him as their representative via the idea of Khilafat. Khilafat (in English the word might be "Caliphate") was the effort to restore power to the caliph, the supreme leader of Islam, who had been the sultan of Turkey. The Muslims of India had begun to turn to Turkey in about 1910, when England ceased to support her against Russia in the Balkan Wars and against Italy when that country attacked Tripoli. Thus, in 1912 an All-Indian Medical Mission went to Turkey, and in 1913 an Anjuman Khuddar i Ka'abah was founded to save the holy places of Mecca, Medina, and Jerusalem. And there developed a cult of Turkey in Indian historical poetry, which was driven underground in 1914 when Turkey became England's enemy in the Great War.

The Khilafat cause was preached mainly by two journalist-orators, the Ali brothers, who were interned for making pro-German (that is, pro-Turkish) propaganda. They had tried to oust from the Muslim college at Aligarh the secular modernists and the Europeans, who were continuing the policy of collaboration with the English begun by Sir Syed Ahmed Khan. The Ali brothers were not the most impressive of politicians, and their credits in the matter of nonviolence were low, yet it was they whom Gandhi tried to make his allies—and for a time he succeeded.

This was because they made a political cause out of Khilafat, a supranational religious issue. Khilafat was the demand that certain territory might be restored to Turkey, so that the sultan, as caliph, might control the holy places of Islam again. If that was not done, the Muslims threatened to walk out of India. And in fact, in 1920, 18,000 did so emigrate, as Muharajins, pilgrims, though most returned. (Some of them formed the backbone of the Indian Communist party.) This was so much Gandhi's kind of politics that he was able to overlook much that was unpalatable to him in what they wanted and how they pursued it.

His friend Charlie Andrews could not agree with Gandhi over Khilafat because he saw it as an imperialist kind of religious movement. But from Gandhi's point of view, it only used imperialist feelings against real empire. Islam was, in 1919, only an *idea* of empire; and Gandhi was sympathetic to the idea of empire, as he was sympathetic to the idea of strength and force. In 1922 he told his followers that Muslims are physically strong. Mustafa Kemal succeeded in Turkey, with the sword, because there is strength in every nerve of the Turk. They have been fighters for centuries. Indians, on the other hand, have followed the path of peace for thousands of years, and Turkey's way is not for India. But Gandhi did not condemn the Muslim way, and he wanted Hindus and Muslims to cooperate and appreciate each other's gifts. Sometimes this happened. In 1919 the Maulana Abdul Bari Sahib (spiritual counselor of the Ali brothers) said that Muslims must reciprocate Gandhi's help in the Khilafat cause, and arranged for there to be no cow sacrifice at Virangi Mahal that spring. Gandhi rushed off a letter to the press about this; it was exactly what he hoped to see happen, what he had so often been disappointed of. We may see his playful comradeship with Shaukat Ali as a continuation in politics of his boyhood friendship with Sheikh Mehtab—and in the long run almost equally disappointing.

As for women, he often said that civilization progressed by men becoming increasingly womanly, by increasing the quantity of the love and self-sacrifice of woman, the mother of man, in circulation. "I have repeated times without number that non-violence is the inherent quality of women. For ages men have had training in violence. In order to become non-violent they have to cultivate the qualities of women. Ever since I have taken to non-violence, I have become more and more of a woman."[31] In *Harijan*, on 14 November 1936, he said women had been deceived into becoming the weaker sex. "As Tolstoy used to say, they are labouring under the hypnotic influence of men."[32] (Indeed, Tolstoy does say things of that kind. In "The Mother" he says that when all women accept the vocation of motherhood, the power over mankind will pass to them, and the world will be saved at their hands—"we men have forgotten the real object of life."[33] But one could not speak of Tolstoy representing women to men in the way that Gandhi did.)

Thus, Tolstoy and Gandhi increasingly opposed the central powers of civilization in the name of all those peripheral groups who are kept subject: some are peripheral socially or sexually rather than geographically or racially; and their subjection is sometimes invisible. But Tolstoy and Gandhi gradually identified themselves with these groups, and so came to realize that the ultimate sanction for *their* political action must be nonviolent—just as the sanction of the central and masculine powers was violence.

XI
Men of Religion and Men of Revolution: 1870–81 and 1915–21

In this period Tolstoy and Gandhi turned away from the culture of violence, which includes a great deal of what we call simply culture. They alienated themselves from ordinary writers and politicians. (This was less true of Gandhi, who developed remarkable skills for cooperating with other nationalist politicians who were poles apart from him in religious and cultural matters; but this was a tour de force on Gandhi's part, and one that kept breaking down, because of that alienation.) They had to make themselves new allies, or rather disciples, in order to build a counterculture of nonviolence. This was harder for Tolstoy, who came to the enterprise later in his life, and who lacked the political projects to involve others. We can think of Gandhi in this period as calling his followers to him, from their various previous pursuits, whereas the support Tolstoy found we have to define as partial sympathies and affinities.

The Russians

Tolstoy's disaffection from conservative nationalism, which developed during the 1870s, had isolated him among Russian writers, cutting him off from those patriotic aristophiles, like Fet and Samarin, with whom he had allied himself after parting from progressive liberals like Turgenev and Nekrasov. He could find no one else who was both interested in religion and radical in politics. The nearest thing to an exception to the rule was Dostoevsky. But it does not seem likely that a significant friendship would have developed between the two great novelists, even if Dostoevsky had not died almost at the moment that Tolstoy's disaffection became absolute, in 1881. Dostoevsky's religion was Church-centered and led his thought towards theological mysteries, not towards the Euclidean reason and moralism which religion meant to Tolstoy. It left him, moreover, nationalist and even imperialist in secular politics—nothing could have been further from Tolstoy's renunciatory radicalism. Dostoevsky wanted to see Constantinople added to the Russian empire, and was a close friend of Pobedonostsev.

The forces at work in Tolstoy can be seen working more crudely in other Russian writers. One of these was Ivan Aksakov (1823–86), one of the sons of the Aksakov from whom Tolstoy learned so much as a writer. He was a member of the same social world as Tolstoy. Later in life, however, he became the leader of the Slavophile movement, by then ultraconservative and ultranationalist. Aksakov made Slavophilism a popular movement, but partly by means of allying it to various sinister political forces. He, too, was a friend of Pobedonostsev; he wanted to drive the Jews out of their positions of economic power in the Western provinces, he whipped up nationalist feeling against the Poles, and he wanted to make Russia the master-leader of a Slavic nation alliance.

The relevant phase of his life from our point of view, however, was religious, and came much earlier, in the 1840s, when (at the same time as Tolstoy's brother Dmitri) he was much under Gogol's influence. He admired the *Selected Passages From A Correspondence with Friends*, and himself agonized over the problems it treated, of how to reconcile art with religion. He thought for a time that he would have to give up the enjoyment of art, but his father, who had been a friend of Gogol but was thoroughly a man of letters, persuaded him that Gogol was crazy. Conservatives as much as liberals rejected the *Selected Passages*, and Ivan Aksakov's experience was a paradigm of the whole culture's.

Gogol himself was, briefly, Tolstoy's contemporary, and a continuing hidden portent for a few; Tolstoy later called him the Russian Pascal. Gogol was of partly priestly descent—his grandfather was the first Gogol not to be a priest. But his talents were not only literary but for acting, mimicry, fantasy, and humor, rather than moralism or philosophy. He met Pushkin in 1831 and admired him just this side of idolatry. He said he wrote his every line with Pushkin's face present to his imagination and with reference to him, though their two temperaments were so dissimilar.

Gogol hoped to teach by his writing, but he did not feel he had succeeded. He was very disappointed with the reception of his play, *The Inspector-General*, in 1836, and went abroad, to travel. In Vienna in 1840 he underwent a spiritual crisis, after which his ascetic Christianity became dominant over his imagination. In 1847 he met Father Matthew Konstantinovsky, a fanatical priest who demanded that Gogol renounce Pushkin, required that he fast, and frightened him with descriptions of hell. In 1848 Gogol made a pilgrimage to the Holy Land, returning in some sense to medieval practices. And in 1852 he starved himself to death.

V. V. Zenkovsky says that Gogol "experienced this tragedy with exceptional force,"[1] the tragedy of the conflict between Christianity and culture. Between 1831 and 1835 he wrote several stories and sketches which posed "the problem of the disparity of moral and aesthetic life."[2] He had hoped to act upon his audience's conscience, to affect their souls, by the means of his great satiric play, *The Inspector-General*. This was a great success on the stage, but its moral-spiritual effect was negligible, so he felt it to have been a failure. His commitment to religious values was so complete that Mochulski has called him a genius in the field of morality (though that title belongs better to Tolstoy).[3] Gogol challenged the aesthetic humanism of Karamzin and the other founders of Russian literature, who taught that humans naturally love the good because they naturally find it beautiful. He, on the contrary, asked: "How can one love human beings? The soul wishes to love only what is beautiful, and the poor are so shabby; there is so little of beauty in them."[4] He felt a conflict between his moral and his aesthetic enthusiasms.

The *Selected Passages* that expressed this doctrine and aroused so much indignation, contained 32 essays, 9 of which deal with literature and 1 with painting; they comprise 91 and 9 pages, respectively, in an edition of 203 pages. In the original edition, though, 5 of the original essays had been suppressed, and a full third of the book dealt with literature. The most often-cited part was "Four Letters on *Dead Souls*," in which Gogol explained his destruction of Part II of his masterpiece, on the grounds that it failed in its purpose of portraying the soul. The destruction of a work of art by an artist for religious reasons—the destruction of a work of reverie and dialectic for reasons of thought and morality—induced a spasm in the mind of the Russian reader not to be repeated until *What is Art?* came out in 1898.

Gogol was still a great admirer of Pushkin, but he now repudiated him as a life-model; Russian writers must subdue their creative powers to their moral obligations. "Now you must forget yourself—no originality of mind, no picturesque personal character, no prideful actions; the poet must now be brought up in a higher Christian education . . . a battle . . . for our soul, which our heavenly Creator Himself regards as the pearl of his Creation. . . . " When we poets have learned to do this, "The anguish of angels will inspire our poetry, and, having struck every string in the Russian, it will move the most hardened soul with a holiness with which no power and no instrument in man can contend."[5]

Tolstoy read this when he was a student, when his brother Dmitri was deeply impressed by the book, but, like other people, Lev Tolstoy then dismissed Gogol as being a narrow and feeble mind when not engaged in imaginative creation—a small and fearful mind, masquerading as a prophet. Not until forty years later, when he re-read it, did he recognize its importance for him. Then he hailed Gogol as a great thinker and declared that the intervening forty years had been wasted or worse, not only by him but by Russian literature as a whole, since Gogol had warned writers against the path they had nevertheless pursued.

The only other fully contemporary writer who took seriously these issues of art and spirituality, and came to conclusions anything like Tolstoy's and Gogol's, was Nikolai Leskov. Born in 1831, he came from a very different sector of Russian life from Tolstoy's. His father was a priest's son, and his mother's family was partly mercantile; one of his mother's sisters married an Englishman, Alexander Scott, who was bailiff to various Russian nobles, and through whom Leskov came in firsthand contact with English culture. He was brought up with another aunt's children, as a noble, until he was eight, and thereafter as a commoner. Thus, his caste was mixed, and he exhibited some of the classical raznochintsy traits. He never read German philosophy, that main element of the nobles' culture, but he could read both Polish and Ukrainian, and he knew from the inside the world of the Russian clergy, about which he wrote.

In subject matter, therefore, he was very remote from Tolstoy, Turgenev, and so on, and in style and form also. He avoided many of the practices that stamped the modern Western novel—for instance, the novel form itself, and its authorial voice or range of voices. Like Gogol, Leskov used shorter forms, with a very obtrusive narrator's voice, which calls into doubt the narrative's authenticity, and a fantastic and elaborate rhetoric.

Leskov was a great liar, in life and in art, and in that way too very unlike Tolstoy. His fiction included elements of truth, historical and personal, but they were inextricably entangled with the invented. Politically, he was hated by the liberals and the radicals, because in 1862 he had written an article about a fire in St. Petersburg, in which he had seemed to entertain the possibility that students had indeed— as the police were saying—started it. He also wrote a satirical novel about revolutionaries, called *No Way Out*, which was bitterly attacked by Pisarev.

In fact, his political opinions were too shifting and eccentric to be called conservative, and one of the functions of the colorfulness and the fantastic character of his fiction was to conceal its politically subversive implications. The liberals felt—as did everyone—that Leskov was untrustworthy. In personal relations, too, he was irresponsible and consequently miserable; he always blamed others, and thus alienated his children and most people he lived with. He was thus not a man Tolstoy could form a personal bond with, though a distant and impersonal bond of great importance did form between them.

From the late 1870s on, Leskov had tried to portray good men, whom he would not need to satirize—he played with the idea of the Three Just Men for whose sake God relented and refrained from destroying the world.[6] He came to know Tolstoy's disciples, Chertkov and Biriukov, in the early 1880s; and in 1887 and again in 1890 he met Tolstoy himself.

He made Tolstoy the last in his series of gurus and father-substitutes. He had much admired *War and Peace* and *Anna Karenina* artistically, and in 1885 had defended Tolstoy and Dostoevsky religiously against Leontiev's attack. The following year he wrote an article exalting Tolstoy above Dostoevsky; the latter had said that the educated could learn from the peasants, but Tolstoy had shown *what* they could learn, which was how to die. Leskov acknowledged the charge often brought against Tolstoy, that he *wanted* to suffer, that he had a "martyr-complex"; however, he was enough in sympathy with Tolstoy's ideas that he straightforwardly admired that—admired his courage in self-sacrifice. In 1886 he published altogether seven articles on Tolstoy.

In 1893 he wrote in a letter about a newspaper article that had called him one of Tolstoy's followers:

> That is quite true. I have said and do say that I long ago sought what he is seeking; but I did not find it, because my light was poor. On the other hand, when I saw that he had found the answer that satisfied me, I felt that I no longer needed my insignificant light, and I am following after him.

I seek nothing of my own, nor do I make a display of myself;
but I see everything in the light of his great torch.[7]

As follower, Leskov wrote for Tolstoy's publishing venture, Posrednik (Intermediary), a firm that published literature for the people,
not for the educated. Leskov's rewriting of Tolstoy's story "God Sees
the Truth But Waits" was one of Intermediary's first four publications;
12,000 copies of it were sold in 1885, and there were new editions in
1886, 1891, 1893, and 1894. He also wrote other things for Posrednik,
for instance, rather overheated contrasts of Roman luxury with early
Christian sufferings, which Tolstoy did not like. Nor did Tolstoy much
like Leskov's letters to him, which he also found overheated and insincere or inauthentic. But they were able to meet each other in a personal
way once or twice—for instance, when Leskov appealed to Tolstoy
for help in facing the idea of death—and there seems no doubt that
in his uneasy way Leskov was a real disciple and adherent. (He might
be called, to use Isaiah Berlin's terms, a fox who wanted to be a
hedgehog—terms which do not apply half so well to Tolstoy.)

In 1881 another famous intellectual besides Tolstoy courageously
challenged the new tsar with an appeal to him to forgive his father's
murderers. This was Vladimir Soloviev (1853–1900), described by
S. L. Frank as "unquestionably the greatest of Russian philosophers
and systematic religious thinkers."[8] He was dismissed from his post
at the university for doing what he did. He was a very different kind
of religious thinker from Tolstoy, for he was a churchman, interested
in organizationally reuniting the separated branches of the Christian
church. But he was also a heretic, who flirted with modern ideas.
Perhaps his most striking heresy derived from three visions, in 1862,
1875, and 1876, of a heavenly feminine Being, Saint Sophia (in one
meaning, holy wisdom), who became his "eternal Friend." Saint Sophia
is the divine basis or essence of all that is not God; and she represents,
within the Christian Godhead, all the female powers otherwise
excluded.[9] Soloviev was, predictably, a friend of Dostoevsky rather
than of Tolstoy, but had talks with the latter, in February and October
1881, in 1884, 1887, 1889, and 1892. Surviving letters between them
cover a period from 1875 to 1894. But their ideas and temperaments
were profoundly discordant. Already in 1881 Soloviev attacked Tolstoyism as a sect. In 1884 he told Strakhov that Tolstoy was insincere
and indirect, and found *What I Believe* insolent and stupid. Recipro-
cally, Tolstoy thought Soloviev's *Lectures of Godmanhood* (1878) rubbish
and childish absurdity.

Soloviev was the nephew of the statist historian of that name, and the grandson of a priest who, just before he died, consecrated Vladimir to the service of the church, at age eight. He thus belonged to the clerical caste, but, like Pobedonostsev, to a secularized professorial branch. At fourteen he repudiated religion and became militantly atheist and materialist; he assembled his friends and solemnly destroyed all his icons. But at eighteen he turned back to Christianity and became the intellectual champion of the Russian church, the man who promised to be able to justify it in the terms of modern thought. He went abroad to study "the gnostic, Indian, and medieval philosophy,"[10] and one of his visions came to him in the British Museum, another in Egypt (holy land of gnosticism). In 1882–84 he published *The Spiritual Foundations of Life*, which offered Christian doctrine couched in terms acceptable to intellectuals.[11]

He is understandable in Anglo-American terms as a Russian equivalent for G. K. Chesterton or C. S. Lewis, since he was essentially a witty and even humorous polemicist; he was different, however, in that he was a heretic—he taught some of the feminine mystique of the New Age. He was a strikingly handsome man who lived a disorderly life and was always falling in love, but was unable to be faithful.

His essay "The Meaning of Love" (written in the early 1890s) sounds like Lewis's *Allegory of Love*, except for its implicit sympathy with mystical and erotic heresy—with the teachings of feminists like Anna Kingsford and Madame Blavatsky. "Both with animals and with men sexual love is the finest flowering of the individual life,"[12] and in men it is the only force able to counteract egotism. This is one kind of antithesis to Tolstoy's teaching in "The Kreutzer Sonata."

Soloviev condemned the abstractness of Tolstoy's Christianity, its lack of love for the person of Christ. In his doctoral thesis, entitled "A Critique of Abstract Principles" (1880), he wrote that abstraction followed from separation from God; in fact, not Christ's teachings but Christ is important. Soloviev taught that men must, like God, seek unity and self-expression in art, personal relations, and creative experience. But his dream of a state-society based on a full affirmation of God-manhood was, in effect, a theocratic idealization of Russian autocracy. Tolstoy naturally was out of sympathy with that in every way.

Soloviev's *Three Conversations*, written in the last year of his life, was directed against Tolstoy's teaching of nonresistance to evil. It concludes with a "Short Story of Anti-Christ," in which a liberal idealist, who suffers from inordinate pride, jealously competes with Christ.

"I shall have to grovel before him, like the most stupid of Christians . . . I, the bright genius, the superman? No, never!"[13] This figure was usually supposed to be based on Tolstoy, and the accusation that Tolstoy wanted to be God was often heard in those years. The story ends with a typical feminist touch: the vision of a woman clothed in the sun, with the moon under her feet and a crown of twelve stars on her head. Thus, Soloviev could be no ally to Tolstoy; nor could he be a significant critic, since he never clearly admitted to himself what Tolstoy was trying to do. But his career does make clear how little hope Tolstoy could have of winning the sympathy of even the cleverest and youngest of churchmen—while the literary men of the Silver Age just beginning, being diabolists rather than Christians, were more in sympathy with Soloviev than with Tolstoy.

So much for the men of religion in the world of Russian letters. Amongst the men of revolution there was an element of diabolism (embodied in Nechaev), but most leaders of that movement were eminently ethical and intellectual men, of whom at least the Populists were quite close to Tolstoy in sympathy.

Alexander Vucinich in *Science in Russian Culture* describes populism as a movement dominated by "repentant nobles"—men like Tolstoy. It was as antimetaphysical as nihilism, but less positivist; Populists did not see science as a social panacea, nor did they want other forms of knowledge to imitate the natural sciences.[14] Their politics were, in fact, a kind of nonecclesiastical piety.

The movement to the people was a pilgrimage, very like the monastic and kenotic movement of earlier Russia, says Billington.[15] This "most original of all the movements of modern Russian history," he continues, was also a revival of all three of the Old Muscovite groups' resistance to modernization: the Raskolniks, the Cossacks, and the conservatives. That seventeenth-century resistance revived in the mid-nineteenth century. "The central fact of the populist era, which haunted the imagination of its creative artists, was that all of Russian life was being materially transformed by modernizing forces from the West."[16] Like the Old Believers of the seventeenth century, the Populists were peaceful in themselves but were allied to violent revolutionaries.

"Going to the people," or "going to the villages," is also an idea that turns up very often in Gandhi's writing in the 1920s; and it was a practice that was very important in the Gandhian movement. Gandhi said students should go to the villages every summer, to study conditions, to preach against untouchability and infant marriage, and to teach the villagers sanitation and spinning, self-help and the assertion of their rights.[17] The vidyapiths, or national schools, which Gandhi established at the beginning of the 1920s, were designed to prepare and motivate their students to go to the villages—just because the government schools' graduates always went to the cities. And what the Indians went for was exactly what the Russians had gone for: to teach the peasants to resist the imperial state, to revive the forms of peasant life, to learn from the peasants the old culture and the virtues it embodied.

The Populists believed, in Russia and in India, that the curse of bigness could still be successfully fought, and federations of self-governing units of producers could be built up. The failure of the European revolutions of 1848 had seemed to prove to the Russian radicals that political revolt could not save a nation. Their main difficulty, at the level of theory, was in deciding how much to learn from the peasants, how much to teach them—which amounted to deciding between immediate action and gradualism. The differences between radicals were largely between different decisions about that. In the mid-1870s the term *Populist* referred to those who believed that revolution would be the work of the people, and not of a few militant radicals. By 1900 it was used by Marxists to describe all non-Marxists, and that has limited, unfortunately, all subsequent use of the term. But it is unmistakably the right term for the Gandhian movement, and the link between the two national movements is also an important link between the two men, Tolstoy and Gandhi. Tolstoy was too far to the right, politically, before 1880 to be called simply a Populist, and too far to the left, religiously, after that. But if one wants to place him on the political map of Russia, then populism is an indispensable aid to definition.

The Indians

The most significant group among Gandhi's contemporaries to emerge during this period were his disciples. The calling of followers was a large part of his work then, and their relations with him, their typology, and the other callings they followed *as* his disciples, together constitute an interpretive context for him in our minds. Though he had had both friends and followers in South Africa, Gandhi's first six years in India were distinguished by a quite different calling of other, younger men to help him in his work. The friends of earlier days had been mostly Englishmen or Europeans, and so were somewhat outside the Gandhian movement proper, while the followers seem to have been too submissive or inarticulate to be called disciples. (In Tolstoy's case the equivalent calling—which was on a much smaller scale in every sense—came later. Tolstoy was slower to assume the role of prophet.)

Among the Gandhians, pride of place may be given to Nehru, on the grounds of his subsequent eminence, though not on the grounds of any greater affinity with or understanding of the Mahatma. In 1919, when Gandhi rose to national fame, Nehru was thirty years old, the youngest of the four who were later to be considered Gandhi's principal lieutenants and possible political heirs: Rajendra Prasad, Vallabhbhai Patel, Chakravarty Rajagopalachari (usually called Rajaji), and Nehru. He was also at that time the only one with no satyagraha experience. Prasad had been thirty-three as a satyagrahi in Champaran, Patel was forty-three as organizer of the Kheda campaign, and Rajaji was forty during the Rowlatt satyagraha. Although we may say that none of the four were fully in accord with Gandhi, it was surely Nehru who was furthest from him, intellectually as well as temperamentally.

He was the son of one of India's most brilliant lawyers, a self-made man and ardent adopter of English styles, who designed his brilliant son's education in order to make him a national leader. Motilal Nehru drove to the law courts with liveried servants behind a fine pair of horses, and lived in a house called Anand Bhavan, equipped with modern English comforts, including wines and cigars. He was a kingly man, with a fierce temper and a hearty laugh. Jawaharlal seems to have loved his father fairly steadily, but he felt the pressure of a powerful will upon him. "I admired Father tremendously. He seemed to me the embodiment of strength and courage. . . . "[18] But he also feared him. He was the instrument of his father's will, though at the same time his own will was cultivated. According to his biographer, the male heir of a Hindu family is "a little idol adored by grandparents, uncles, aunts and sisters; his wayward will is a law unto itself."[19] We are bound to guess that Jawaharlal Nehru's attraction to Gandhi was in part a rebellion against his father. (On 5 July 1920 Motilal wrote to him: "So far as your following the request of Gandhiji is concerned, there is nothing to be said. That is more or less a matter of sentiment of a kind which does not enter into my composition."[20])

For Nehru, to choose Gandhi was to refuse his heritage of luxury and worldliness. This became true in a literal sense: when Motilal followed Jawaharlal into Gandhi's camp, everything in his life-style had to change—cars, clothes, food, and drink—from Englishness to

Indianness, from modernity to tradition, from splendor to simplicity. The Anand Bhavan bonfire of foreign cloth must have been one of the biggest and most sacrificial. Even the legal practice had to go. Motilal said to Gandhi: "You have stolen my son; let me keep my practise." But Gandhi replied: "No, I want everything from you." And Motilal was, like his son, able to appreciate that answer, that sense of style. (Jawaharlal very much appreciated that style; he says Gandhi was "in his best dictatorial vein. He was humble but also clear-cut and hard as a diamond."[21]) There can be no doubt, however, that there was a struggle between father and son. Going to Calcutta by train, Motilal had been used to take a whole first-class compartment to himself; when one day he saw Jawaharlal traveling third class on the same train, he said to Rajendra Prasad, with tears standing in his eyes: "Look at this boy. . . . This is a time when he should be enjoying himself but he has given up everything and has become a Saddhu."[22]

Moreover, for Nehru to choose Gandhi was also to rebel against Motilal ideologically, or religiously. Motilal is supposed to have said to Gandhi: "I don't believe in your spirituality, and am not going to believe in God, at least in this life."[23] In the long run, however, Jawaharlal was to follow his father in this, but not without some continuing loyalty to Gandhi. In a letter to Gandhi in 1933, about Gandhi's crusade for the Harijans, he begins: "Not being a man of religion, my interest is largely confined to the social aspect and to the wider issues involved. . . . " But he continues that his jail solitude and the sight of the Himalayas from jail have driven him in upon himself, "and I have grown a little contemplative, in defiance of heredity and family tradition and personal habit! But that is a thin veneer which I am afraid will rub off at a little provocation. How can the Ethiopian change his skin?"[24] He thinks of Buddha's grief about Brahma's indifference to the world he has created.

That last reflection is typical of what "religion" meant to Nehru, and it was quite unlike what it meant to Gandhi. But Gandhi was able to respond to Nehru, and his reply to this letter catches something of Nehru's tone. "I have dashed to pieces all Vallabhbhai's hope of becoming a good Sanskrit scholar. He can't concentrate on his studies in the midst of the excitement of Harijan work and the daily dish of spiced criticism which he enjoys like the Bengal footballers their game."[25] That gay and gallant tone was very modern-British, and in Nehru it went along with comparable qualities of character, which Gandhi much appreciated. It was a British and a modern-world style, and Gandhi's romance with Nehru is one of the signs of the degree to which he was in tune with that modern world.

Motilal Nehru rose to the challenge. He formed a genuine alliance with Gandhi, and engaged in poverty and simplicity as if they were great adventures and the newest and most elite forms of privilege. He wrote a letter to Gandhi in 1921, comparing the trip he was then taking to Mussoori with his old hunting trips, on which he had brought English food and so on. "The *Shikar* has given place to long walks and the rifles and guns to books, magazines and newspapers (the favorite book being Edwin Arnold's *Song Celestial* which is now undergoing a third reading). . . . 'What a fall, my countrymen!' But, really, I have never enjoyed life better."[26] The Nehrus were a family like the Kennedys, and it is thus we can imagine the Kennedys' dealing with their cardinals. Jawaharlal remained a Nehru. He came round from that initial rebellion, no doubt because of his father's tactful response to it, and his own tone of voice to and about Gandhi soon became Motilal's.

Handsome, intelligent, brave, sensitive—Nehru had to worry at all times about having more advantages than the rest of the world. He was continually praised in the most extravagant terms by Tagore, Sarojini, and even by Gandhi. He had moreover a kind of princely carelessness, which echoes even in his writings; he writes letters to his daughter to pass the time, and other people insist that they be published as a book. He can't suppose they are of any value, and certainly has no time to rewrite them, "but if they mean so much to you. . . ."

He was full of the spirit of adventure, much cultivated in England then. He talks of the "exciting adventure of Man" and asks Indira to imagine the Aryans: "Can you not see them trekking down the mountain passes into the unknown land below? Brave and full of the spirit of adventure, they dared to go ahead without fear of the consequences. If death came, they did not mind, they met it laughing. But they loved life and knew that the only way to enjoy life was to be fearless. . . . "[27] And he makes a confident claim on happiness, for himself and for his daughter. "This letter has become much too dismal for a New Year's Day letter. That is highly unbecoming. Indeed, I am not dismal, and why should we be dismal? . . . And you, my darling one, on the threshold of life, must have no dealings with the dismal and the dreary."[28]

There were periods of Jawaharlal's life, however, especially periods in prison when he was young, when he was quite Gandhian, when perhaps he seriously doubted his career and his calling. One outward sign of that is that he became an expert spinner. On 1 September 1922 he was sending home 10,000 yards of fine-spun yarn; he was not interested in any but fine-spun, he tells us. (Vinoba, so much closer to Gandhi, in 1932 suggested that Gandhians should only spin coarse yarn.)

Among Gandhi's other disciples, one of the first to get to know him was J. B. Kripalani, who met him at Santiniketan in 1915. Kripalani also was not of a Gandhian temperament, being confessedly severe, cynical, angry, an intellectual and moralist of politics—but in fact that temperament is to be found in many of Gandhi's most faithful followers. (Because it is to be found, concealed, and subdued in Gandhi himself; amongst his followers, Vinoba and Rajaji may be pointed to as other examples.)

Kripalani was a practical idealist. In 1915 he was giving away Rs360 out of the 400 he earned every month. But he was not at ease with goodness or with himself. Leaving Gandhi at Agra, after serving with him in a position of some authority in a campaign, he said gruffly: "I have neither the heart nor the aptitude for offering apologies. I do my duty as I know how and there my task ends. You should offer all the necessary apologies for me."[29] Pyarelal said, in *Harijan* on 15 March 1952, that Kripalani followed Gandhi when he found that the latter was "the rebel and revolutionary he himself aspired to be."[30] (There was something of this dialectic—Gandhi saying "*I* am really what you claim to be"—between him and many of his followers. Louis Fischer says Nehru once declared he wanted revolution and Gandhi replied: "When your exuberance has subsided and your lungs are exhausted, you will come to me, if you are really serious about making a revolution."[31])

An early friend of Kripalani's was Dattatreya Kalelkar, who had a somewhat parallel career as a Gandhian, joining the movement at the same time, never becoming an Ashramite, and belonging to the educational wing of the movement. He was, however, less interested in politics—at least, after his first youth—and has been called Gandhi's heir in matters of culture, as Nehru was in politics and Vinoba in religion. He was born in 1885, a Maharashtrian brahmin, in the very month that Congress was founded. From 1899 he was a student at Ferguson College, the old home of Tilak and Gokhale, but seems to have been more impressed by the former, whose magazines he read. He was also influenced by Western ideas, decided to become an engineer, read the Rationalist Free Press publications, and in 1905, under Ibsen's influence, vowed never to have a career but always to investigate and experiment.

In 1906 he took another vow, not to rest until the British were driven out of India. He decided to join a band of terrorists, and took an oath before a picture of Shivaji: "I dedicate my life to the service

of the Motherland. I will obey all orders. I will divulge no secrets."[32]
He was already a good shot, and now he learned the formulas for
bomb explosives. He worked for Tilak's *Rastramat* in Bombay, and
was briefly in the Savarkar group. (His exuberant, hearty, and full-
blooded temperament seems to have supported extreme opinions and
actions with less of what is called "fanaticism" than most people could
achieve.) In 1910 he went to work in a school in Baroda, founded by
Arabindo, where he became a friend of K. G. Deshpande, who had
known Gandhi in London. Kalelkar still harbored terrorists, and was
ready to shoot and make bombs, but he now deprecated terrorism.

In 1911, when the school was closed, he set off on a two-year
pilgrimage to the holy places of Hinduism and the Himalayas. He
visited traditional swamis in the hills, and Vivekananda and the disciples of Ramakrishna. He was then known as the Saddhu Dattatreya.
Hearing of Gandhi via Deshpande, he came to Shantiniketan to meet
him and had to run the experiment there in doing without servants
when Gandhi left. In 1915 Harilal Gandhi asked him why he did not
join the Ashram, and he explained that he had dedicated his services
to Deshpande; Gandhi approved of this answer, and his approval won
over Kalelkar.

Mahadev Desai, on the other hand, was of an artistic-poetic type,
physically delicate and charming, sympathetic and responsive, and
always in danger of being seduced. He became Gandhi's secretary,
and wanted to become his Boswell. We find Gandhi reproving him
in 1921: "If extensive notes of Johnson's talks were taken, they have
conferred on the world no incomparable benefit that I know of. We
do not at all look at this matter merely from the point of view of
literature."[33] Desai became Gandhi's favorite son, replacing Harilal.

He was chosen by Gandhi in 1917 in Ahmedabad, where he had
been a lawyer and inspector of cooperatives. Not being very successful
at law, he had taken to collecting folk songs and examples of the
dialect of the peasants of his district, like a Populist ethnographer.
Gandhi wrote to him: "I have found in you the young man I have
been searching for these two years. I have spoken like this to only
three people before—to Mr. Polak, Miss Schlesin and Shri Maganlal.
Leave everything else and come to me. But go to Hyderabad and
enjoy yourself for a year, and the moment you feel you are losing
yourself, come and join me."[34] This is Desai's account of Gandhi's
letter, given to his friend Parikh, who wrote his biography. Desai
added that he had felt tired of life, but now (a day or two after getting
Gandhi's letter) everything seemed worthwhile. Desai's wife, on the
other hand, felt herself deserted; and Gandhi was often hard on him;

but it seems clear that on the whole Desai was reassured by the discipline and never deeply doubted that he had found his vocation.

A very different type, a proud mind, was Rajagopalachari, the brahmin leader of Madras. Born in 1878, he was an intellectual and a wit (an admirer of G. Bernard Shaw) but also a prohibitionist and khadi-man, being morally and religiously conservative. He never left India or, one might say, the nineteenth century; but his familiarity with English literature, and his temperamental Englishness, were complete. He is one of the best examples of Indian high culture meeting the West in the mid-twentieth century without yielding to it—sophisticated but not Europeanized. He says that when he met Gandhi he had lost faith in Congress and moderation, but could not accept organized violence. Thus, Gandhi saved him from the dilemma of choosing either terrorism or cynicism. Rajaji says Gandhi saved all India from that choice—and thus from the terrorist movement. He understood Gandhi very well, but his own mind was fundamentally ironic.

The son of a village Sanskrit scholar who knew no English, he was brought up a Vaishnavite and a brahmin, yet he refused to wear the thread of his caste. Monica Felton has described his beautiful slow voice, his bald, high-domed head, lean face, and dark glasses.[35] She speaks of his incisive directness on issues, but also of his elaborate evasiveness, both encouraging and discouraging her attempts to write a book about him. She presents him as a master politician, whose natural element was a committee, and as one who would envelop and reject the whole world—except Gandhi—in a web of pessimism and cynicism. Even on the subject of Gandhi he allowed himself, to Ved Mehta, the remark that Gandhi had starved himself of good conversation by surrounding himself with disciples. Thus, Rajaji was always potentially the intellectual aristocrat, deploring ethical enthusiasm.

He told Monica Felton that the basis of the Hindu religion is the idea that life is a play; that if you try to right the wrongs of the world, you spoil the play; and that our ideas of right and wrong are only illusions which arise from thinking ourselves the center of the universe.[36] At the same time, he was ethically conservative and clung to the world of nineteenth-century English literature—which he accused her, as a twentieth-century Englishwoman, of not believing in. He said he liked even Thackeray's goody-goody characters—because he was one himself.[37] And in terms of international politics, he developed Gandhi's heritage more than any of the other lieutenants. He campaigned against the bomb and called upon the rich to become poor and simplify their lives. But he had no hope of succeeding. He said that nowadays *no one* could resist the lure of development and technology, and that God was soon going to spray the world with DDT.

Finally, the greatest of Gandhi's disciples in most ways was Vinoba Bhave, who carried on the Gandhi work in India in the 1950s and 1960s, concentrating on land reform. He is vividly described by Hallam Tennyson, in *India's Walking Saint*, where the slender, smooth-skinned figure with bedraggled hair and unkempt beard comes alive on the page. He was more of an intellectual than Gandhi was, being a mathematician and knowing fifteen languages, and more of an ascetic, having lived upon curds almost exclusively for most of his life. Having aimed at reducing the 1 to 0 (Gandhi's metaphor for self-denial in every sense of self), he had in a sense no personal relations; he never married; and in 1918 he refused to attend the funeral of his mother—to whom he was deeply attached—because the professional priest would chant hymns.

He heard Gandhi's speech at Benares Hindu University in 1916. He had just left home, at the age of twenty-one, to make his way either to Bengal (and revolution) or to the Himalayas (and mystical retreat). He found in Gandhi, he says, "not only the peace of the Himalayas but also the burning fervour of revolution typical of Bengal. I said to myself that both of my desires had been fulfilled."[38] After questioning Gandhi about his speech by letter, Vinoba appeared at the ashram on 7 June 1916, and from that time devoted himself to Gandhi—though most often he kept himself at a certain distance. "It was indeed God's boundless grace that brought me to Gandhiji, impelled me to sit at his feet. . . . "[39] "My heart and life are firmly established at Gandhiji's feet. . . . I kept testing him, whether or not he tested me. . . . I met Bapu and at once fell in love with him. That was because of the unity of his inner and outer state. Then again, it was Bapu who initiated me into the philosophy of karma-yoga. . . ."[40] He talked as a mother, responded as a mother, and so people unhesitatingly ran to him. . . ."[41]

Vinoba was a Chitpavan brahmin, like Savarkar and the assassins, and felt the call to the same destiny. He used to read Tilak's magazine, *Kesari*, aloud to his mother. "Only I can know what I have got in the ashram. It was an early ambition of mine to distinguish myself by a violent deed in the service of the country. But Bapu cured me of that ambition. It is he who extinguished the volcano of anger and other passions in me." He was relieved to find in Gandhi someone who outreached and encompassed him. "Deprived of your blessings I find the world a howling desolation. Pray commend me to God so that he may make me a worthy offering for the great Sacrificial Fire you have lighted. . . . "[42]

On the other hand, Gandhi never considered himself a guru, nor did Vinoba consider himself a disciple. But he found in Gandhi the "man of steadfast mind" described in the *Gita*; and Gandhi called him the son who outdoes the father. He wrote to Vinoba in 1918: "I do not know in what terms to praise you. . . . I accept your own estimate and assume the position of a father to you. You seem almost to have met a long-felt wish of mine. In my view a father is, in fact, a father only when he has a son who surpasses him in virtue. . . . "[43] He told Mahadev Desai that Vinoba was a great man, a phrase he applied to no one else.

Gandhi found all these variously gifted men, called them to him, and involved them in his movement, in somewhat the same way as Tolstoy found his characters (who were based on people he knew or sought out) and wove them into his novels. The Gandhi followers are as much Gandhi's achievement—in a sense, creation—as his characters are Tolstoy's. The men of religion and the men of revolution, the men of letters and the politicians, were woven together to form the Gandhian movement.

XII
Tolstoyans and Gandhians: 1881–94 and 1921–31

In 1881 Tolstoy appealed to Tsar Alexander III to pardon the revolutionary assassins of his father on Christian principles; from that time on, he was committed to nonviolence and religious radicalism. Tolstoy had been stimulated to the change by conversation with his eldest son's tutor, Alekseev, who had himself been a revolutionary. In the same year, moreover, the Tolstoy family moved from their country seat to Moscow, and there Tolstoy had to face the misery of that city's proletariat. As described earlier, he took part in the Moscow Census of 1881, he wrote *What Then Must We Do?* in 1886, and, parallel with that attack on the civic conscience, he delivered another on the religious teaching of the Church.

Already in 1881–82 he was writing his *Critique of Dogmatic Theology*, in which he rendered judgment on a series of the Church's most important documents. His judgment was that these works were more blasphemous and faithless than those of Voltaire and Hume, because they adapted the Gospel message to quite opposite meanings, and perverted it morally and intellectually. Dogmata, such as that God is both one and three, meant nothing to Tolstoy. He dismissed the sacraments as "savage customs" suited to an earlier phase of civilization. Reading these books of theology would have made him an atheist had he not independently found his way to a faith in Christ's message. "I had intended to go to God, and I found my way into a stinking bog, which evokes in me only those feelings of which I am most afraid: disgust, malice, and indignation."[1] Church Christianity stirred Tolstoy's most sardonic self to life.

As for his political views, in a short pamphlet of 1882, entitled "Church and State," he declared the phrase *Christian State* to be as paradoxical and nonsensical as *hot ice*; either such a state is no state, or—more likely—its Christianity is no Christianity. Kings, after all, are simply anointed robbers. Christ's teaching is hostile to the state, and Christians, though not called on to destroy it, are called on not to support it or to comply with many of its demands. This phase of his work culminated in *The Kingdom of God is Within You*, the book which he finished in 1893 and Gandhi read in 1894.

In 1915 Gandhi returned to India, and after a year's interval of quiet observation (imposed on him by Gokhale) he engaged in a series of satyagraha campaigns on a variety of political issues, which—together with some more conventional cooperation with other national leaders in Congress—carried him with amazing speed to the position of supreme national leader. In 1917 he took up the cause of the peasant indigo growers of Champaran, in the north of India, who were being economically exploited by the white plantation owners there. Gandhi assembled an enormous amount of evidence as to what was happening—in defiance of official orders to leave the district—and persuaded the government to intervene against the planters.

In 1918 he led the striking mill-hands of the cotton mills of Ahmedabad in their labor dispute. Here, for the first time in India, he engaged in a fast; it was directed against his own followers, who were failing to observe the discipline he required of them, but it also exerted pressure upon the mill-owners, and they came to the settlement he wanted.

And then he led the nationwide agitation against the Rowlatt Acts of 1919, which the government had introduced to allow it to maintain in time of peace certain wartime measures of arrest and imprisonment without proof of guilt. Gandhi exhorted India to "noncooperate" with the government: to refuse to use government schools and colleges, or lawcourts and tribunals, or titles and honors—in sum, to withdraw from the whole structure of British civilization in India, and to build up a purely Indian civilization instead. This was satyagraha on the very largest scale.

Thus, in their old age, both men were public leaders, threatened by the governments of their respective countries, and the object of popular reverence (and also hatred). They had a following, they were a cause, and so one most significant group of their contemporaries was their disciples. Thus in Russia it is the Tolstoyans we shall study. But since we have already discussed the most famous Gandhians, those who were the leaders of the nationalist movement in India, or of his religious or other reforms, this section will concentrate on Gandhi's European followers, often women, who came to India because of him, and usually to the ashram.

Tolstoy's Followers

On the whole we can take Tolstoy's most significant contemporaries in this period to be those who clustered around, those who took him as their prophet. There were Tolstoyans in the 1880s, just as there were to be Gandhians in the 1920s. In the 1880s his ideas were propagated by M. S. Gromeka and L. E. Obolenski. (In the 1890s he rather receded from public view, but re-emerged when violent insurrection was checked in 1905.) Gromeka, whose book of 1884 went into five editions before 1894, drew out Tolstoy's forbidden ideas in the form of an imaginary dialogue with Levin, the hero of *Anna Karenina*.

There was even a Tolstoy movement, though it was not a national phenomenon on a scale one could compare with the Gandhi movement in India. But then the latter was a wave of nationalist activity, which included only a minority of true Gandhians. Tolstoy was not a nationalist, nor a politician, even in the sense that Gandhi was. But still there was enough political substance to Tolstoyism for both the Russian government and the revolutionary movement to spend some energy fighting it. Numbers are not easy to estimate, but in the mid-1880s there were several Tolstoyan agricultural communes: one in the Caucasus, founded by N. L. Ozmidov; one at Tver, founded by Mikhail Novoselov; one at Kharkov, founded by Mitrofan Vasilievich Alekhin (who had been a professor of chemistry); one at Smolensk, founded by Alekhin's brother, Arkady; and one at Kherson, founded in 1890 by Feinermann and Butkevich. By 1895 S. N. Krivenko listed five in Tver, three in Smolensk, and others as far apart as Samara, Chernigov, and Perm.[2]

Unlike Gandhi, Tolstoy did not found or join a commune or ashram himself. He showed few signs of wanting to: he condemned monastic self-segregation and distrusted any kind of group-self; he located or centered all the changes he wanted in the individual. He did not believe in Tolstoyism, he often said. But neither did Gandhi believe in Gandhism—his life was his message, he said; he, too, located every valuable change in the individual. The difference is rather that Gandhi had great gifts as a politician, and a political situation in some ways susceptible of influence by religion. Another difference is certainly that Tolstoy was incarcerated among the lilacs and nightingales of Yasnaya Polyana, and *had* to invest his energies in making that imprisonment his sadhana.

Some of his disciples were peasants. Like Gandhi, Tolstoy felt a vocation to speak out on large issues because he felt himself closer than others to the peasants of his country, the simple, selfless people.

Most educated people of course rejected Tolstoy's claims of that kind; being his disciple was perhaps mostly a matter of accepting them. Mikhail Engelhardt (1861–1915), who was exiled to the country for his part in student disorders, wrote to Tolstoy in 1881 as to someone who could save the peasantry. Engelhardt saw everywhere in his exile the breakdown of the peasant commune and wrote to Tolstoy in great distress, suggesting that *he* could reorient the sectarian movement towards making propaganda and constructively preventing the disintegration of the old peasantry.[3]

That was not something Tolstoy could do, but it is significant that two of the men from whom he learned something in this period, and whom he helped to utterance, were sectarian peasants. This was much remarked on at the time. The French scholar Leroy-Beaulieu said that Tolstoy's credo was a kind of Christian nihilism which assembled together all the ideas of the village apostles—that he had condensed and codified the teaching of the sectarians.[4]

One of these men, Syutaev, was a small man with a thin red beard who wore a sheepskin when he came to Moscow. He was a muzhik from Tver who worked as a stonemason in St. Petersburg during the season. Illiterate until after marriage, but pious, he became a searcher of texts, and by 1880 had repudiated the sacraments and rebelled against the village priest's authority. He refused to have his grandson baptised, or another grandson buried, and he devised his own form of marriage ceremony for his daughter. (Unlike Tolstoy, Syutaev had the full support of his family.) He defined "truth" just as Gandhi might have done, as "love in communal life." He expected the coming of the New Jerusalem and tried to interpret the imagery of the Apocalypse, but his teaching had political bearings, too. He refused to pay taxes or to lock doors or to prosecute thieves; his son refused military service, was imprisoned, and later worked for *Posrednik*.

In 1880 the *Tversky Vestnik* announced the formation of a new sect, of Syutaevtsi, in Shevelino. In the fall of 1881 Tolstoy went to see Syutaev, in his north-Russian village. A railway had recently been built that reached to nearby, but the area, as described by E. M. de Vogüé, was still remote, dominated by a sad and implacable sky, with a sense of immense distances, low hills, pines, marshes, everything poor and pale, and no walls, hedges, or stone houses. There was nothing for Syutaev to read but the Bible, and he read that very slowly, said de Vogüé.[5] Tolstoy was very interested and admiring, and the two men had long and earnest talks together, both there and in Moscow. Syutaev taught him the evil of upper-class philanthropy, as Tolstoy says in *What Then Must We Do?*

Syutaev was not a writer, and except when he spoke to fashionable audiences, as at the Tolstoys' house, his influence was confined to his own circle. Timofei Bondarev *was* a writer; his manuscript, which Tolstoy got into print, was entitled *Industry and Idleness, or the Glory of the Agriculturist.* It had been deposited unpublished in a museum at Minusinski, and there read by G. I. Uspensky, who wrote about it in *Ruskaya Misl* in 1884, which Tolstoy read. He got in touch with Bondarev soon after, via some political prisoners exiled to that area, V. S. Lebedev and L. N. Zhebynev. His efforts to get the manuscript published failed with two magazines, but succeeded with a third, *Ruskaya Beseda*, in 1888, only to have the issue confiscated by the censors. It finally got published abroad, in French in 1890 and in English in 1896. Tolstoy wrote to Lebedev that no Russian university book or journal had said anything as important as Syutaev and Bondarev.[6]

Bondarev had read in the Book of Judges of the time when the Jews had no kings, and everyone ploughed and cultivated; and he took that as his ideal state. But in many ways his doctrine was a stern reversal of Gospel Christianity. For him, Cain was the first born, the first farmer, and the model to imitate. The true trinity, which can save us from death, is God, bread, and the laborer. But in some towns in the 1880s a measure of bread cost no more than one of dry muck; a cold shiver ran through Bondarev at the thought of this insult to all farmers. He had organized a successful farm economy in Iudino, his village of Subbotniks (Sabbatarians), but had then abandoned it to live alone in a small hut. He wrote on scraps of paper, and then began chiseling on limestone. On his tombstone he had written: "I shall not come to you, but you shall all come to me."[7] He said he had petitioned for twenty-two years, and now lay in his grave like ripe wheat harvested in time and ready for a new sowing. He was in many ways a Russian Whitman, with the representative difference that he lacked the self-expansive life-orientation.

Syutaev and Bondarev were not so much Tolstoyans as sources for Tolstoy and confirmation of his own views and of their fitness for the peasants. But there were peasant Tolstoyans: V. D. Liapunov (1873–1905), a peasant poet of Tula whose poems Tolstoy liked; Afanasi Aggeev, a free-thinker from Yasnaya Polyana, exiled to Siberia in 1903, where he died five years later; S. P. Chizhov, from Umansk, exiled to Poland and then to Siberia; K. N. Zyabrev, nicknamed Bely, of Yasnaya Polyana, whom Tolstoy talked to; M. P. Novikov, to whom Tolstoy turned for help in disappearing from his family; P. V. Olkhovik, who refused military service and got three years in a disciplinary battalion, and then joined the Dukhobors. And besides these, who all in some way distinguished themselves, in some way or other "spoke," there was the mass of the speechless. It was them above all who Tolstoy felt called upon to represent, and the peasant Tolstoyans were important as a bridge to them.

But Tolstoyans, like Gandhians, fall into many groups; there were some primarily interested in education or literature, some in politics or social action, some in religion or self-realization. And, again like Gandhians, they came from many different parts of society. At the opposite extreme from the peasants, it was the aristocracy that gave birth to the two men who were personally closest to Tolstoy and his family, V. G. Chertkov and P. I. Biriukov.

Chertkov's father was adjutant-general to the tsars Alexander II and Alexander III, and his mother was a personal friend of the tsarina Maria Alexandrovna. The Chertkovs owned 30,000 desyatinas in the south of Voronezh, but they lived in St. Petersburg because they were court nobility—by most social standards, they stood considerably higher than the Tolstoys. On his mother's side, Vladimir Grigorevich was related to the Decembrists Chernyshev and Muraviev, and on his father's side to P. A. Shuvalov, one of the most powerful (and reactionary) of Alexander II's ministers. (Through Shuvalov, Chertkov was able to set up a *Posrednik* bookstore in St. Petersburg and hold weekly teas for Tolstoyans—an amazing concession.) His father's brother had been Ataman of the Don Cossacks, then governor-general of Kiev, and then governor-general of Warsaw.

Chertkov said later that his personal character derived from his situation within his family, and his family's situation in the world. He always knew of their power and position, and he was denied nothing as a child. He had two brothers who died young, and he remembered the younger of them as his only real intimate. He did not go to school but had English tutors; he visited England often, and stayed with the Duke of Bedford and Lord Northampton. In 1883 he had an income of Rs 10,000 a year. There is much in his upbringing that can remind one of Vladimir Nabokov and—*mutatis mutandis*—of Osbert Sitwell; perhaps if he had been born forty years later, he would have followed a path like theirs, but the path he did follow could hardly have been more different.

He grew up tall and handsome, a gilded youth, indulging in wine, women, and gambling. "Everything he wanted, he wanted very much," we are told.[8] At nineteen he entered the Life Guards, but he had always taken an interest in serious things and was shocked by the cruel treatment of patients in military hospitals. His mother, who was unhappy in her marriage, was herself something of an intellectual and interested in religion. She met abroad some of the followers of an English evangelist, Lord Radstock, and was converted by his revivalist preaching. She invited Radstock to Russia, where he preached to fashionable gatherings with great success. (Tolstoy describes such preaching in *Resurrection*.) Her brother-in-law, Colonel Pashkov, devoted his life to propagating Radstock's kind of Christianity, and was punished by the authorities for creating a new sect, the Pashkovites. Thus, Chertkov's Tolstoyism can be seen as an "overcoming" of his family tradition: he could both defy his mother, who thought Tolstoy irreligious, and at the same time show himself more serious than she; by almost any standards, Tolstoy was a greater man than Radstock, and working among the peasants was in better taste than preaching to fashionable congregations.

Chertkov resigned his commission after the assassination of Alexander II, and went to live on one of his properties, Lisinovka, where he set up a model farm, a trade school, a surgery, a credit and savings cooperative, and local industries. (Lisinovka had a population of about 5,000.) He met Tolstoy in 1883, and immediately took on the task of running *Posrednik*. He was skillful at dealing with the censors and with other forms of authority, and he had many private connections with them via his family and friends. He presented himself as a commanding and efficient personality, and in the first years of their acquaintance had some influence over Sonia and the older Tolstoy children, persuading them to take Tolstoy's ideas more seriously, or at least more civilly.

In later years he quarreled bitterly with them, and that quarreling caused Tolstoy a great deal of grief. There came a time when Tolstoy complained (to others) that Sonia and Chertkov were tearing him apart with their contrary demands, especially to hand over his diaries; and Chertkov has generally been regarded by those who write about Tolstoy as a troublemaker. But Tolstoy himself respected and liked him, and saw a great similarity between them. On 6 April 1884 he wrote in his diary that he and Chertkov were "wonderfully concentric."[9] And on 7 December 1883 the latter had written to him, "In almost everything I agree with you, and I see in you the exponent of my best striving."[10]

Altogether Tolstoy wrote him 928 letters, which was one for every ten days of their acquaintance. Chertkov wrote even more to Tolstoy, and his letters were more like a diary of his most intimate thoughts (which he begged Tolstoy to let no one else see). He had a tense and stormy and self-divided nature, which he presented to others as serene, masterful, and impassive, but which Tolstoy understood to be like his own. (That Tolstoy also on one occasion compared that nature with Peter the Great's, in warning to Chertkov, throws an extra illumination on his own interest in Peter.) Clearly, theirs was a relationship somewhat like that of guru (Tolstoy) to chela (Chertkov), and within it, this (to others) cold and haughty man abandoned his defenses. In their work for their common cause, however, he acted more like an equal; even in the matter of Tolstoy's writing, he criticized everything Tolstoy wrote, and elicited new work from him by copying out fragments Tolstoy had abandoned and leaving large blank spaces around what was copied, to induce Tolstoy to expand upon it. Sometimes he interfered and was a burden; sometimes Tolstoy reproached him, and no doubt much more often he groaned to himself. On the whole, though, he seems to have been grateful to have found an equal and a collaborator, rather than yet another disciple.

Pavel Biriukov seems to have been a soft and malleable nature by ordinary standards, as well as by comparison with Chertkov. Olga Biriukov, in her "Introduction" to his correspondence with Tolstoy, calls him serene and gentle, and says he could peacefully embody what Tolstoy only passionately strove after all his life. By the same token, perhaps, Tolstoy and others did not take Biriukov's opinions and decisions as seriously as they did Chertkov's. This may be why Tolstoy rather discouraged Biriukov from marrying his daughter, Masha, while he positively encouraged Chertkov to marry; he felt that Biriukov could be governed and shaped.

Born in 1860, the son of a general, Biriukov entered the Page Corps (a very elite institution) and then went to the Naval Academy to study science. He was appalled by the death sentence imposed on some mutineers aboard ship, resigned, and looked for a new direction in life. He had read Dostoevsky's novels with enthusiasm, and identified with Alesha in *The Brothers Karamazov*, but was disillusioned by *The Diary of a Writer*. Chertkov had him read *Confession* and *What I Believe*, and then took him to meet Tolstoy, in November 1884. He worked with the peasants on his property in Kostroma, giving them training in medicine and general education, and then took part in *Posrednik*. He ran the book deposit in St. Petersburg, while Chertkov was editor. He sold copies of the Gospels to those who came in to ask for prayer books and church canticles. Together with Chertkov, he was sent into exile in 1896 for his part in leading the agitation about the Dukhobors. And in subsequent years, one of his major activities on behalf of Tolstoyism was the writing of Tolstoy's biography.

Gandhi's Followers

We can choose to concentrate mostly on a group of those Western disciples of Gandhi's who were drawn to him personally and to work for his cause. Nearly all came to live in India with him.

The first, and in some ways the most spectacular, case was that of Madeline Slade. Her father, Sir Edmund Slade, had been commander in chief of the East Indies Fleet of the Royal Navy and, after his retirement, chairman of the board of Anglo-Iranian Oil. He was thus an important figure in the complex of British authority and exploitation in the East, and his daughter's defection was a vivid gesture of repentance by (in the name of) British culture as a whole. She chose Gandhi to be her real father; she addressed him and referred to him as "Bapu," and when they first met in 1925 she knelt at his feet, and he raised her, saying: "You shall be my daughter." Even more dramatically than C. F. Andrews, Madeline Slade chose to be Gandhian and Indian rather than English; she took the name Mirabai (or Mirabehn), wore the sari, shaved her head, took a vow of celibacy, and so on.

Born in 1892, Mira had always been a misfit in her family and class—though she clung to her mother—and developed immoderate enthusiasms for trees and animals and everything that represented something opposite. As she grew older, it was the masters of art she adored—notably Beethoven and one particular executant of Beethoven's music, and then Romain Rolland, who had written about him.

In 1924 she read Rolland's book about Gandhi and immediately booked her passage to India. (She had spent the years 1909 to 1911 there, when her father commanded the Eastern Fleet.) She also wrote to Gandhi, and soon realized that she was being too precipitate, so deferred her passage for a year, during which time she prepared herself, learning to spin, to speak Urdu, to sleep on the floor, and so on.

Once at the Ashram, Mira made herself very useful to Gandhi in many aspects of his work and correspondence, notably in the organization of khadi work and later in setting up model dairies and centers of village regeneration. Gandhi sent her on many missions through the country, partly because she was so independent, with great practical capability, and partly because she was so dependent on him, in terms of emotional attachment.

He devoted considerable effort to freeing her from that

dependence. Thus he wrote on 22 March 1927: "I want you to be a perfect woman. I want you to shed all angularities . . . do throw off the nervousness. You must not cling to me as in this body. . . . "[11] She seems to have had hysterical fits at the thought of his fasting and at having to leave him. She was denied access to him once when he was ill; her intensity made her dangerous to a patient with high blood pressure, as Sonia was dangerous to Tolstoy on his deathbed; and even telling of the incident, her language indicates how she reacted— "The words hit me like a thunderbolt. . . . "[12]

She became, one might say, Gandhi's Chertkov, because of her anxious possessiveness and her instinct for conflict, as well as her executive ability and authoritative training. Gandhi, too, was drawn into a troubled love relationship, though this was less of a burden to him than Chertkov was to Tolstoy because it did not bulk so large in his life. He sent her away and then wrote: "Now that you are away from me, my grief over having grieved you is greater. No tyrant has yet lived, who has not paid for the suffering he has caused. No lover has ever given pain without being more pained. Such is my state. What I have done was inevitable. Only I wish I did not lose temper. But such is my brutality towards those I love most."[13] So he offered her tenderness, allowed her a special relationship. But he told her, for instance, in 1931: "I was on a bed of hot ashes all the while I was accepting your service."[14]

Theirs was, finally, a love relationship, a spiritual marriage. On 23 September 1932, during his fast, he wrote to her: "The thought of you corrodes me. I wish you could be at peace. Do write daily and wire tomorrow your condition."[15] And later: "The seven years [of their relationship] seem like a dream. As I recall the terrible scoldings I tremble. . . . As I look back upon the past I realize that my love was impatient. . . . "[16] And she replied, when he was about to begin a fast, in 1933: "God gave me light to recognize His messenger . . . in you. He will therefore give me strength to go through everything and anything for the fulfilment of His word through you. . . . My love would be a poor thing, if it failed at this supreme moment and gave way to misery and desperation. And that is my cry, borne on the wings of a love which knows no bounds."[17]

Another disciple who knew Gandhi during the same years was the American Nilla Cram Cook. In most ways unlike Madeline Slade, she, too, had psychological problems relating to her father, and sought out Gandhi, who gave her, temporarily, a solution to her problems. In *The Spirit's Pilgrimage*, Madeline Slade wrote:

Nilla was a sprite, dancing and singing her way through life like a bird. Earnest she was too, but it was an earnestness of exaltation, and one fine morning we found that she had flown from the nest. . . . [She was found] dancing all alone in the woods of Lord Krishna. . . . [In other words, she had suffered, much more quickly and theatrically than Madeline Slade, a relapse to the way of life she had followed before meeting Gandhi, accompanied by a mental disturbance, so it was decided to send her home to America.] Bapu was pained. It was clear to me that, in spite of the extraordinary escapades, he had seen much more in that passing spirit than the rest of the world at that time.[18]

To understand Nilla Cram Cook, it is well to begin with her father, George Cram Cook, for in many ways her relationship to India and to other things was a continuation and fulfillment of his. George Cram Cook, famous in theater history as a founder of the Provincetown Players and the early producer of Eugene O'Neill, followed a standard course of intellectual self-emancipation in the 1890s, discarding an early transcendentalism for an erotic philosophy of life. This eroticism did not present itself as the enemy, rather as the ally, of spiritual values like anarchism and pacifism. Teaching at Stanford, Cook read Tolstoy and Kropotkin, and left teaching for farming. Next followed his pioneering work with the Provincetown Players and, after the Great War, his move to Greece, where he hoped to revive and adapt the ancient Greek theater. He now also began to make a cult of India, as an even older culture.

George Cram Cook died in Greece in 1922, but his daughter Nilla soon made her way from there to India, in a gesture of cultural repentance like, though also unlike, Madeline Slade's. She had grown up in Provincetown and California, traveling between divorced parents, imbibing the spirit of Greenwich Village, espousing the dance and eroticism, and compared by her peers with Isadora Duncan.

In Greece she had helped revive ancient arts, woven her own cloth, married a poet at seventeen and borne him a child at nineteen (by her own account). But soon she left him, and traveled further east with her baby. In Kashmir she persuaded the brahmins to accept her as a Hindu. In Bangalore she produced a performance of Nataraja dances, in the spirit of her father, but then involved herself in the picketing of temples, in protest against their exclusion of untouchables. When her activity of this kind was reported in the press, she came to Gandhi's attention, and he wrote asking her to come to see him in Yeravda Jail in 1932.

The first letter preserved from him to her is dated 18 January 1933 and begins: "My Dear N., I have your two interesting and instructive letters. It is very great work you are doing. . . . "[19] (This work is street cleaning, in which she was helped by a group of young men; they were taking on themselves the dharma of the outcastes.) Gandhi said he wanted to meet her when she could.

But on 12 February he wrote to say that he had heard an attack upon her character, that the friend she had sent to see him—one of the young men—seemed unbalanced, and that her own letter smelled of the hysteric. He then wrote to various people whose names she had given him, to ask about her. In March he wrote to Ramachandra, the secretary to the Mysore Board of the Servants of the Untouchables Society, saying; "She has led for years an utterly immoral and extravagant life and has been an utter stranger to truth."[20] Now she had promised to make a public confession, and to lead a beggar's life in Harijan quarters, abstaining from all public activity. He continued: "Some of the young men at least who have surrounded her do not seem to have behaved well."[21]

By her own account, she had written him that her life had been a moral hell from his point of view, since he disapproved of "the sensual world" while she adored it.[22] She was her father's pupil in the philosophy of eroticism. "I did not relish these reminders of Protestant puritanism," she writes in *My Road to India*.[23] However, she went to Yeravda, where she found Gandhi so ugly that she "nearly ran away"; when charged, however, she "confessed everything to him" and accepted his message that she should embrace poverty.

Gandhi was as shocked by her financial as by her sexual sins. He told someone else: "She was open to the advances of practically every person, and she was no better after her acceptance of Hindu religion. She has debts amounting to nearly Rs 10,000 spread over Europe and India. She has travelled under a false name. . . . "[24] And her public confession, which was addressed to "Dear Mahatmaji" and written for him, laid the stress on her unpaid debts. "And I want the general public to know that as an aspirant to social service I have been a great hypocrite."[25]

From our point of view, however, the erotic dimension of her style is very interesting. She called herself a mother to these young men, and indeed to Gandhi. (He wrote to her, "I did not like the subscription to your note." " 'Your son' looks unnatural and theatrical

. . . you ought to shed all hysteria and unnaturalness."[26]) Her motherhood was that of Magna Mater, the great female deity whose lovers
are her children. Gandhi wrote to Rudramuni, a Harijan priest, "N.
tells me that you are talking about spiritual marriages or spiritual
friendships bordering on marital relations. This is nothing but playing
with fire and an echo of very subtle sensuality."[27] And later: "You
were all working together, the central attraction being N. Devi, at that
time not a fountain of purity. You cannot divest yourself of all responsibility for all that happened during that period."[28] And to another
correspondent in April, who claimed to have been unmoved by any
animal passion whatsoever while passing the night with Nilla, he said
this was "impossible for any person who is not utterly impotent or
who is not a God. . . . You were no baby, nor was N. playing the part
of mother when she forgot herself and the limitations of sex which
God has imposed on us human beings."[29]

Gandhi was concerned because the Untouchable work was his
work, and any scandal would be to its disadvantage; also, he felt, as
he said, like a father to all these young men, whom he must have met
while he was in Bangalore. But he was also impressed by Nilla, saying
that she had great capacity for sacrifice and service, and that she had
great ability and wide knowledge. He was impressed with her knowledge of the *Mahabharata* and her potential as a teacher. He was also
moved by the moral mess she had gotten into. In a statement in
Harijan, following on her confession, he said her life had been one
of lewdness, untruth, and extravagance, because she was brought up
in a bohemian family, where the very name Jesus was taboo. "One
word to the young men who fell under N.'s spell . . ." he wrote; "it
shows the need for the young to maintain brahmacharya up to the
age of twenty-five.[30] Brahmacharya in this context means chastity.

His encounter with Nilla inspired him—unconsciously—to undertake a fast in 1933. "I can see that she has had a large share in
persuading me to undertake this fast. I did not know this. If there is
anything which can give her strength, it will be this fast, and, if I have
made any mistake in sending her there [to the Ashram], the fast is
the only thing which can undo it."[31] He wrote to her with some of
the emotion he showed to Mira. At first: "My spirit hovers about you
as a mother's about her lost child. I would love to own you as a child,
but I have not got that Faith in you yet. It may be no fault of yours,
but there it is. . . . "[32] But soon: "I can't put you out of my mind."[33]

She went back to Bangalore, now seeing herself as a great sinner,
and gave away all her saris and jewels, shaved her hair, wore a monk's
robe, and wrote Gandhi a letter every day. Going further to extremes

(of course against his advice), she went to live in an Untouchable temple in a poor village of Mysore, where, by her own account, she ceased to menstruate, so completely had she renounced her former Aphroditean self. When her health began to break down, Gandhi ordered her by wire to return to Yeravda, and sent her from there to the Ashram. Like Madeline Slade, she was devoted to Gandhi personally and exclusively, uninterested in the rest of the Ashram, and upset by the scavenging (lavatory cleaning) imposed on her there. She speaks of the "terrible consciousness of human physiology" this forced upon her; of course, her earlier philosophy had focused upon human physiology, but under the aspect of Eros, of beauty and pleasure. Now she had to see death and the dying—she had to see all the things she had avoided seeing before. She refused to look after herself, and no one could do anything with her.

When Nilla ceased to menstruate, she thought it was because she had transcended the sexual condition, but Gandhi thought she was merely pregnant, and was glad of it. He said a new child would be a test for her and for the Ashram. But he had no doubt that she could in time become entirely spiritual. "You have in you the making of such a woman."[34] At this point we might compare Nilla with Natasha Rostov after Prince Andrei's death—an erotic woman called to a spiritual destiny—but while Tolstoy called his character back to marriage and motherhood, Gandhi encouraged Nilla to move away from them.

He could not, however, give her the time and devotion that would have been needed to confirm her in her new vocation. Quite apart from her psychological and moral instability, her mind and imagination were harnessed to other life choices. Soon he was writing to her: "I wish you will forget Pythagoras, Bacchus, and the *Mahabharata*. Why should you brood over the past when you have to re-enact the Mahabharata at the Ashram?"[35] He wanted her simply to move forward, morally; but her imagination needed huge spaces of freedom. Her letter of 13 May was "too imaginative and poetic for me. You have plenty of poetry in you. Your imagination knows no bounds. I want you to transmute these into an inexhaustible power for real service. We have all to aspire after being childlike."[36] But she relapsed psychologically, fell ill, and eventually ran away from the Ashram.

When Gandhi was released from jail, he ordered her to eat and wash and to sleep on a bed; he nursed her himself, as he nursed Madeline Slade when she suffered from typhoid in 1936. He taught Nilla, she says, "to be a girl again," and told her she must dance again. One more reliably recognizes his voice in his remark: "Nilla has lost the tenant in her upper storey. But let's hope we will be able to rent it out again soon."[37] In many ways, he played father to her, as he had to Madeline Slade, and Nilla acknowledges this. "In the role of Bapu's daughter I straightened out an uncompleted relation to Kyrios Kook."[38] This is how she refers to her father, for it was the name the Greek peasants had given him. Finally, she and her little boy were sent home to the care of relatives in America.

There were other women, the patterns of whose relations with Gandhi were quite different. Among the early names we may mention a German, Helene Haussding, an Englishwoman, Mary Barr, and a Frenchwoman, Antoinette Mirbel.

There were also three or four other categories of Gandhi-disciple, besides the white woman who came to live with him; however, these cases will illustrate both the effort and the skill this disciple relationship extorted from Gandhi, and the variety of response he elicited from those who followed him.

XIII
Anti-Tolstoyans and Anti-Gandhians: 1894–1910 and 1931–48

In the last period of their lives, Tolstoy and Gandhi had national and even international fame, as leaders of nonviolence and of anti-imperial resistance. Tolstoy's movement may be said to have focused upon the simplification of life and the refusal to serve in an army—it made its main appeal to those born into the ruling classes of great empires—while Gandhi's movement focused on political action by the oppressed nations of the lands colonized by those empires. But the two movements were twin manifestations of the same idea, twin progeny of the same enthusiasm, the same conviction, the same commitment.

Tolstoy and Gandhi were in some ways the principal enemies of, on the one hand, the Russian Empire, on the other the British. Their lives in this period were great moral dramas, in which the men of peace were threatened and punished from above, and supported from below by the adoration of the oppressed.

Since their deaths that drama has often been rehearsed to give aid and comfort to those who would like to see nonviolent values prevail. But because of the risk of sentimentalizing the idea of nonviolence, and masking its essential core of bitter and painful paradox, in this chapter I will focus upon the less exalting and ennobled aspects of the two stories.

In this last period of his life, Tolstoy was tormented by bitter quarrels with his wife and, to a lesser extent, with his children. They knew that he felt chained to them against his will, and that he disapproved of the family's extravagant and idle life-style. He anticipated both his own and his society's death—he anticipated political revolution; and in some sense he wanted it to happen, while the prospect also horrified him. He yearned to change his life to that of a pilgrim, or of an ascetic, waiting for death in quiet concentration. But his family frustrated that desire, believing it to be a proof of feeble-mindedness or a hypocritical itch for notoriety.

His writing was heavily censored, and in 1901 the Russian church authorities excommunicated him. Thereafter he received a lot of mail from pious Christians who regarded him as the Anti-Christ—though he also got angry letters from revolutionaries who wanted him to give up his prayers and to take up a rifle. And even among his own disciples, as we have seen, there was much dissension and complaint, against each other and against him.

Gandhi's last years were, of course, dominated by the tragic drama of India's internal conflicts and the refusal of the Muslims to form a part of the united free India. Because the liberation of India had been Gandhi's life work, and its achievement through nonviolence against the British had been *his* triumph, the violence that broke out between the Hindus and the Muslims, on such an enormous scale, was *his* tragedy. All his enemies in some sense gloated over the bloodshed that he had promised, and failed, to avert.

He had moreover to watch his hopes and plans for a nonviolent free India pushed aside by his heirs, Nehru and Patel. In the first few months of office, they set up military academies and engaged in military aggression, like that in Kashmir. Gandhi wrote Nehru that he wanted to keep India a village society because only on such a social basis could truth and nonviolence flourish; but Nehru replied he had never understood why Gandhi thought that. He set about industrializing and modernizing India as fast as he could.

In this final chapter, we can concentrate mostly upon Tolstoy's and Gandhi's enemies, in order to give the reader some sense of the atmosphere of indifference or antagonism in which they ended their days. They were, of course, highly revered by the general publics, in Russia and India and the world at large, but amongst those "professionally" close to them, the situation was different. Though there were exceptions, their very fame, their success with the public, above all the sanctified character of that fame, provoked a marked reaction of resistance or hostility in others who would have been ready enough to welcome them as colleagues—even to admire them as stars—if they had stayed in the socially defined fields of literature and politics.

Tolstoy's Enemies

In the last period of his life, Tolstoy was becoming old-fashioned, intellectually speaking. He had been old-fashioned before, in the 1860s, but then he was himself still young and changing, and still believed in his own version of literature and the intellectual life. Moreover, the tides of artistic fashion were then liable to sweep back in his direction, as they did quite soon. In the 1890s (when, oddly enough, he was thinking more like "a man of the 60s") none of those was true. He was established as a Grand Old Man in the field of literature, and he had his disciples, the Tolstoyans, among whom were to be counted some men of talent and mind, though usually such men were only briefly discipular; but so far as the world of ideas was concerned, Tolstoy offered only stale wares.

The orthodoxy in the world of ideas was liberal. In the 1890s, as James Billington points out in *The Icon and the Axe*, liberalism finally acquired a broad basis of support in Russia, due largely to the work of professors like Miliukov and Vinogradov. The constitutionalism associated with work in the zemstvos coalesced with the Kadets' idea of "liberation" from old social forms, in the thinking of those who founded the Liberal party in 1903. And for Liberals, engaged in the work of modernizing Russia, Tolstoy's moralistic Christian anarchism could only seem quaint or reactionary.

We can divide Tolstoy's contemporaries into three groups, literary, religious, and political, who all show similar patterns of response to the fact of his picturesque eminence: a pattern of general neglect and repudiation, interspersed with episodes of personal tribute. Amongst men of letters, a writer with a somewhat enigmatic relation to Tolstoy was Anton Chekhov (1860–1904), who wrote to his friend Suvorin in March 1894: "The Tolstoyan morality has stopped stirring me, and in the depths of my soul I feel badly disposed towards it . . . [but it] had a powerful effect on me, governed my life for a period of six or seven years. . . . [Now] prudence and justice tell me there is more love in natural phenomena than in chastity and abstinence from meat. . . . I am not an isolated case, as I have noted just this kind of mood all about me. It is as though everybody had fallen in love, had got over it, and was now looking for some new distraction."[1]

The values Chekhov "now" believed in were a kind of modern, science-respecting humanism, in most ways opposed to Tolstoy's. In a letter of 4 October 1889, he wrote:

Any trade-mark or label to me means a prejudice. Sacrosanct to me is the human body, health, reason, talent, inspiration, love, and absolute freedom. . . . [I]n electricity and steam there is more real humanity than in chastity and abstinence from meat. . . . Modern culture is the beginning of the work to be performed in the name of the great future, while the religious movement is a survival, almost the end, of that which is dead or dying.[2]

On the other hand, Chekhov saw Tolstoy quite often after 1895 (especially when Tolstoy was recuperating in the Crimea in 1901) and had very friendly personal relations with him. He wrote to Mikhail Menshikov on 28 January 1900 that Tolstoy's illness

... frightened me and made me very tense. I fear Tolstoy's death. His death would leave a large empty space in my life. First, I have loved no man the way I have loved him. I am not a believer, but of all beliefs I consider his the closest to mine and most suitable for me. Second, when literature has Tolstoy, it is easy and gratifying to be a writer. Even if you are aware that you have never accomplished anything, and are still not accomplishing anything, you don't feel so bad, because Tolstoy accomplished enough for everyone. His activities provide justification for the hopes and aspirations that are usually placed on literature. Third, Tolstoy stands firm, his authority is enormous, and as long as he is alive, bad taste in literature, all vulgarity in its brazen-faced or lachrymose varieties, all bristly or resentful vanity, will remain far in the background. His moral authority alone is enough to maintain what we think of as literary trends and schools at a certain minimal level. If not for him, literature would be a flock without a shepherd or an unfathomable jumble.[3]

One sees in this example how much importance was attributed to Tolstoy by other writers, and how much responsibility for Russian literature was thrust upon him. Many others, who can be represented as a group by the mystical poet, Alexander Blok, had similarly strong feelings about all that Tolstoy had done and been, without having the personal relation with him that Chekhov had. In 1908 Blok wrote: "It often enters one's head that nothing matters, everything is still straightforward and not fearfully relativistic so long as L. N. Tolstoy is alive. . . . So long as Tolstoy is alive and walks down the furrow behind the plough and his white horse, the morning is still dewy, fresh, unfrightening, the vampires are drowsing, and God be praised. Tolstoy walks—it is the sun that moves. And if the sun sinks and Tolstoy dies, *the last genius departs*—what then?"[4]

Of course, Blok's phrasing also in its own way suggests that Tolstoy was old-fashioned; and his own imaginative work belonged to the opposite literary party, and had nothing in common with Tolstoy's. In 1903 Blok admitted to being a Decadent, though he deplored everything that went by that name. By 1911 he called himself a Symbolist, which he and his friends thought just the opposite, but was just as bad from Tolstoy's point of view. Like Soloviev he believed in an Eternal Feminine that was both spiritual and sensual and always in conflict with itself, to which he added Christ and Russia (Russia the violent and primitive) to make his Trinity. All this could not be further from Tolstoyism.

The most interesting relationship maintained with Tolstoy by an adherent of the new literature was that of D. S. Merezhkovsky (1865–1941), though this relationship was all on Merezhkovsky's side and to some degree inexplicit. Dmitri Merezhkovsky, the youngest of six sons, grew up protected by his mother and estranged from his father, a Karenin-like privy councillor. His mother later figured in *his* Trinity (he, like Blok, was influenced by Soloviev) as goddess and muse. For a time the young Merezhkovsky wanted to become a Narodnik poet and village teacher, in the old style which was compatible with Tolstoy's principles. But he was also early inspired by pagan and classical images and themes. (This material was something common to most Symbolist poets, and carried with it anti-Christian implications.) Visiting the Crimea in 1878, he found "all of Greece" there—he found the groves of mighty pagan Pan. Implicit within this paganism, as within the Renaissance kind, was eroticism and heroism. In the 1890s Merezhkovsky read Nietzsche and began to theorize about both Superman and sexuality. He began to contrast Christ with the gods of Olympus, and though he looked beyond both to "the unknown God," the force of his eclecticism was much more pagan than Christian.

After his stay in Paris he became a Symbolist and a propagandist for Symbolism. He now rejected everything Tolstoy had written since 1880, and saw him as having been even before then a betrayer of art, a writer divided between creating and preaching. All life is a struggle between Christ and Anti-Christ, but the two are synthesized in the great artists, like Plato, Pushkin, and above all da Vinci. In his early work Tolstoy also performed this synthesis. In "The Cossacks" Merezhkovsky saw Yeroshka as "a pagan wood-god," and in *Anna Karenina* he saw both Anna and Kitty as divine manifestations of the cruel but fertile Aphrodite, and thought Tolstoy only *wanted* to favor the opposite kind of woman, the daughters of the kind but barren Artemis.

Merezhkovsky's idea was that both of life's opposing principles should be reconciled in "Christianity," which he, like his friend Rozanov, held to be a fusion of the morality of the Sermon on the Mount with the carnal wisdom of the pagans. This idea was of course incompatible with the Christianity of the late Tolstoy. Merezhkovsky gave lectures on "Tolstoy and Dostoevsky" in which he said—even before Tolstoy's excommunication—that the latter was no Christian. He contrasted the two writers as the seer of the flesh (Tolstoy) and the seer of the spirit (Dostoevsky), and the latter had the advantage. This essay was developed into a book in 1902.

In *Tolstoy as Man and Artist* Merezhkovsky described Tolstoy's face as "powerful in ruggedness, the face of a blind subterranean Titan. . . ." He saw on it "the mark of Cain, of anguish and dark pride."[5] This is very like the language Merezhkovsky was to use to describe Peter the Great in his novel; it is also very like the language Gorki was to use for Tolstoy. "No, he has found nothing, no faith, no God."[6] He insisted on seeing Tolstoy as a pagan sensualist—only tormented by the aspiration to be spiritual, too. "In all literature, there is no writer equal to Tolstoy in depicting the human body . . . [and that] side of the flesh which approached the spirit and that side of the spirit which approached the flesh."[7] He compared Tolstoy with Michelangelo, Dostoevsky with da Vinci.

There is no denying the truth of this vision of Tolstoy as artist, or the power of the contrast drawn with Dostoevsky. On the other hand, it is an account of Tolstoy which brushes aside everything he had been since 1880—Tolstoy as a man of religion, not a man of art; and this is the way the world has since dealt with the late Tolstoy's challenge to it—the world as represented by writers like Merezhkovsky, Gorki, Thomas Mann, and others. The stress has fallen on Tolstoy's titanism, his power and carnality, his "Luciferean pride of appetite" (Prince Mirsky's phrase), in order to put out of order the far more disturbing questions raised by his meekness and humility.

Turning from literature to religion, the Russian church's reactions to the late Tolstoy were dramatic, since they included excommunicating him, but they were less interesting intellectually. Pobedonostsev was at the end of his long career as procurator of the Holy Synod. He denounced the disturbances of 1905 very harshly in a "Message to all Children of the Orthodox Church," and then resigned—and so disappeared from the scene of Tolstoy's last years. Symbolically, though, he remains of the greatest importance to understanding Tolstoyism and anti-Tolstoyism.

Konstantin Pobedonostsev was born in Moscow in 1827, the son of a professor who was himself the son of a priest. He was therefore the same age as Tolstoy, but he belonged to a secularized subdivision of the clerical caste—very unlike the nobles. As such we can link him in our minds with two of the most harshly treated characters in Tolstoy's fiction, Karenin and Speransky. In fact, Pobedonostsev was often compared with Speransky, both by contemporaries and by later students, as Robert Byrnes tells us in *Pobedonostsev*. And like Speransky, though a staunch supporter of the tsar and the state, Pobedonostsev had no sympathy for nobles. The Slavophiles were too aristocratic for his taste.

His father was a professor of literature, and though Konstantin turned to the law for his career, he remained a writer and a man of learning. He began as the historian of Russian civil law; during twenty years of service in the Senate, he did a great deal of research into various humanities and social science topics, and between 1858 and 1868 he produced thirty-two books and articles, many of them surveys of contemporary learning. In this way he resembled the seemingly opposite Chernyshevsky, and in his early years Pobedonostsev, too, was something of a reformer; the legal system he helped introduce in 1864 brought the jury system to Russia. But he was always close to the court and the government. In 1861 he was appointed special tutor to the heir to the throne; in 1863 he accompanied the tsarevich on a tour of Russia, which he described in a book; and in 1865 he was appointed tutor to the new heir, who became Alexander III. By the late 1870s he was Alexander's grey eminence.

Pobedonostsev was very alert to the contemporary world, especially the Western countries, but he thought that if Russia (and most of Europe) tried to imitate the Anglo-Saxons, disaster would result. Always in love with stability and quiet, he wrote religious poetry and meditations, and translated Thomas a Kempis. This love of the past and of quietude (Tolstoy felt a similar nostalgia) turned into something more sinister when, in 1880, he replaced D. A. Tolstoy at the Holy Synod and began to attend the Council of Ministers. He drafted the tsar's Manifesto of 1881, which postponed all reforms. Chicherin, who had been a close friend from the early 1860s, said that after 1881 Pobedonostsev became a dishonest, cynical manager of men.[8] Leroy-Beaulieu called him the Russian Torquemada, and it is impossible to dissociate him from the ideal type Dostoevsky depicted as the Grand Inquisitor; though there is no evidence that Dostoevsky made that connection, the two men had discussed the themes of *The Brothers Karamazov* together quite intensively.

By 1890 Pobedonostsev had decided that the distribution of Tolstoy's manuscripts could not be prevented, but that they were having a profoundly deleterious effect on Russian society, belief, and on the state. In 1901 he published the excommunication without getting the tsar's permission; and in January 1902, when Tolstoy was so ill, he plotted to have a priest join the Tolstoy household secretly, in order to proclaim afterwards that the great heretic had repented and rejoined the church on his death bed. All of this was just what Dostoevsky had described in his Grand Inquisitor legend, a prolonged and remorseless persecution of a man in search of Christianity's essence by a man in control of church apparatus.

Pobedonostsev never met Tolstoy, but the relationship between the two vividly corresponds to Dostoevsky's fable. Pobedonostsev admired *War and Peace* as a great intellectual achievement, and took a great interest in the development of Tolstoy's Christian anarchism; when he had all fifty copies of the first printing of *What I Believe* confiscated, he had two of them reserved for his own reading. After 1881, however, he decided that Tolstoy was a dangerous fanatic who would destroy the bases of the Russian state if he were not controlled.

When, despite his efforts, Tolstoy's letter of 1881 reached the tsar, Pobedonostsev denounced it. He alerted the censors always to Tolstoy's preparation of each new book or article. He got the play *The Power of Darkness* denied performance because it would persuade the city-educated that "the masses wallowed in sin" and foreigners that "Russia was a foul and decadent country."[9]

Gorki's major statements about Tolstoy come in the form of a brilliant essay in his *Reminiscences*. He often hated Tolstoy, he said, because the other man's "disproportionately over-grown individuality is a monstrous phenomenon, almost ugly, and there is in him something of Sviatogor, the bogatyr whom the earth cannot hold." Tolstoy's loneliness and nihilism "are beyond everyone else's"[10] and so is his pride. That is why he thinks he might be immortal, having already outreached everyone else in every other way.

Gorki implicitly dismissed the idea that Tolstoy was a Christian, by creed or by aspiration. He said that Tolstoy spoke of Christ very poorly, with "no enthusiasm, no feeling in his words, and no spark of real fire. I think he regards Christ as simple and deserving of pity. . . . It is as though he were uneasy; if Christ came to a Russian village, the girls might laugh at him."[11] Here we can surely say that it was Gorki rather than Tolstoy who was thinking these thoughts; he attributed them to the other man to save himself from the challenge represented by what Tolstoy *was* thinking. He insisted that Tolstoy had "very suspicious relations" with God: "they sometimes remind me of the relations of 'two bears in one den.'" [12] Tolstoy was like those Russian pilgrims who keep on the move all their lives, existing as "terribly homeless and alien to all men and things. The world is not for them, nor God either. They pray to him from habit, in their secret souls they hate him—why does he drive them over the earth, from one end to the other? What for? People are stumps, roots, stones on the path . . . but it is pleasant sometimes to surprise a man with one's own unlikeness to him, to show one's difference from him."[13]

Despite the imaginative and descriptive language, it is an ideological difference between the two men that appears in what Gorki says. He is speaking for "men"—normal men, who like to show they are similar to each other, who are comrades in their deepest identity, where all religious and other differences are lost. He is speaking against "souls"—who have to struggle against their bodies, and love God, and seek salvation by release from the human condition. Avvakum and Tikhon Zadonsky are the only exceptions he admits to the rule that "preachers" are cold men who teach others salvation doctrine in order that *they* may be left alone.[14] (This reproach to Tolstoy—and a similar one to Gandhi—is to be found again in Orwell's essays.)

Gorki gives some vivid descriptions of Tolstoy, which are strikingly like Merezhkovsky's. He had "wonderful hands—not beautiful, but knotted with swollen veins, and yet full of a singular expressiveness and the power of creativeness. Probably Leonardo da Vinci had hands like that. . . ."[15] Also, Tolstoy was like a Russian god—"not very majestic but perhaps more cunning than all the other gods."[16] (It is surely clear that the animating force behind Gorki's tangle of feelings is his dismay at seeing Tolstoy to be what he, Gorki, wanted to be—a great Promethean and Protean artist—but finding that that was not what Tolstoy wanted to be.) Seeing Tolstoy on the seashore—again seeing him as a nature-god—Gorki says: "I am not an orphan on the earth, so long as this man lives on it."[17] Tolstoy was his father, but a rejecting father.

But what has this imagery of bears and bogatyrs and river gods and immortality got to do with the man whom we see weeping daily over his humiliation by his family and his impotent yearning to disappear from Yasnaya Polyana and find a different identity? Tolstoy told E. J. Dillon in 1890 of two peasants who had come to consult him as a wise man, and turned and left when they saw his house, upbraiding him as a hypocrite. He said: "Look upon me as a finger-post at a cross roads, which points the way but does not follow it,"[18] and surely that was no more than the truth? Surely Tolstoy's behavior during the last thirty years of his life is striking in its weakness, not in its strength? Surely the contrast with Gandhi, who did what he wanted to do, makes that clear? And the fact that one cannot imagine Gorki's or Merezhkovsky's response to Gandhi tells one that they just refused to imagine the styles of personality and behavior which are entailed by a creed like the Sermon on the Mount. Gorki and Merezhkovsky make, of course, a queer pair of allies—being so naturally opposed in every other way; but allies, against radical religion, is just what they were. Gorki's *Reminiscences* are one of the world's more striking pieces of propaganda on behalf of secularism and hearty "normalness," as against religion and spiritual ascesis. Even today its palpably misleading arguments are followed by writers on Tolstoy like Edward Crankshaw and Isaiah Berlin.

In the political sphere, however, the prime witness has to be Lenin, and the encounter has to be hostile, though it is not only that. Between 1908 and 1911 Lenin wrote seven essays on Tolstoy, and together they constitute an important step in the development of Lenin's theory of the relation of art and ideas to social reality, his theory of "reflection."

The first essay, "Tolstoy as Mirror of the Russian Revolution" (referring to the events of 1905 primarily but also to the revolutionary movement), asks the crucial question of what causes the crying inconsistencies of Tolstoyism and which inadequacies and weaknesses of the revolution are reflected in it. Lenin divided Tolstoy in two: on the one side is the artistic genius who produced not only unrivaled pictures of Russian life, but also first-class productions of world literature; on the other side, the landowner playing the fool in Christ. On the one side, a remarkably powerful, direct, and sincere protest against the general lying and falsehood—on the other, the Tolstoyan, the worn-out hysteric called the Russian *intelligent*, who publicly beats his breast and says, "I am bad, I am disgusting, but I am trying to perfect myself morally . . . [;] on the other, the prophet of one of the most disgusting things in the world, namely religion, the attempt to replace the military-service priests with priests of moral conviction, that is, the cult of the most subtle and therefore most fatal clericalism."[19]

Tolstoy could not understand the working-class movement and its role in the fight for socialism, says Lenin. And his inconsistencies reflect those of the Russian revolutionary movement—they reflect the

resistance of the patriarchal peasants to the capitalism that was await-
ing them; and when he expressed the ideas and feelings of such
peasants, Tolstoy was a great writer. Tolstoy expressed both the boiling-
over hatred and the fatal softness of purpose of the Russian revolution; Tolstoyism is our historical sin.

But the essays can give a false impression of Lenin's basic attitude;
in them a major motive was Lenin's desire to appropriate Tolstoy
(suitably corrected) as an ally for the revolutionary movement—to
show that he could appreciate literature; at other times he essentially
shared Gorki's hostility to Tolstoy's late self-manifestations. And when
Gorki's essay came his way he read it at one sitting, and told B. Malkin:
"There you have Tolstoy to the life; no one has written about Tolstoy
so honourably and boldly."[20]

Perhaps the key word Lenin used about Tolstoy was "Eastern."
In his last essay on that subject he said that Tolstoy's essays on education and progress attacked the West in the name of the "unchanging
nations of the East." From the East Tolstoy took his asceticism, his
nonviolent resistance to evil, the deep notes of his pessimism, and his
conviction that everything material is unreal—his beliefs that the origin of everything is a spirit, and that man's duty is to save his soul.
Lenin says: "1905 was the beginning of the end of Eastern immo-
bility."[21] And the essay ends: "In our day, every attempt to idealize
Tolstoy's teaching, every justification and softening of his nonresistance, his appeal to the Spirit, his calls to moral self-perfection, his
doctrines of conscience and universal love, his preaching of asceticism
and quietism, etc., bring with them most immediate and profound
evil."[22] Thus, Lenin is to be counted among the anti-Tolstoyans, and,
indeed, as one of their leaders.

Gandhi's Enemies

The major anti-Gandhians were deeply involved in the actual death
of our other subject, Jinnah by raising the temperature of that communal violence that eventually claimed Gandhi's life as its climax, and
Savarkar via the actual assassins.

Of these assassins, Nathuram Godse was thirty-eight and his main
co-conspirator, Narayan Apte, was thirty-four, in 1948. Both were
Chitpavan brahmins (like Savarkar himself) and members of the Hindu
Rashtra Dal, founded by Savarkar in 1942 as the secret society at the
heart of the Rashtra Swayamsevak Sangh, which was the paramilitary

arm of the Hindu Mahasabha. All the members of the Hindu Rashtra Dal had to be Chitpavan brahmins and took an oath of loyalty to Savarkar as dictator.

Godse was puritanical, hypersensitive, afraid of women. He was, according to Manohar Malgonkar, brought up as a girl, to ward off evil fate, because his older brothers had all died. "Born in a devotional Brahmin family," he said in the dock, "I instinctively came to revere Hindu religion, Hindu history, and Hindu culture."[23] He was the theoretician among the conspirators, the intellectual. He was taught tailoring by American missionaries but long found no practical career for himself.

In 1929, however, his family moved to Ratnagiri, which was Savarkar's place of exile within India, once he returned from the Andamans. Godse made acquaintance with Savarkar and soon became his secretary. In 1937 the new Bombay government of congressmen (installed, to some degree, by Gandhi) released Savarkar from his sentence and he returned to Poona, with Godse still his secretary. Savarkar became twice president of the Hindu Mahasabha, whose membership was one million and whose doctrine was explicit Hindu imperialism. He taught that all but Hindus should leave India, that Gandhi had usurped Tilak's position and perverted his mission, that nonviolence was a coward's philosophy.

Apte had had plans to blow up Jinnah and his assembly in Delhi, to blow up a Pakistan ammunition train, and to lead a commando raid into Hyderabad. His violence was more multidirectional. In 1946 he already knew one of the other conspirators-to-be, Vishnu Karkare, an illiterate but political brahmin who ran a boarding house in Ahmednaggar. Karkare and six other Hindu Mahasabha workers had gone to Noakhali at the same time as Gandhi did. They, too, were rallying the Hindus there, with their own message of militant Hinduism, opening Vir Savarkar relief centers and wearing chain mail under their shirts for protection. Karkare had returned humiliated by the failure of their efforts, which were counteracted by Gandhi's, and talking of revenge.

The leaders of the group were clearly Godse and Apte. But it was in Savarkar that the idea of Hindu nationalism had been embodied and became infectious. He had hated Gandhi and fought Gandhism for forty years. The conspirators themselves were in one sense or another his agents, perhaps carrying out his orders or advice, probably carrying his blessing, certainly inspired by the hatred he had generated. But that hatred was a vortex swirling around Gandhi, and sustained by cross currents from Jinnah and Ambedkar and many other sources. For instance, Godse and Apte sought arms and got advice from Dada Maharaj, the head of an affluent Vaishnava sect in Bombay, the Pushtimarg Vaishnavites. But above all they visited Savarkar in his Bombay home, Savarkar Sadan (guarded by armed men day and night), immediately before the assassination.

Besides these men, we can look at some of Gandhi's new enemies, and listen to their testimony against him, and then turn to those of his disciples who tried to answer the call to nonviolence despite a heritage and training in violence.

In the first category we find Dr. B. R. Ambedkar (1891–1956), born a Maharashtrian Untouchable, educated at the expense of the Gaekwar of Baroda, trained as a lawyer in England, and a great enemy of Gandhism. When Ambedkar heard of the assassination in 1948, he was at first silent, and then said: "My real enemy has gone; thank goodness the eclipse is over now."[24] And in the 1957 B.B.C. program "Talking of Gandhiji," in which many contemporaries were interviewed, Ambedkar said: "I've a feeling I knew him better than most other people, because he had opened his real fangs to me, you see, and I could see the inside of the man."[25] This is the tone and the image (the wolf in sheep's clothing) that one guesses to lie behind the discretion of Gandhi's other enemies, like Savarkar and Jinnah. Its plausibility depends upon the audience's sharing the assumption that the surface of Gandhi's personality—the meekness—*could* not be true to the depths.

Ambedkar wanted to modernize India, and to destroy Hinduism. He often quoted Harold Laski, and was in sympathy with Laski's London School of Economics socialism. In his opposition to Hinduism, he supported the splitting off of Pakistan, and ordered his followers to convert to Buddhism. Temperamentally he admired, and aspired to be, the bold and manly and realistic leader. "Napoleon always charged from the front," he often said.[26] Treachery and deceit were the weapons of the weak, he said, and he ascribed them to Gandhi— the "most dishonest politician in Indian history," with his "pernicious saintly idiosyncracies. . . . If a man with God's name on his tongue and a sword under his armpit deserved to be called a Mahatma, then Gandhi was one."[27] He often called Gandhi a "humbug" and compared him with Uriah Heep; Ambedkar's rhetoric was in some ways nineteenth century. He compared Gandhi's attitude toward the Untouchables with Lincoln's toward the negroes, as expressed in his 1862 letter to Horace Greeley, where Lincoln said it was the Union he really cared about, not the slaves. In other words, it was the glorification of India that Gandhi really cared about, and his love for the

Untouchables and the rest of his protestations were propaganda. (This is of course what Jinnah felt, too.)

Ambedkar accused Gandhi of looking to the past and not the future; of not making Congress-membership conditional upon acceptance of Harijans; of failing in 1933 to keep a promise to fast to death if the Guruvayar Temple were not opened; of keeping the control of the Harijan Seva Sangh in the hands of caste Hindus; of treating the Muslim and Sikh minorities differently from the Untouchables, because they were the heirs to old ruling castes; and of pretending that there were no minorities in India. We must remember the pressure put upon Ambedkar by Gandhi's 1932 fast, which Ambedkar described as "foul and filthy," "vile and wicked."[28] At that time he received letters written in blood, threatening his life if he did not yield or compromise with Gandhi.

But, finally, what strikes one most in his testimony is the intensity of hatred he directed at the other man, which helps us to understand the situation in which Gandhi lived and died—the bubble of adoration and service, transparent and lit up to attract everyone's attention, while outside it the storms of jealousy and hatred lashed towards him. Ambedkar wrote: "Is Gandhi a Mahatma? I am sick of this question. There are two reasons why this question annoys me. Firstly, I hate all the Mahatmas, and firmly believe that they should be done away with . . . because they try to perpetuate blind faith in place of intelligence and reason."[29]

Amongst Congress rivals, the most striking new figure was Subhas Chandra Bose (1897–1945). Bose was born into the Kayastha caste in Bengal—the caste which ran Calcutta and had grown rich on British trade. His father was a lawyer and a social reformer, his mother "a Hindu wife and mother"; in other words, he had the same sort of family background as Nehru. He grew up an introverted rebel against his family's Edwardian and seigneurial style; he decided to become a sanyasi statesman, and cut everything else out of his life.

He went to Cambridge in 1918 to prepare himself for the Indian Civil Service examinations, and became very English in style. In 1921 he began to write to C. R. Das, offering to devote himself to the nationalist cause, and recommending that Congress keep a research staff. He met Gandhi at this time, but did not like what he saw, although he always admired Gandhi's power to arouse the masses.

In 1928 he became president of the All-India Trade Union Congress, and at the Congress meeting in Calcutta led a procession accompanying President Motilal Nehru in a triumphal chariot, Bose wearing the semimilitary uniform of his Youth Movement, the members of which later demonstrated with black flags against Gandhi. By 1930 he was mayor of Calcutta. He followed the model of the nineteenth-century Italian independence movement, but with the semimilitarist style also of contemporary fascism in Italy and Germany.

The issues between him and Gandhi always included violence, and generally political "realism" or "unscrupulousness." In April 1939 Gandhi wrote Bose: "I wholly dissent from your view that the country has never been so nonviolent as now. I smell violence in the air I breathe. . . . We seem to differ as to the amount of corruption in Congress. My impression is that it is on the increase. I have been pleading in the past many months for a thorough scrutiny."[30]

Arrested in July 1940, Bose was released in November when he threatened to go on hunger strike. In January 1941 he disappeared and made his way to Germany, where he gave broadcasts over Radio Berlin in April 1942. He then left Europe by German submarine, and made his way to Japanese-held Singapore. There he formed the Indian National Army from units of Indians that had surrendered with the rest of the British army in Southeast Asia. The Indian National Army fought in Burma, and was intended to lead an invasion of India itself, but the defeat of the Axis powers frustrated that scheme. Bose himself died with his hopes, in 1945.

What he stood for may be summed up as efficiency, in the party and in the state. He was not a great orator, but was a good organizer and disciplinarian, just as in the world of the mind he was efficient but not profound. He admired the German army and liked to see men, in or out of uniform, looking spruce and well-turned-out. He clearly had some of the potential to become a dictator like his con-temporaries in Europe, and in his conflict with Gandhi, we see how the latter might have met the challenge of, for instance, Mussolini.

Turning now to Gandhi's disciples, there is a great variety of types to be found among them, as can be seen merely by juxtaposing such names as Rajendra Prasad with Sardar Patel, Sarojini Naidu with Mira Behn, Birla with Vinoba, or Rajagopalachari with Bhansali. One of the most remarkable of Gandhi's skills was his ability to work with all of them—to "get work from them," as he put it. In "Gandhi's Lieutenants—Varieties of Followership" Suzanne Hoeber Rudolph compares Bajaj and Birla, Nehru and Patel, and Gandhi's relations with each. All except Patel were sons to Gandhi, she says. Even with Patel, Gandhi concerned himself with the health, education, and so on, of his children. Patel often wished Gandhi would leave him alone, especially on Hindu-Muslim matters, but Gandhi insisted on intimacy, and built up an important relationship thereby. His knack for matching men with projects was also shown in the way he involved Birla in Harijan matters.

Among the Indian disciples prominent in this period, perhaps the most striking was Abdul Ghaffar Khan, the Frontier Gandhi. Born into a wealthy Pathan family in 1890, he attended a mission school and was inspired by its teacher, the reverend Wigram, to dedicate his life to serving the people. When he heard of Gandhi's work for Khilafat, he transferred his devotion to him. Though the Pathans were the very epitome of a martial race, of Kipling's India, Abdul Ghaffar Khan founded the Khudai Khitmagar, the Servants of God, among them, and practiced nonviolence.

In May and again in October/November of 1938, Gandhi toured the North-West Frontier Province with Abdul Gaffar Khan. This province was 38,000 square miles, and included settled districts, a tribal belt, and an independent territory. The population was mostly Pathan, including the Afridis, a tribe famous for its cruelty, which had been the preserve of military and political officers. There had been trouble there in 1924, 1927, and 1930. Gandhi would have liked to have tested the efficacy of satyagraha by settling in that province if the viceroy would have let him.

The Khan brothers had launched their Gandhian movement of Khudai Khitmagars in 1930. The elder brother had gone to London to study medicine, returning in 1920, and Abdul would have liked to have gone there to study engineering, but his mother objected. He turned his attention to politics. He was jailed more than once in 1919, and became a leader of the Khilafat movement, founding national schools. In 1921, having been given a three-year jail sentence, he began teaching religion in jail. He met Gandhi at the 1931 Congress, and in 1934 he came to stay at Wardha, and gave his daughter to Mira Behn to educate.

Two other of the late disciples can be aligned with Abdul Ghaffar Khan, Prithvi Singh and Balvantsimha, inasmuch as they were all three by birth and temperament men of violence, who submitted themselves to Gandhi. Prithvi Singh developed revolutionary ideas in Canada before the Great War, and in 1914 led a band of revolutionaries back to India; he received a life sentence for his part in the Lahore Conspiracy Case in 1915, and he began to serve it in the Andamans, but he escaped in 1922. For the next fifteen years he lived in hiding. A powerfully built man, he taught gymnastics and trained young revolutionaries. Converted to nonviolence, he came to Gandhi on 18 April

1938, entrusting him with his fate. Gandhi wrote to his district magistrate, offering him back to justice but also accepting responsibility for him if he were set free. He had in fact to go to jail again, where he occupied himself at the spinning wheel for a year, and thereafter played a prominent part in the Gandhian movement for a time. (Mira Behn proposed marriage to him, but he was not willing.)

Balvantsimha first heard of Gandhi while in the army at Aden during the First World War. He wrote of when he and his friends heard of the Amritsar massacre: "We therefore discussed among ourselves the possibility of our returning to India by land, after massacring our few British officers."[31] In 1921 he began to read Gandhi's newspapers, and in 1928 he made his way to him, to ask "What should a man do for his spiritual development?" By his own account, he was a harsh man, full of self-hatred and self-love, but "My relations with Bapu were like those of a child with his mother."[32] When a police inspector pounced on him like a wildcat, seized his throat, and sat on his chest, showering obscenities on him, Balvantsimha laughed, he says, reciting Gandhi's name in his mind. He looked after the cows at Sevagram, and often threatened to leave for the jungle, angry at some pettiness or some insult. Gandhi treated him humorously; when Balvantsimha protested about something in a letter "as a representative of the cow," Gandhi replied (in December 1940), "I have heard the roar of the lion and the wail of the cow."[33] This was a reference to the name "simha," which means lion. Balvantsimha was not as public a figure as Prithvi Singh, but within the ashram he was a vivid symbol of Gandhi's power to subdue psychological types opposite to himself.

Like Tolstoy in the equivalent period, Gandhi discussed Marx and the difference between violent and nonviolent revolution. He told Pyarelal in August 1942: "I think I could have written Marx better than Marx, provided, of course, I had his scholarship, which I do not have. He has the knack of making simple things appear difficult."[34] Marxism, he said, is not a science but a tool, used to produce a certain effect. When Pyarelal said that Gandhi's stress on hand-work was like the Marxists', Gandhi said no, because Marx wanted to abolish the hand in favor of the machine. Thinking of the great experiment in Russia, in 1944, he said: "What a great difference between that experiment and our spinning wheel . . . as different from each other as East from West or North from South."[35] Gandhi insisted, against Marxism, on the historical importance of individuals, such as Hitler. But above all, he wrote, "the difference between violence and nonviolence is fundamental. It cuts at the very root of the Marxist theory. If you alter the foundation the whole superstructure will have to be changed."[36] All this is essentially what Tolstoy had said.

The divergence of the two forms of radicalism was conscious, and complete. Tolstoy and Gandhi offered a dissent from the prevailing mode of change as profound as their dissent from the status quo.

Epilogue

When did I first get interested in this subject? Of the many moments I might cite, perhaps the closest to a tap on the shoulder and a beckon was the half hour when I first heard of Gandhi's death. I was twenty, in my last year of studying English at Cambridge. I had gone to look at a notable church—I think it was the one in St. Neots—and I read the news when I went for a cup of coffee afterwards.

I was sitting next to the window in one of those empty and echoing rooms so frequently found in English pubs and restaurants, with a wilderness of tables and shiny cutlery—a stage-set for Angst. To be honest, I don't remember if the news came in the form of a broadcast or in the morning's paper which I hadn't seen before setting off. And I don't recall what I thought or felt about Gandhi, but the news added a strong resonance to my feelings about myself. I was alone and feeling lonely—feeling self-conscious about my church-going.

Church-going was such an important thing then, such a typical thing, such a clue, to people like me—who were quite a number, as Philip Larkin's poem with that title shows. "Another church: matting seats and stone, / And little books: sprawlings of flowers, cut / For Sunday, brownish now . . . " and so on. "The same neat organ; / And a tense, musty, unignorable silence." There were so many like Larkin and me, sent out on our mission by kind and clever schoolmasters—our mission of self-alienation. We were sent out, to churches and other such places, to look for something other than the life around us—other than and better than the vacation office job, the football game, the Saturday dance, or our Basic Training. We were looking for something nobler but less massive, finer but less threatening, something implicitly transparent. And unfortunately we knew we were supposed to welcome danger and carnality; earlier teachers had taught us that, so our values were undermined in advance. It has taken these thirty-seven years to demonstrate that what we called "threatening" was really threatening.

I mean that our church-going was in the name of culture, of appreciating and discriminating the colors of past life; Early English, Perpendicular, St. Thomas Aquinas, *Murder in the Cathedral*. Of course, if we and those teachers had had the courage of our convictions ("convictions") we would have been looking for something beyond the stonework, expecting to find something behind the altar, through the rose window. We *were* looking for it, but without expecting to find it; our most actual conviction, our best intelligence, told us that the church was empty. "Grass, weedy pavement, brambles, buttress, sky / A shape less recognizable each week, / A purpose more obscure." Presence and substance we knew we must seek elsewhere, in bodies and personal relations, in "life itself," as Tolstoy amongst others told us.

It happened that I had in those years a close friend who was what Tolstoy must have been like—what he is like in his novels: a high-spirited, high-colored, excitable person; with many gifts but confused about his convictions, confused about himself, and solving his uncertainties by forwarding his excitement, flourishing his physical presence—the brightening eye, the flushing cheek, the stammering voice; exploiting his naïveté, rooting reality in the shared sensation of physical process. Knowing him, I knew the world of Tolstoy in advance, and barely noticed the Russian names. I was, I knew even then, in love with him, and that was another part of the loneliness. He was, of course, another church-goer.

As for Gandhi, I didn't know much about him, and I had no convictions about nonviolence. How could I imagine there ought not to be a war when there so obviously was one? Where would I find the force to deny such an overwhelming fact? But the frail, bowed figure, the wire-rimmed glasses, the loincloth, and the spinning wheel, stayed with me on the bus back to Cambridge; the upper deck of a country bus, again empty and echoing. The simplicity of his image, the sobriety and despatch of the murder itself, the lack of tanks and bombs, the absence of goose-stepping Nazis or liberating Americans, both seemed familiar, and I felt at ease with them. The bus was shivering and creaking on my behalf, and I was feeling myself too small, too rabbitty, for any of the destinies I would have wanted. Gandhi and his murder associated themselves with that perception but calmed it; and I now see that that was very appropriate. For he, too—for instance, in his London years—knew himself as a lonely and timid person who recoiled from crowds and fights and big bangs. But he went on to conquer the realms of danger for the rest of us, so he is our patron saint.

So that was the call, thirty-seven years ago. But what matters is the landscape now, the lifescape of the future, if there is to be one.

We all know that Shiva is now dancing the Tandava, the most famous of his hundred and eight dances, in which the angry god, surrounded by his drunken attendants, beats out the wild rhythm which jars apart the world's joints and smashes the ground from under us. Muriel Lester described Gandhi's ashram as the burning focus of a historical era, where the Place, the Time, and the Man of Destiny came together. "And as a result our poor old earth was given another reprieve, another chance to get saved from self-destruction." The Man of Destiny is a modern notion, full of the drama and excitement of historicism. The older notion was the one Leskov made use of, the just men for whose sake God would save the world. We could rely more quietly on Tolstoy and Gandhi as our two just men, but we have lost the providential world-view which could make that notion real to us.

Tolstoy and Gandhi represent the purest form of "religious radicalism." In that combination, the term *radical* can refer to the alliance between religion and politically radical elements in a creed or movement, and this certainly applies to them. But it can also refer—and this is more important in their case—to a radically religious, an antipolitical and anticultural, element. They both repudiated the term *anarchist* on occasion, claiming *religious* as the only adjective for what they were preaching. But both, on other occasions, accepted *anarchist*, which is indeed the only political term that fits them even roughly. They wanted to diminish the importance of state authority, with all its allies, like big business, big cities, big banks, and big bangs; high explosives, high culture, tall buildings; orchestras, armies, and novels. Both knew very well out of how widespread and valuable human propensities all these things developed, and how unlikely was their renunciation. But they felt it their calling to tell men that they should renounce them, could renounce them, and must renounce them or die.

This is a teaching directed against common sense, against probability, against our knowledge of what human nature is and what our history has been. Tolstoy and Gandhi declared that all that knowledge was illusory—that the way men had been did not illustrate any laws of nature but was the result of feebleness and failure. This is also, by the same token, a teaching that recommends itself to a few people only—to those who, for good or bad reasons, doubt the way of the world and recognize themselves (or everybody else) as misfits. It recommends itself only to a few; and yet offers itself to all. It promises salvation to the human race as a whole; and yet addresses only those who will renounce normality—the gratification of normal appetites and normal ambitions. Most men must hear such an appeal as addressed to others, not themselves. This was true even in the case of Gandhi's mass movement, and even of such intimates of his as Nehru. Because Gandhi's doctrine was radically religious, it was politically nonsense, and was quietly ignored. It did not even address itself to men as men.

Nevertheless, he and Tolstoy have a potentially large constituency. I don't mean only the "sick, aged, and infirm" (though these are indeed in that constituency), but some of the most gifted individuals among the ruling classes and countries, and whole oppressed classes and tribes—all those who will not engage in conquest and domination, and only endure it and acquiesce in it unwillingly. For "political manhood" is a matter of conquest and domination; to become a man is to join those who engage in that, at least by delegation and in imagination. *Men* have been taken to be or to represent humanity as a whole. To suggest that some other group could replace them goes against common sense; but not beyond the bounds of possibility; and that is the direction in which Tolstoy and Gandhi point. Thus, they are the heroes and martyrs of radical religion at its purest, and if the political leaders of the West are to understand the world opposition they meet—and if that opposition is to understand itself—they will have to be studied.

We all now stand at a crossroads. And if we cannot make a right-angled turn, by an act of faith, we stand on the edge of a precipice. It is the moment before we fall—before *they* fall, the missiles. For this moment we can look both ways, both forwards and down into the blinding chasm of annihilation, and backwards, along the stretched out march of invention and creativity that has brought us to where we are. It is not literal annihilation that we expect, but it seems likely to be cultural annihilation. There will probably be no continuity between us and whatever comes after. There will be no more books; the authorial voice, which we have passed from one to another, will finally fall silent.

It is a dizzying moment, and in its way exhilarating. We should at least take this last chance to pay tribute to the two men who could have saved us, the two men in whom the holy spirit was manifest to us. The holy spirit did not transform them empirically; they remained angry, despotic, vacillating, at times ugly; but if those are the features we see when we look at them—if we prefer Sonia Tolstoy and Harilal Gandhi to represent us—we shall have failed to use the one opportunity we have left, failed to redeem this moment, too.

Notes

Chapter I

1. Leo Tolstoy, *The Kingdom of God is Within You*, trans. Leo Wiener, 286.
2. Ibid., 291.
3. Ibid., 293.
4. J. H. Billington, *Fire in the Minds of Men*, 3.
5. Ibid., 5.
6. Leo Tolstoy, *Collected Works* 19:310.
7. Ibid., 20:17.
8. J. F. Baddeley, *Russia, Mongolia, China*, lxix, lxxiii.
9. Gandhi, *Collected Works* 39:203.
10. Ibid., 230.
11. Ibid., 497.
12. C. Brontë, *Jane Eyre*, 454–55.
13. Leo Tolstoy, *Tolstoy's Love Letters*, 29.
14. Ibid., 26.
15. Ibid., 51.
16. Ibid., 56.
17. Leo Tolstoy, *Letters of Tolstoy and Alexandra Tolstoy*, 107.
18. Gandhi, *Collected Works* 4:112–13.
19. Ibid., 7:7–8.
20. Ibid., 6:358.
21. Ibid., 5:476–77.
22. Ibid., 469–70.
23. Ibid., 6:480–81.
24. Ibid., 38:275.
25. K. Marx, *On Colonialism*, 41.
26. Ibid., 40.
27. J. Nehru, *The Discovery of India*, 42.
28. Ibid., 72.
29. F. Nietzsche, *On the Genealogy of Morals*, 19.
30. Leo Tolstoy, *On Life*, trans. A. Maude, 71.
31. N. Weisbein, *L'Evolution Réligieuse de Tolstoi*, 408.
32. A. Tolstoy, *Tolstoy, a Life of my Father*, 285.
33. Gandhi, *Collected Works* 48:434.

34. D. G. Tendulkar, *The Mahatma* 3:110.
35. *Young India*, 31 Oct. 1924.
36. Gandhi, *My Dear Child*, 22.
37. V. Bhave, *The Steadfast Wisdom*, 18.
38. Tolstoy, *Collected Works* 20:242.
39. Gandhi, *Collected Works* 51:115.
40. Tolstoy, *Collected Works* 20:242.

Chapter II

1. W. H. Parker, *An Historical Geography of Russia*, 27–28.
2. J. Morris, *Pax Britannica*.
3. J. H. Billington, *The Icon and the Axe*.
4. V. T. Bill, *The Forgotten Class*, 216.
5. G. M. Carstairs, *The Twice Born*.
6. Gandhi, *Collected Works* 5:6, 31.
7. A. Herzen, *My Past and Thoughts*, 1578.
8. Bill, 64.
9. S. F. Starr, *Decentralization and Self-Government in Russia 1830–1870*, 12–15.
10. Tolstoy, *Tolstoy's Letters*, 106.
11. Ibid., 110.
12. F. Venturi, *The Roots of Revolution*, 136.
13. E. C. Thaden, *Conservative Nationalism*.
14. Ibid., 69.
15. R. A. Huttenback, *Racism and Empire*, 14–15.
16. R. Orme, *History of the Military Transactions of the British Nation in Indostan* 1:5–6.
17. J. D. Hunt, *Gandhi in London*, 49.
18. Gandhi, *Collected Works* 16:358.
19. Ibid., 359.
20. Ibid., 5:326.
21. Morris, 41.
22. Gandhi, *Collected Works* 48:134.
23. Ibid., 33:41.
24. H. Tinker, *A New System of Slavery*.
25. Ibid., xiv.
26. Ibid., 163.
27. Ibid., 113.
28. Ibid., 178.
29. G. D. Bearce, *British Attitudes Towards India 1784–1858*, 7.
30. Ibid., 160.
31. Ibid., 162.
32. Ibid., 163.
33. Ibid., 180.
34. Ibid., 187.
35. Ibid., 184.
36. Quoted by E. Morton in *The Women in Gandhi's Life*, 285.
37. Quoted by L. Collins and D. LaPierre in *Freedom at Midnight*, 70.

38. Ibid.
39. Ibid., 72.
40. Ibid., 73.
41. Ibid., 68.
42. N. Weisbein, 287.
43. Ibid., 364.
44. D. Gillard, *The Struggle for Asia 1828–1914*, 118.
45. J. F. Baddeley, *The Russian Conquest of the Caucasus*, xxxviii.
46. Ibid., 97.
47. Gillard, 2, 4.

Chapter III

1. E. J. Simmons, *Pushkin*, 7.
2. T. Wolff, ed., *Pushkin on Literature*, 63.
3. A. Yarmolinsky, ed., *Works of Pushkin*, 646.
4. S. Aksakov, *Tales of Childhood*, 264, 280.
5. Simmons, 7.
6. P. Miliukov, *Outlines of Russian Culture*, 33.
7. R. E. Matlaw, *Belinsky, Chernyshevsky, Dobroliubov*, 12.
8. R. Hingley, *Russian Writers and Society*.
9. R. Gopal, *How India Struggled for Freedom*, 106.
10. S. Wolpert, *Tilak and Gokhale*, 45.
11. Ibid., 86.
12. Ibid., 291.
13. Gandhi, *Collected Works* 16:491.
14. *Indian Opinion* 8:418.
15. L. L. Rai, *Autobiographical Writings* 1:139.
16. Ibid., 78.
17. G. M. Birla, *In the Shadow of the Mahatma*, 20.
18. Rai, 203.
19. J. H. Broomfield, *Elite Conflict in a Plural Society*.

Chapter IV

1. C. J. Hogarth and A. Simes, trans., *Tolstoy's Diaries 1847–1853*, 37.
2. R. Fülöp-Miller, ed., *Tolstoy: New Light on his Life and Genius*, 55–57.
3. Tolstoy, *Collected Works* 19:76.
4. Leo Tolstoy, *Childhood, Boyhood, Youth*, 67.
5. Leo Tolstoy, *The Portable Tolstoy*, 457.
6. Tolstoy, *Collected Works* 1:398.
7. P. Biriukov, *Leo Tolstoy: His Life and Work* 1:155.
8. V. Shklovsky, *Leo Tolstoy*, 100.
9. Biriukov, 56.

10. Quoted in J. F. Baddeley, *The Russian Conquest of the Caucasus*.
11. Fülöp-Miller, 58.
12. E. J. Simmons, *Leo Tolstoy* (1973), 32.
13. E. Crankshaw, *The Shadow of the Winter Palace*, 112.
14. Bestuzhev-Marlinsky, *Ammalet Bek*, quoted in L. Kelley, *Lermontov*, 77.
15. Shklovsky, 422.
16. Baddeley, 34.
17. J. Morris, *Pax Britannica*, 115.
18. Ibid., 46.
19. J. Bowle, *The Imperial Achievement*, 301–2.
20. Ibid., 296.
21. E. Maitland, *The Life of Anna Kingsford* 1:37.
22. A. Kingsford and E. Maitland, *The Perfect Way*, iii–iv.
23. Ibid.
24. Ibid., 23.
25. Ibid., 54.
26. E. Carpenter, *My Days and Dreams*, 243.

Chapter V

1. J. T. Baker, *St. Petersburg: Industrialization and Change*, 1.
2. Ibid., 9.
3. T. Szamuely, *The Russian Tradition*, 169.
4. Ibid., 241.
5. Ibid., 166.
6. N. Riasanovsky, *The History of Russia*, 483.
7. A. Vucinich, *Science in Russian Culture* 2:18.
8. Szamuely, 229.
9. A. Gleason, *Young Russia*, 102.
10. Ibid., 297.
11. F. Dostoevsky, *Short Novels*, 132.
12. Leo Tolstoy, *Anna Karenina*, trans. D. Magarshak, 160.
13. Ibid., 261.
14. Leo Tolstoy, *War and Peace*, trans. R. Edmonds, 401.
15. Tolstoy, *Tolstoy's Letters*, 60.
16. A. Tolstoy, *Tolstoy, a Life of my Father*, 83.
17. E. J. Simmons, *Leo Tolstoy* (1973), 42.
18. Tolstoy, *Collected Works* 19:50.
19. L. Wiener, ed., *Tolstoy's Works* 3:250.
20. Tolstoy, *Collected Works* 19:50.
21. B. Eikhenbaum, *Lev Tolstoy* 1:132.
22. Ibid., 24.
23. Gandhi, *Satyagraha in South Africa*, 3.
24. J. Doke, *M. K. Gandhi*, 6.
25. C. W. DeKiewiet, *History of South Africa*, 154–55.
26. Quoted in Pyarelal, *Mahatma Gandhi: the Early Phase* 1:353.
27. "South Africa," in *Encyclopaedia Britannica* (1911), 25.

28. Gandhi, *Collected Works* 5:4.
29. Ibid., 40.
30. Ibid., 3:347.
31. Ibid., 355.
32. Ibid., 4:1.
33. Ibid., 5:167.
34. Gandhi, *Satyagraha in South Africa*, 15.
35. Ibid., 71.
36. Ibid.
37. Ibid., 33.
38. R. Gopal, *How India Struggled for Freedom*, 42.
39. Ibid., 64.
40. S. Roy, *The Restless Brahmin*, 97.
41. Ibid.
42. Ibid., 123.
43. Ibid., 100.
44. Ibid., 103.
45. Ibid., 115.

Chapter VI

1. B. Eikhenbaum, *Tolstoy in the Sixties*, xiv–xv.
2. Tolstoy, *Collected Works* 19:167.
3. Ibid., 165.
4. Ibid., 166.
5. Tolstoy, *Tolstoy's Letters*, 115–16.
6. Ibid., 96.
7. H. Troyat, *Tolstoy*, 172.
8. John Keats, *Letters of John Keats*, 48.
9. Ibid., 226.
10. Tolstoy, *Tolstoy's Letters*, 182.
11. Eikhenbaum, 66.
12. Ibid., 69.
13. Leo Tolstoy, *Tolstoy on Education*, 198.
14. Ibid.
15. Ibid., 200.
16. G. Woodcock, *Who Killed the British Empire?* 159.
17. Gandhi, *Collected Works* 1:159.
18. Ibid., 2:120–21.
19. Ibid., 38.
20. Ibid., 3:223.
21. P. A. Sergeenko, *Tolstoy in the Memory of his Contemporaries*, 13–14.
22. D. Brogan, *Proudhon*, 10.
23. Ibid., 11.
24. E. Schuyler, *Selected Essays*, 274.
25. Eikhenbaum, 73.
26. Gandhi, *Collected Works* 13:204.

27. Gandhi, *Satyagraha in South Africa*, 50.
28. S. Koss, *Nonconformity in Modern British Politics*, 73.
29. Ibid.
30. M. Watts, *The Dissenters* 1:4.
31. Ibid., 3.
32. Koss, 71–73.

Chapter VII

1. K. Mashruwala, *Gandhi and Marx*, 15.
2. C. J. S. Sprigge, *Karl Marx*, 28.
3. F. J. Raddatz, *Karl Marx: A Critical Biography*, 18.
4. I. Berlin, *Karl Marx: His Life and Environment*, 24.
5. Ibid., 2, 7, 119.
6. D. McLellan, *Karl Marx: His Life and Thought*, 299.
7. Ibid., 53.
8. Berlin, 78.
9. McLellan, 177.
10. Berlin, 119.
11. Raddatz, 34.
12. R. Fülöp-Miller, *Lenin and Gandhi*, vii.
13. Ibid., viii.
14. R. H. W. Theen, *Lenin*, 45.
15. Ibid., 59–60.
16. B. D. Wolfe, *Three Who Made a Revolution*, 150–51.
17. Raddatz, 229.
18. Ibid., 147.
19. Berlin, 182.
20. K. Marx, *Capital*, trans. E. Paul and C. Paul, 1:113.
21. Ibid., trans. B. Fowkes, 1:503.
22. Raddatz, 273.
23. Szamuely, 19.
24. McLellan, 203.
25. Ibid., 214.
26. Ibid., 258.
27. D. R. Gandy, *Marx and History*, 20.
28. Sprigge, 64.
29. McLellan, 270.
30. Raddatz, 70.
31. McLellan, 331.
32. "Lenin," *Encyclopaedia Britannica*, 15th ed., 10:794.
33. Leo Tolstoy, *Recollections and Essays*, 183.
34. C. M. Breitburg, ed., *V. I. Lenin o L. N. Tolstom*, 18.
35. J. Nehru, *Glimpses of World History*, 643.
36. Ibid., 547.
37. Ibid., 645.

Chapter VIII

1. I. Spector and M. Spector, *Readings in Russian History and Culture*, 150.
2. T. Masaryk, *The Spirit of Russia*, 5.
3. Ibid., 4.
4. N. Weisbein, *L'Evolution Réligieuse De Tolstoi*, 17.
5. P. Biriukov, *Leo Tolstoy: His Life and Work*, 91.
6. G. P. Fedotov, *The Russian Religious Mind*, 94.
7. N. Zernov, *Three Russian Prophets*, 37.
8. Gandhi, *Autobiography* (1960), 19–21.
9. Prabudas Gandhi, *My Childhood with Gandhiji*, 17.
10. H. Spodek, "On the Origins of Gandhi's Political Methodology: the Heritage of Kathiawad and Gujarat," *Journal of Asian Studies* 30 (Feb. 1971): 361–72.
11. Gandhi, *Collected Works* 12:92.
12. Ibid., 126.
13. Ibid., 127.
14. G. Freeze, *The Russian Levites*, 218.
15. V. T. Bill, *The Forgotten Class*, 69.
16. Freeze, vii.
17. T. Szamuely, *The Russian Tradition*, 168.
18. Gandhi, *Collected Works* 53:258.
19. Ibid., 455.
20. Ibid., 56:47.
21. Ibid., 59:62.
22. Ibid., 58:219.
23. Ibid., 19:174.
24. Ibid., 175.
25. Quoted in B. Eikhenbaum, *Tolstoy in the Sixties*, 36.
26. Ibid., 32.
27. Ibid., 36.
28. Ibid., 37.
29. Ibid., 44.
30. D. R. Dudley, *History of Cynicism From Diogenes to the Sixth Century A.D.*, 170.
31. G. Florovsky, *Christianity and Culture*, 84.
32. Ibid., 88.
33. Dudley, 207.
34. M. Detienne, *Dionysos Slain*, 24.
35. Ibid.
36. G. Bataille, *Eroticism*, 47–48.
37. Ibid., 74.

Chapter IX

1. B. Eikhenbaum, *Tolstoy in the Sixties*, 13.
2. Ibid., 16.
3. Ibid., 17.

4. Efim Etkind, "Leo Tolstoy and Afanasy Fet," *Russia 4* 1:980.
5. Ibid.
6. P. Biriukov, *Leo Tolstoy: His Life and Work* 1:281.
7. Gandhi, *Satyagraha in South Africa*, 250.
8. L. Gerstein, *Nikolai Strakhov*, 4.
9. Tolstoy, *Tolstoy's Letters*, 280.
10. Ibid., 336.
11. D. Fanger, *Dostoevsky and Romantic Realism*, 133.
12. Durga Das, *India from Curzon to Nehru and After*, 76.
13. A. Smedley, *Battle Hymn of China*, 14.
14. Some words in the manuscript are hard to read.
15. Letters in the National Archives in Delhi by Sarojini Naidu.
16. P. Sengupta, *Sarojini Naidu*, 79.
17. Ibid., 338.
18. Gandhi, *Collected Works* 51:71.
19. Smedley, 12.
20. Ibid., 15, 23.
21. Ibid., 13–14.
22. Ibid., 12.
23. B. N. Pandey, *Nehru*, 140.
24. S. Roy, *The Restless Brahmin*, 94.

Chapter X

1. Tolstoy, *Tolstoy's Letters*, 236.
2. S. Tolstoy, *Diary of Tolstoy's Wife*, 67.
3. Leo Tolstoy, *Journal of Leo Tolstoy*, 58.
4. V. Shklovsky, *Leo Tolstoy*, 411.
5. M. Raeff, "Pugachev's Rebellion," in *Preconditions of Revolution in Early Modern Europe*, ed. R. Forster and Jack P. Green, 181.
6. S. Aksakov, *A Russian Gentleman*, 8.
7. Ibid., 14.
8. Gandhi, *Collected Works* 10:308.
9. Gandhi, *Satyagraha in South Africa*, 241.
10. Ibid., 244.
11. Sir Percy Fitzpatrick was a leader of the Progressive party and the author of several books about South Africa.
12. Gandhi, *Collected Works* 12:381.
13. Gandhi, *Satyagraha in South Africa*, 246.
14. Ibid., 247.
15. Gandhi, *Collected Works* 11:124.
16. Ibid., 12:23.
17. Ibid., 60:86.
18. Madan C. Gandhi, *Gandhian Aesthetics*, 61.
19. Gandhi, *Collected Works* 59:9.
20. Ibid., 296.
21. D. Lessing, *Going Home*, 19.

22. Ibid.
23. F. Venturi, *The Roots of Revolution,* 113.
24. N. K. Bose, *Lectures on Gandhism,* 112.
25. D. G. Tendulkar, *The Mahatma* 5:131.
26. Ibid., 2:85.
27. Gandhi, *Collected Works* 53:461.
28. Ibid., 36:263.
29. Ibid., 279.
30. Ibid., 297.
31. N. K. Bose, *My Days with Gandhi,* 1–2.
32. Pyarelal, *The Last Phase,* 45.
33. Leo Tolstoy, *Church and State,* 149–50.

Chapter XI

1. V. V. Zenkovsky, *History of Russian Philosophy* 1:175.
2. Ibid., 174.
3. Ibid., 175.
4. J. Zeldin, "A Reevaluation of Gogol's *Selected Passages,*" *Russian Review* 37 (Oct. 1968): 425–26.
5. Ibid., 426.
6. Volume 2 of Leskov's *Collected Works* (1889/90) was entitled *Pravedniki,* The Just Men.
7. W. B. Edgerton, "Leskov and Tolstoy: Two Literary Heretics," *American Slavic and East European Review* (Dec. 1953): 525.
8. S. L. Frank, *A Solovyov Anthology,* 9.
9. Ibid., 12.
10. Ibid., 15.
11. Ibid., 16.
12. Ibid., 154.
13. Ibid., 230.
14. A. Vucinich, *Science in Russian Culture,* 22.
15. J. H. Billington, *The Icon and the Axe,* 204.
16. Ibid., 402.
17. Gandhi, *Collected Works* 42:316–17.
18. J. Nehru, *Towards Freedom,* 21.
19. B. R. Nanda, *The Nehrus,* 62.
20. J. Nehru, *A Bunch of Old Letters,* 17.
21. Nehru, *Towards Freedom,* 53.
22. M. Saksena, *Motilal Nehru,* 7.
23. L. Fischer, *Gandhi: His Life and Message for the World,* 92.
24. Gandhi, *Collected Works* 53:504–5.
25. Ibid., 310.
26. Saksena, 103.
27. J. Nehru, *Glimpses of World History,* 13.
28. Ibid., 477.
29. *Harijan,* 15 March 1952.

30. Ibid.
31. Fischer, 92.
32. M. Prasad, *A Gandhian Patriarch*, 48.
33. Gandhi, *Collected Works* 20:501.
34. N. D. Parikh, *Mahadev Desai's Early Life*.
35. M. Felton, *I Meet Rajaji*.
36. Ibid., 70.
37. Ibid., 138.
38. S. R. S. Radhakrishnan, *Vinoba and his Mission*, 14.
39. *Vinoba on Gandhi*, ed. K. Shah, ix.
40. Ibid., 3.
41. Ibid., 8.
42. *Gandhi Marg* 2:64.
43. Gandhi, *Collected Works* 14:188.

Chapter XII

1. Tolstoy, *Collected Works* 13:188.
2. W. B. Edgerton, "The Artist Turned Prophet," *American Conference of the Sixth Congress of Slavists*, 74.
3. V. Shklovsky, *Leo Tolstoy*, 536–37.
4. A. Leroy-Beaulieu, "La Religion en Russie," *Revue des Deux Mondes*, 15 Sept. 1888.
5. E. M. de Vogüé, *Revue des Deux Mondes*, 1 Jan. 1883, 60.
6. Shklovsky, 540–41.
7. Ibid., 544.
8. M. V. Muratov, *Tolstoi u Chertkov*, 32.
9. Ibid., 79.
10. Ibid., 73.
11. M. Slade, *The Spirit's Pilgrimage*, 93.
12. Ibid., 197–98.
13. M. Slade, *Letters to a Disciple*, 61.
14. Ibid., 88.
15. Gandhi, *Collected Works* 51:131.
16. Ibid., 298.
17. E. Morton, *The Women in Gandhi's Life*, 200.
18. M. Slade, *The Spirit's Pilgrimage*, 179–80.
19. Gandhi, *Collected Works* 53:84.
20. Ibid., 54:7.
21. Ibid.
22. N. C. Cook, *My Road to India*, 307.
23. Ibid.
24. Gandhi, *Collected Works* 54:27.
25. *Harijan*, 6 May 1933.
26. Gandhi, *Collected Works* 54:26.
27. Ibid., 121.
28. Ibid., 230.
29. Ibid., 124.

30. Ibid., 55:8–9.
31. Ibid., 153.
32. Ibid., 54:102.
33. Ibid., 55:164.
34. Ibid., 190.
35. Ibid., 167.
36. Ibid., 209.
37. Cook, 399.
38. Ibid., 411.

Chapter XIII

1. H. Gifford, ed., *Tolstoy: Penguin Critical Anthology*, 99.
2. P. Miliukov, *Outlines of Russian Culture*, 52.
3. S. Karlinsky, *Anton Chekhov's Life and Thought*, 374.
4. Gifford, 126.
5. D. S. Merezhkovski, *Tolstoy as Man and Artist*, 91.
6. Ibid., 43.
7. Ibid., 174, 187.
8. R. Byrnes, *Pobedonostsev*, 40.
9. Ibid., 256.
10. M. Gorki, *Reminiscences of Tolstoy, Chekhov, and Andreev*, 312.
11. Ibid., 6.
12. Ibid., 11.
13. Ibid., 7.
14. Ibid., 45.
15. Ibid., 4.
16. Ibid., 4.
17. Ibid., 39.
18. E. J. Dillon, *Count Leo Tolstoy*, 178 ff.
19. C. M. Breitburg, *V. I. Lenin o L. N. Tolstom*, 18–19.
20. Ibid., 96.
21. Ibid., 50.
22. Ibid., 52.
23. R. Payne, *The Life and Death of Mahatma Gandhi*, 637.
24. B. R. Ambedkar, *Gandhi and Gandhism*, Introduction by Bhagwan Das.
25. F. Watson and M. Brown, *Talking of Gandhiji*, 10.
26. Ambedkar, 121.
27. Ibid., Introduction.
28. Ibid., 70.
29. Ibid., 119.
30. B. N. Pandey, *The Indian Nationalist Movement 1885–1947*, 131.
31. Balvantsimha, *Under the Shelter of Bapu*, 3.
32. Ibid., 40.
33. Ibid., 132.
34. Gandhi, *Collected Works* 73:236.
35. Ibid., 76:466.
36. Ibid., 77:277.

Glossary of Russian and Indian Words

Arya Samaj (Indian). A society founded to reform Hinduism by making it more nationalist

ashram (Indian). A place to which a group retreats from the world for spiritual purposes

bania (Indian). Of the commercial caste

Bashkirs (Russian). The tribal inhabitants of the Asian borders of central Russia

bhakti (Indian). Devotional piety

bitovoye blagochestie (Russian). The inherited values embodied in traditional ways of doing things

brahmacharya (Indian). Renunciation of sexual activity

Brahmo Samaj (Indian). A society founded to reform Hinduism by making it more transcendental

Chandala (Indian). An Untouchable

chela (Indian). A disciple

Cherkess/Chechen (Russian). The tribal peoples of the Caucasus

chin/chiny (Russian). Official rank/ranks

desyatina (Russian). About 2.7 acres of land

dharma (Indian). A duty or law

Durga (Indian). Also Kali and Shakta. The goddess partner to Shiva, the god of destruction

guru (Indian). A teacher

hartal (Indian). A general strike

intelligent (Russian). A member of the intelligentsia

Jain (Indian). A religion which teaches respect for animal life

jati (Indian). A caste

karma (Indian). Action, in its moral character

krepostnik (Russian). A supporter of serfdom

kshattriya (Indian). Of the warrior caste

kumys (Russian). Fermented mare's milk

mandir (Indian). A temple

Maratha (Indian). A part of northern and western India with a patriotic military tradition

Modh bania (Indian). A kind of bania, the kind to which Gandhi belonged

narodnik (Russian). A populist

pochva/pochvennik/pochvennost (Russian). Soil/enthusiast for the soil and roots/rootedness

posad (Russian). A city's trading quarter

rajas (Indian). One of the three aesthetic qualities; associated with passion, splendor, and excitement

raskol (Russian). Schism

raskolnik (Russian). Schismatic or dissenter

raznochintsy (Russian). Of mixed caste

saddhu (Indian). An ascetic

sadhana (Indian). Method

sanyasi (Indian). A religious wanderer

sattva (Indian). Another of the aesthetic qualities; associated with purity, peace, innocence, and reason

shakti (Indian). Female power

shudra (Indian). Of the agricultural caste

soslovie (Russian). Social class or estate

swadeshi (Indian). Locally made

swaraj (Indian). Home rule

tamas (Indian). Another of the aesthetic qualities; associated with gloom, chaos, and turbidity

vaishnavite (Indian). A worshipper of Vishnu, the preserver god

varna (Indian). A caste

varnashrama (Indian). Division of life into developmental stages

Vedas (Indian). Traditional religious poems

verst (Russian). About 3,500 feet

yurodivi (Russian). God's fool

zemstvo (Russian). Elective district council

Bibliography

Aksakov, Sergei, *Chronicles of a Russian Family*. Translated by M. C. Beverley. London, 1924.

———. *A Russian Gentleman*. Translated by J. D. Duff. London, 1917.

———. *Tales of Childhood*. Translated by Alec Brown. New York, 1960.

Ambedkar, B. R. *Gandhi and Gandhism*. Introduction by Bhagwan Das. Jullundur, 1970.

Anand, M. R. *The Humanism of M. K. Gandhi*. Bombay, 1967.

Armytage, W. H. R. *Heavens Below*. London, 1961.

Ashe, Geoffrey. *Gandhi*. New York, 1968.

Asquith, Cynthia. *Married to Tolstoy*. 1961. London, 1964.

Baddeley, John F. *Russia, Mongolia, China*. New York, 1967.

———. *The Russian Conquest of the Caucasus*. London, 1908.

Baig, Tara Ali. *Sarojini Naidu*. New Delhi, 1974.

Baker, James H. *St. Petersburg: Industrialism and Change*. Montreal, 1976.

Balvantsimha. *Under the Shelter of Bapu*. Ahmedabad, 1962.

Bandhyopadhyaya, J. *Mao Tse Tung and Gandhi*. Bombay, 1973.

Barr, Mary. *Bapu*. Bombay, 1949.

Basham, A. L. *The Wonder That Was India*. New York, 1954.

Bataille, Georges. *Eroticism*. London, 1962.

Bearce, George D. *British Attitudes Towards India 1784–1858*. New York, 1961.

Bedford, C. H. *The Seeker: D. S. Merezhkovsky*. Lawrence, Kans., 1975.

Behrs, C. A. *Recollections of Count Tolstoy*. London, 1893.

Benson, Ruth Crego. *Women in Tolstoy*. Urbana, Ill., 1973.

Berlin, Isaiah. *Karl Marx: His Life and Environment*. New York, 1978.

Bernal, J. D. *The World, the Flesh, and the Devil*. Bloomington, 1967.

Bhattacharya, J. N. *Hindu Castes and Sects*. Calcutta, 1968.

Bhave, Vinoba. *The Steadfast Wisdom*. N.p., 1966.

———. *Talks on the Gita*. N.p., 1970.

———. *The Third Power*. N.p., 1972.

Bill, Valentine T. *The Forgotten Class*. New York, 1959.

Billington, James H. *Fire in the Minds of Men*. New York, 1980.

———. *The Icon and the Axe*. New York, 1966.

———. *Mikhailkovsky and Russian Populism*. London, 1958.

Biriukov, P. *Leo Tolstoy: His Life and Work*. New York, 1906. (See also Tolstoy, *Socialisme et Christianisme*.)

Birla, G. D. *In the Shadow of the Mahatma*. Bombay, 1953.

Bodelsen, C. A. *Studies in Mid-Victorian Imperialism*. London, 1968.

Bolitho, Hector. *Jinnah*. London, 1954.

Bondarev, Timothy, and L. N. Tolstoy. *On Toil*. Chicago, 1891.

Bose, N. K. *Lectures on Gandhism*. Ahmedabad, 1971.

————. *My Days With Gandhi*. Calcutta, 1953.

————. *Selections From Gandhi*. Ahmedabad, 1947.

Bowle, John. *The Imperial Achievement*. Boston, 1975.

Boyer, Paul. *Chez Tolstoi*. Paris, 1950.

Breitburg, C. M., ed. *V. I. Lenin o L. N. Tolstom*. Moscow, 1969.

Brogan, Denis. *Proudhon*. London, 1934.

Broido, Vera. *Apostles into Terrorists*. New York, 1977.

Brontë, Charlotte. *Jane Eyre*. New York, 1950.

Broomfield, J. H. *Elite Conflict in a Plural Society*. Berkeley, 1968.

Brower, Daniel R. *Training the Nihilists*. Ithaca, 1975.

Brown, Emily C. *Har Dayal*. Tucson, Ariz., 1975.

Brown, Judith M. *Gandhi and Civil Disobedience*. Cambridge, 1977.

————. *Gandhi's Rise to Power*. Cambridge, 1972.

Bulgakov, V. G. *The Last Year of Leo Tolstoi*. Translated by Ann Dunnigan. New York, 1971.

Bunin, I. *Memoirs and Portraits*. Translated by Traill and Chancellor. New York, 1951.

Byrnes, Robert. *Pobedonostsev*. Bloomington, 1968.

Carpenter, Edward. *My Days and Dreams*. London, 1921.

Carstairs, G. Morris. *The Twice Born*. Bloomington, 1961.

Chertkov, Vladimir. *The Last Days of Tolstoy*. London, 1922.

Clarke, Arthur C. *Prelude to Space*. London, 1951.

Collins, Larry, and Dominique LaPierre. *Freedom at Midnight*. New York, 1975.

Confino, Michael. *Daughter of a Revolutionary*. LaSalle, 1974.

Cook, Nilla Cram. *My Road to India*. New York, 1939.

Coomaraswamy, A. K. *Selected Works*. Edited by Roger Lipsey. Princeton, 1977.

Crankshaw, Edward. *The Shadow of the Winter Palace*. New York, 1976.

Curtiss, John S. *The Russian Army Under Nicholas I*. Chapel Hill: University of North Carolina, 1965.

de Custine, M. *Journey for Our Time*. Translated by P. P. Kohler. New York, 1951.

De Kiewiet, C. W. *A History of South Africa*. New York, 1940.

De Lubac, H. *The Un-Marxian Socialist*. Translated by R. E. Scantlebury. London, 1948.

Desai, Mahadev. *Day to Day with Gandhi*. Ahmedabad, 1968.

————. *The Diary of Mahadev Desai*. Vol. I. Ahmedabad, 1953.

————. *Gandhiji in Indian Villages*. Madras, 1927.

————. *The Story of Bardoli*. Ahmedabad, 1929.

Detienne, M. *Dionysos Slain*. Baltimore, 1979.

Devanesen, C. D. S. *The Making of the Mahatma*. Madras, 1969.

Dillon, E. J. *Count Leo Tolstoy*. London, 1972.

Dimock, Edward C. *The Thief of Love*. Chicago, 1963.

Doke, Joseph J. *M. K. Gandhi: An Indian Patriot in South Africa*. London, 1909.

Dolgoff, Sam. *Bakunin on Anarchy*. New York, 1972.

Donnelly, Alton S. *The Russian Conquest of Bashkiria*. New Haven, Conn., 1968.

Dostoevsky, F. *Crime and Punishment*. New York, 1968.

Dudley, Donald R. *History of Cynicism From Diogenes to the Sixth Century A.D.* London, 1937.

Dumas, Alexandre. *Impressions de Voyage*. Vol. I. Paris, 1900.

Durga Das. *India from Curzon to Nehru and After*. London, 1969.
Dwarkadas, Kanji. *Gandhiji Through My Diary Leaves*. Bombay, 1950.
Eikhenbaum, B. *Lev Tolstoy I*. Leningrad, 1928.
———. *Tolstoy in the Seventies*. Ann Arbor, Mich., 1981.
———. *Tolstoy in the Sixties*. Ann Arbor, Mich., 1981.
———. *The Young Tolstoy*. Ann Arbor, Mich., 1972.
Elwin, Verrier. *The Tribal World of Verrier Elwin*. Bombay, 1966.
Elwin, V., and J. Winslow. *Gandhi: The Dawn of Indian Freedom*. New York, 1930.
Erikson, Erik. *Gandhi's Truth: On the Origin of Militant Non-Violence*. New York, 1969.
Fanger, Donald. *Dostoevsky and Romantic Realism*. Cambridge, Mass., 1967.
Fedotov, G. P. *The Russian Religious Mind*. Cambridge, Mass., 1960.
Feuer, K. B. "The Genesis of War and Peace." Ph.D. diss., Columbia University, 1965.
Field, Daniel. *The End of Serfdom*. Cambridge, Mass., 1976.
———. *Rebels in the Name of the Tsar*. Boston, 1976.
Figner, Vera. *Memoirs of a Revolutionist*. New York, 1922.
Fischer, Louis. *Life of Mahatma Gandhi*. New York, 1950.
———. *Life of Mahatma Gandhi*. New York, 1954.
Florovsky, George. *Christianity and Culture*. Belmont, Mass., 1978.
Forster, R., and Jack P. Green. *Preconditions of Revolution in Early Modern Europe*. Baltimore, 1970.
Frank, J. *Dostoevsky*. Princeton, 1976.
Freeze, Gregory L. *Russian Levites*. Cambridge, Mass., 1977.
Fülöp-Miller, R. *Lenin and Gandhi*. London, 1927.
———. *Tolstoy: New Light on His Life and Genius*. New York, 1931.
Gallie, W. B. *Philosophers of Peace and War*. Cambridge, 1978.
Gandhi Marg. (A quarterly journal of Gandhian thought.) Vol. I. Bombay, 1957.
Gandhi, M. K. *An Autobiography*. Washington, D.C., 1948 (Boston, 1960).
———. *Collected Works*. Vol. I. Ahmedabad, 1958.
———. *My Dear Child*. Ahmedabad, 1956.
———. *Satyagraha in South Africa*. Stanford, Cal., 1954.
Gandhi, Madan C. *Gandhian Aesthetics*. New Delhi, 1969.
Gandhi, Prabhudas. *My Childhood With Gandhiji*. Ahmedabad, 1957.
Gandy, D. Ross. *Marx and History*. Austin, Tex., 1979.
Ganguly, B. N. *Gandhi's Social Philosophy*. New Delhi, 1973.
Gerstein, Linda. *Nikolai Strakhov*. Cambridge, Mass., 1971.
Gifford, Henry, ed. *Leo Tolstoy: Penguin Critical Anthology*. London, 1971.
Gillard, David. *The Struggle for Asia*. London, 1977.
Glaspell, Susan. *The Road to the Temple*. New York, 1927.
Gleason, Abbott. *European and Muscovite*. Cambridge, Mass., 1972.
———. *Young Russia*. New York, 1980.
Gogol, N. *Taras Bulba*. Translated by John Cournos. London, 1954.
Goldenveizer, A. B. *Talks with Tolstoi*. Translated by S. S. Koteliansky and V. Woolf. London, 1923.
Goncharov, I. *Oblomov*. Translated by D. Magarshack. London, 1954.
Gopal, Ram. *How India Struggled For Freedom*. Bombay, 1967.
Gorky, M. *Reminiscences of Tolstoy, Chekhov and Andreev*. New York, 1946.
Gudzy, N. K. *History of Early Russian Literature*. New York, 1970.
Gupta, A., ed. *Studies in the Bengal Renaissance*. Calcutta, 1958.
Gusev, N. N., and V. S. Mishin, eds. *Tolstoy in the Memory of his Contemporaries*. Leningrad, 1955.

Haimsun, Leopold H. *The Russian Marxists and the Origins of Bolshevism.* Cambridge, Mass., 1967.

Haithcox, J. G. *Communism and Nationalism in India.* Princeton, 1971.

Hammond, Dorothy, and Alta Jablow. *The Africa That Never Was.* New York, 1970.

Hay, S. N. *Asian Ideas of East and West.* Cambridge, Mass., 1970.

———. "Gandhi's First Five Years." In *Encounter With Erikson,* edited by D. Capps, et al. Missoula, Mont., 1977.

Herzen, A. *My Past and Thoughts.* New York, 1968.

Hingley, R. *A New Life of Anton Chekhov.* New York, 1976.

———. *Russian Writers and Society.* New York, 1969.

Hobsen, J. A. *Imperialism.* London, 1902.

Hunt, J. D. *Gandhi in London.* New Delhi, 1978.

Hutchins, F. *The Illusion of Permanence.* Princeton, 1967.

Huttenback, R. A. *The British Imperial Experience.* New York, 1966.

———. *Gandhi in South Africa.* Ithaca, 1971.

———. *Racism and Empire.* Ithaca, 1976.

Hutton, J. M. *Caste in India.* New York, 1963.

Huxley, Aldous. *Jesting Pilate.* London, 1948.

James, William. *The Writings of William James.* Edited by John J. McDermott. New York, 1967.

Jules-Verne, J. *Jules Verne.* New York, 1976.

Kalelkar, D. *Stray Glimpses of Bapu.* Ahmedabad, 1950.

Karlinsky, Simon. *Anton Chekhov's Life and Thought.* New York, 1973.

Keats, John. *Letters of John Keats.* Edited by S. Colvin. London, 1891.

Kelly, Laurence. *Lermontov.* New York, 1978.

Kenworthy, John C. *A Pilgrimage to Tolstoy.* 1896.

Kipling, R. *The Light That Failed.* New York, 1969.

Klyuchevsky, V. O. *Peter the Great.* London, 1958.

Koestler, A. *Darkness at Noon.* London, 1941.

Korolenko, V. G. *History of My Contemporary.* London, 1972.

Koss, Stephen. *Nonconformity in Modern British Politics.* Hamden, Conn., 1975.

Kravchinsky, Serge. *Underground Russia.* New York, 1883.

Krishnadas. *Seven Months With Mahatma Gandhi.* Ahmedabad, 1959.

Kropotkin, P. *Selected Writings on Anarchism and Revolution.* Cambridge, Mass., 1970.

Kumar, R., ed. *Essays on Gandhian Politics.* New York, 1971.

Kuzminskaya, T. S. *Tolstoy As I Knew Him.* New York, 1948.

Lensen, G. A. *Russia's Eastward Expansion.* Englewood Cliffs, N.J., 1964.

Lester, Muriel. *Entertaining Gandhi.* London, 1932.

Lipsey, Roger. *Coomaraswamy: His Life and Work.* Princeton, 1977.

Lomunov, K. M. *L. N. Tolstoy in the Memory of His Contemporaries.* Moscow, 1978.

Lyons, John D. *The Invention of the Self.* Carbondale, Ill., 1978.

McLean, Hugh. *Nikolai Leskov.* Cambridge, Mass., 1977.

McLellan, David. *Karl Marx: His Life and Thought.* London, 1973.

Mahabharata, The. 18th ed. Translated by C. Rajagopalachari. Bombay, 1976.

Maitland, Edward. *Life of Anna Kingsford.* 2 vols. London, 1895.

Maitland, Edward, with Anna Kingsford. *The Perfect Way.* London, 1890.

Malgonkar, Manohar. *The Men Who Killed Gandhi.* New Delhi, 1978.

Mali, Martin. *Alexander Herzen and the Birth of Russian Socialism.* Cambridge, Mass., 1961.

Markovitch, Milan I. *Tolstoi et Gandhi.* Paris, 1928.

Marx, K. *Capital.* Translated by E. Paul and C. Paul. London, 1972.

————. *Capital.* Translated by B. Fowkes. New York, 1977.

Marx, K., with Friedrich Engels. *On Colonialism.* New York, 1972.

Masaryk, T. G. *The Spirit of Russia.* London, 1919.

Mashruwala, K. *Gandhi and Marx.* Ahmedabad, 1951.

Matlaw, R. E., ed. *Belinsky, Chernyshevsky, and Dobrolyubov.* Bloomington, 1976.

Maude, Aylmer. *Family Views of Tolstoy.* Boston, 1926.

————. *Life of Tolstoy.* London, 1908.

————. *Tolstoy and His Problems.* London, 1901.

Mehta, Ved. *Mahatma Gandhi and His Apostles.* New York, 1977.

Melotti, U. *Marx and the Third World.* Translated by P. Ransford. Atlantic Highlands, New Jersey, 1972.

Mendel, Arthur P. *Dilemmas of Progress in Tsarist Russia.* Cambridge, Mass., 1961.

Merezhkovsky, D. S. *Peter and Alexis.* London, 1905.

————. *Tolstoy as Man and Artist.* London, 1902.

Miliukov, Paul. *Outlines of Russian Culture.* Translated by Ughet and Davis. Philadelphia, 1948.

————. *Russia and Its Crisis.* New York, 1962.

————. *Origins of Ideology.* Translated by J. L. Wieczynski. Gulf Breeze, Fla., 1974.

Miller, Wright. *Russians As People.* New York, 1961.

Moon, Penderel. *Gandhi and Modern India.* New York, 1969.

Morris, James. *Heaven's Command.* New York, 1973.

————. *Pax Britannica.* New York, 1978.

Morton, Eleanor. *The Women In Gandhi's Life.* New York, 1953.

Mukherjee, H. U. *Bipin Chandra Pal and India's Struggle for Swaraj.* Berkeley, 1958.

Munshi, K. M. *I Follow the Mahatma.* Bombay, 1940.

Muratov, M. V. *Tolstoi i Chertkov.* Moscow, 1934.

Nag, Kalidas. *Tolstoy and Gandhi.* Calcutta, 1950.

Nanda, B. R. *Gokhale, Gandhi, and the Nehrus.* London, 1974.

————. *The Nehrus.* New York, 1963.

Nehru, Jawarhalal. *A Bunch of Old Letters.* New York, 1960.

————. *The Discovery of India.* New York, 1960.

————. *Glimpses of World History.* New York, 1962.

————. *Towards Freedom.* Boston, 1958.

Nikitenko, A. L. *Diary of a Russian Censor.* Amherst, Mass., 1975.

Norman, Dorothy. *Nehru: The First Sixty Years.* New York, 1965.

O'Flaherty, W. D. *Hindu Myths.* London, 1975.

Orme, Robert. *History of the Military Transactions of the British Nation in Indostan.* London, 1980.

Pal, Bipin Chandra. *My Life and Times.* Calcutta, 1932.

Pandey, B. N. *Indian National Movement.* New York, 1979.

————. *Nehru.* New York, 1976.

Parikh, Narahari D. *Mahadev Desai's Early Life.* Ahmedabad, 1953.

Parker, W. H. *An Historical Geography of Russia.* Chicago, 1968.

Payne, R. *The Life and Death of Mahatma Gandhi.* New York, 1969.

Phelps, G. *The Russian Novel in English Fiction.* London, 1955.

Philipp, F. H. *Tolstoj und der Protestantismus.* Giessen, 1959.

Philipson, M. *The Count Who Wished He Were a Peasant.* New York, 1967.

Pomper, Philip. *Peter Lavrov and the Russian Revolutionary Movement.* Chicago, 1972.

————. *Sergei Nechaev.* New Brunswick, N.J., 1977.

Prabhu, R. K. *This Was Bapu.* Ahmedabad, 1954.

Prasad, Madho. *A Gandhian Patriarch.* New Delhi, 1965.
Prasad, Rajendra. *At the Feet of Mahatma Gandhi.* New York, 1957.
————. *Autobiography.* Bombay, 1957.
Presniakov, A. E. *Emperor Nicholas the First of Russia.* Gulf Breeze, Fla., 1974.
Proffer, C., and E. Proffer. *The Silver Age of Russian Culture.* Ann Arbor, Mich., 1975.
Purves, J. G., and D. A. West. *War and Society in 19th Century Russia.* Toronto, 1972.
Pushkin, A. *Pushkin on Literature.* Edited by Tatina Wolff. London, 1971.
————. *Works of Pushkin.* Edited by Yamolinsky. New York, 1936.
Putnam, A. G. *Russian Alternatives to Marxism.* Knoxville, 1977.
Pyarelal. *Mahatma Gandhi. Volume I: The Early Phase.* Ahmedabad, 1965.
————. *Mahatma Gandhi. Volume II: The Last Phase.* Ahmedabad, 1956.
Raddatz, Fritz J. *Karl Marx: A Political Biography.* Boston, 1978.
Radhakrishnan, S. R. S. *Vinoba and His Mission.* Wardha, 1948.
Radhakrishnan, S., ed. *Mahatma Gandhi.* London, 1949.
————. *One Hundred Years.* New Delhi, 1968.
Raeff, M. *The Decembrist Movement.* Englewood Cliffs, N.J., 1966.
————. *Michael Speransky.* The Hague, 1969.
————. *Origins of the Russian Intelligentsia.* New York, 1966.
Raeff, M., ed. *Peter the Great.* Boston, 1963.
Rai, Lala Danpat. *Life Story of Lala Lajpat Rai.* New Delhi, 1976.
Rai, Lala Lajpat. *Autobiographical Writings.* New Delhi, 1965.
Ramachandran, G. *Gandhigram Thoughts and Talks.* Bombay, 1964.
————. *A Sheaf of Gandhi Anecdotes.* Bombay, 1945.
Ramachandran, G., ed. *Gandhi: His Relevance For Our Times.* Bombay, 1964.
Ramayana, The. Translated by C. Rajagopalachari. Bombay, 1975.
Rao, G. Ramachandra. *An Atheist With Gandhi.* Ahmedabad, 1951.
Rao, M. B., and S. G. Sardasai, eds. *The Mahatma.* New Delhi, 1969.
Ray, S., ed. *Gandhi, India, and the World.* Bombay, 1970.
Reynolds, R. *A Quest for Gandhi.* New York, 1952.
Riasanovsky, N. "Nicholas I and the Course of Russian History." In A. E. Presniakov,
    Emperor Nicholas I of Russia. Gulf Breeze, Fla., 1974.
————. *History of Russia.* New York, 1977.
————. *Nicholas I and Official Nationality in Russia.* Berkeley, 1969.
————. *A Parting of the Ways.* New York, 1976.
————. *Russia and the West in the Teaching of the Slavophiles.* Cambridge, Mass., 1952.
Rice, Martin F. *Valery Briusov and the Rise of Russian Symbolism.* Ann Arbor, Mich., 1975.
Riha, Thomas. *Readings in Russian Civilization.* Chicago, 1964.
Rolland, R. *Inde: Journal 1915–43.* Paris, 1951.
————. *Prophets of The New India.* New York, 1936.
————. *Rolland-Gandhi Correspondence.* New Delhi, 1976.
————. *Tolstoy.* New York, 1911.
Rousseau, J. J. *Reveries of a Solitary Walker.* Translated by Peter France. London, 1979.
Roy, D. K. *Among the Great.* Bombay, 1945.
Roy, M. N., and P. Spratt. *Beyond Communism.* Bombay, 1947.
Roy, Samoyen. *The Restless Brahmin.* Bombay, 1970.
Rudolph, L., and S. Rudolph. *The Modernity of Tradition.* Chicago, 1967.
Saksena, M. *Motilal Nehru.* New Delhi, 1961.
Schuyler, Eugene. *Selected Essays.* New York, 1901.
Schwartz, B. *In Search of Wealth and Power.* Cambridge, Mass., 1964.
Sergeenko, P. *Tolstoy and His Contemporaries.* Moscow, 1911.

Shah, Kantilal, ed. *Vinoba on Gandhi.* N.p., 1973.
Shahani, R. *Mr. Gandhi.* New York, 1961.
Shaw, Nellie. *Whiteway: A Colony on the Cotswolds.* London, 1935.
Shklovsky, V. *Leo Tolstoy.* Translated by Olga Shartse. Moscow, 1978.
Shub, David. *Lenin.* New York, 1948.
Shukla, Chandrashankar. *Incidents of Gandhiji's Life.* New Delhi, 1949.
———. *Reminiscences of Gandhiji.* N.p., n.d.
Simmons, E. J. *Leo Tolstoy.* Boston, 1946.
———. *Leo Tolstoy.* Boston, 1973.
———. *Pushkin.* Cambridge, Mass., 1937.
Singham, S. D. R. *Ananda Coomaraswamy: Remembering and Remembering Again and Again.* Petading Jaya, 1974.
Sinha, M. P. *The Contemporary Relevance of Gandhi.* Bombay, 1970.
Slade, Madeline. *Letters to a Disciple.* London, 1951.
———. *The Spirit's Pilgrimage.* London, 1978.
Smedley, Agnes. *Battle Hymn of China.* London, 1978.
Snyder, Louis. *The Imperialism Reader.* Princeton, 1962.
Soloviev, V. *A Solovyov Anthology.* Edited by S. L. Frank. Translated by N. Duddington. New York, 1950.
Spear, P. *The History of India.* Vol. II. London, 1973.
———. *The Nabobs.* Oxford, 1963.
Spector, I., and M. Spector. *Readings in Russian History and Culture.* Boston, 1965.
Spratt, P. *Blowing Up India.* Calcutta, 1955.
Sprigge, C. J. S. *Karl Marx.* New York, 1962.
Starr, J. F. *Decentralization and Self-Government in Russia 1830–1870.* Princeton, 1972.
Sukhotina-Tolstoy, Tatiana. *The Tolstoy Home.* Translated by Alec Brown. London, 1950.
———. *Tolstoy Remembered.* Translated by Derek Coltman. London, 1977.
Sumner, B. H. *Survey of Russian History.* London, 1944.
———. *Tsardom and Imperialism.* New York, 1968.
Swinson, A. *Six Minutes to Sunset.* London, 1964.
Szamuely, T. *The Russian Tradition.* London, 1974.
Tagore, R. *Creative Unity.* Calcutta, 1971.
———. *A Tagore Reader.* Edited by A. Chakravarty. Boston, 1966.
Tandon, Prakash. *Beyond Punjab.* New Delhi, 1971.
Tendulkar, D. G. *The Mahatma.* Vol. I. New Delhi, 1951.
Tennyson, Hallam. *India's Walking Saint.* New York, 1955.
Thaden, E. C. *Conservative Nationalism in 19th Century Russia.* University of Washington, Seattle, 1964.
Theen, Rolf H. W. *Lenin.* New York, 1973.
Thompson, Edward. *The Other Side of the Medal.* Westport, Conn., 1974.
Thompson, E. P. *William Morris.* New York, 1977.
Tinker, Hugh. *A New System of Slavery.* New York, 1974.
Tolf, R. W. *The Russian Rockefellers.* Stanford, Calif., 1976.
Tolstoy, Alexandra. *Tolstoy: A Life of My Father.* Translated by E. R. Hapgood. New York, 1953.
———. *The Tragedy of Tolstoy.* London, 1933.
Tolstoy, Ilya. *Reminiscences of Tolstoy.* London, 1914.
Tolstoy, Leon L. *The Truth About My Father.* London, 1924.
Tolstoy, L. N. *Anna Karenina.* Translated by D. Magarshack. New York, 1961.

——. *Childhood, Boyhood, Youth*. Translated by Rosemary Edmonds. London, 1964.

——. *Church and State*. Boston, 1891.

——. *Circle of Reading*. New York, 1911.

——. *Complete Works of Tolstoy*. Edited by L. Wiener. Boston, 1904.

——. *The Cossacks*. Translated by A. R. McAndrew. New York, 1961.

——. *Diaries 1847–1852*. Translated by C. J. Hogarth and A. Smith. London, 1917.

——. *Diary, 1853—1857*. Translated by A. Maude. New York, 1927.

——. *Essays from Tula*. London, 1948.

——. *Father Sergius, and other stories and plays*. Edited by Hagberg Wright. New York, 1911.

——. *Forged Coupon*. Edited by Hagberg Wright. New York, 1912.

——. *Journal of Leo Tolstoy 1895–1899*. Translated by Rose Strunsky. New York, 1917.

——. *The Kingdom of God is Within You*. New York, 1961.

——. *Law of Love and the Law of Violence*. New York, 1970.

——. *Letters of Tolstoy and Alexandra Tolstoy*. Translated by Leo Islavin. London, 1929.

——. *On Life*. Translated by Aylmar Maude. London, 1934.

——. *The Pathway of Life*. Translated by Archibald Wolfe. New York, 1919.

——. *Polnoe Sobranie Khudozhestvennykh Proizvedenii Lva Tolstovo*. Edited by I. I. Glivenko and M. A. Tsuavkivskii, beginning in Moscow, 1928. (The Jubilee Edition.)

——. *Portable Tolstoy*. Edited by Bayley. New York, 1978.

——. *Les Quatre Livres De La Lecture*. Paris, 1928.

——. *Recollections and Essays*. Translated by A. Maude. London, 1937.

——. *Rede gegen den Krieg*. Frankfurt, 1968.

——. *Resurrection*. London, 1916.

——. *Sebastopol*. Ann Arbor, Mich., 1961.

——. *Short Stories*. Introduction by L. Leonov. Moscow, 1960.

——. *Sobranie Sochinenii Lva Tolstovo*. Moscow, 1960.

——. *Socialisme et Christianisme: Correspondence Tolstoi-Birioukoff*. Paris, 1957.

——. *Tolstoy on Art*. Edited by Aylmer Maude. Boston, 1924.

——. *Tolstoy's Letters*. Translated by R. F. Christian. New York, 1978.

——. *Tolstoy's Love Letters*. Translated by S. S. Koteliansky and V. Woolf. London, 1923.

——. *Tolstoy's Writings on Civil Disobedience and Non-Violence*. New York, 1967.

——. *War and Peace*. Edited by G. Gibian. New York, 1966.

Tolstoy, Sergei. *Tolstoy Remembered by His Son*. Translated by M. Budberg. London, 1961.

Tolstoy, Sonia. *Autobiography of Countess Sophie Tolstoy*. Translated by S. S. Koteliansky and L. Woolf. London, 1922.

——. *Countess Tolstoy's Later Diary*. Translated by A. Werth. New York, 1929.

——. *Diary of Tolstoy's Wife*. Translated by A. Werth. London, 1928.

——. *The Final Struggle*. Edited and translated by A. Maude. New York, 1936.

Tolstoy, Tania. *Tolstoy Remembered*. London, 1977.

——. *Tolstoy Remembered*. New York, 1967.

Troyat, H. *Tolstoy*. New York, 1967.

Tulsidas. *The Holy Lake of the Acts of Rama*. Translated by W. Douglas Hill. Cambridge, 1952.

Twain, M. *Roughing It*. New York, 1962.

Tyler, J. E. *The Struggle for Imperial Unity*. London, 1938.

Ulam, A. *In the Name of the People*. New York, 1977.

Upadhyaya, J. M. *Mahatma Gandhi—A Teacher's Discovery*. Ahmedabad, 1969.

Venturi, F. *The Roots of Revolution.* New York, 1960.

Vucinich, A. *Science in Russian Culture.* Stanford, Calif., 1963.

———. *Social Thought in Tsarist Russia.* Chicago, 1976.

Watson, F., and M. Brown. *Talking of Gandhiji.* London, 1957.

———. *The Trial of Mr. Gandhi.* London, 1969.

Watts, M. *The Dissenters.* Oxford: Oxford University Press, 1978.

Weisbein, Nicolas. *L'Evolution Réligieuse De Tolstoi.* Paris, 1960.

Wellock, W. *Off the Beaten Track.* Varanasi, 1963.

Winsten, Stephen. *Salt and His Circle.* London, 1951.

Wiser, W. W., and C. V. Wiser. *Behind Mud Walls.* Los Angeles, 1963.

Wolfe, B. *Three Who Made A Revolution.* Boston, 1948.

Wolpert, S. A. *Tilak and Gokhale.* Berkeley, 1962.

Yajnik, I. K. *Gandhi As I Knew Him.* New Delhi, 1943.

Yule, H., and A. C. Burnett. *Hobson-Jobson: a Glossary of Anglo-Indian Words.* London, 1905.

Zenkovsky, V. V. *A History of Russian Philosophy.* Translated by G. L. Kline. New York, 1953.

Zernov, N. *Three Russian Prophets.* London, 1944.

Index